THE GOOD HOUSEKEEPING
INTERNATIONAL COOKBOOK

THE GOOD HOUSEKEEPING INTERNATIONAL COOKBOOK

OFFICIAL WORLD'S FAIR EDITION

EDITED BY Dorothy B. Marsh, *DIRECTOR OF FOODS AND COOKERY, GOOD HOUSEKEEPING MAGAZINE*

ILLUSTRATIONS BY BILL GOLDSMITH

HARCOURT, BRACE & WORLD, INC.   NEW YORK

Photographs by James Viles and Paul D'Ome

FOREWORD

One of the world's great writers, Joseph Conrad, once said: "The intention of every other piece of prose may be discussed and even mistrusted; but the purpose of a cookery book is one and unmistakable. Its object can conceivably be no other than to increase the happiness of mankind." We agree with Mr. Conrad—and in our interpretation "happiness" includes "understanding"—for we believe that the more understanding the countries of the world have of each other, the greater our chances for peaceful and happy coexistence.

This particular "cookery book" is the result of many factors: the heritage of cookery lore brought to us by the several young women of countries other than our own who have graced our staff; our readers' interest in the recipes of other countries; our own travels and our insatiable curiosity about the foods of the world.

Like all other *Good Housekeeping* cookbooks, this one bears the imprint of each member of our Foods and Cookery staff. Largely responsible for collecting and testing and adapting many of the recipes was Margrit Hoehener—a member of our staff who came to us from Switzerland. Guiding its course and giving our official pledge of accuracy to results was our Director of Foods and Cookery, Dorothy B. Marsh.

Every recipe has been adapted to American standards of measuring, and has been checked and rechecked for accuracy and dependable results before being included in this book. There are tables on pages 228–30 for converting measurements into terms of other countries.

Our only regret in preparing this book is that we did not have space enough to do justice to each country. Every traveler finds his own favorite food among a country's offering; every native has his opinion of which of his country's foods are best, and each always feels an injustice has been done if his choice is not included in such a compilation as this. We share that feeling of injustice, and indeed, had our own friendly arguments about which recipes should be included. So we trust that readers will understand the limitations of space and will look on this collection of recipes as a tribute to great food and to the countries that make it possible.

The book can take you on exciting travels to many lands. Do not be afraid to try new flavors and strange combinations. Among them you are sure to find new delights and increase your stature as a cook and hostess.

With every recipe come good wishes from *Good Housekeeping* in America.

WILLIE MAE ROGERS, *Director*
Good Housekeeping Institute

CONTENTS

NORTH AMERICA 187

SOUTH AMERICA 207

EUROPE

AUSTRIA	*FRANCE*	*POLAND*
BELGIUM	*GERMANY*	*PORTUGAL*
CZECHOSLOVAKIA	*GREECE*	*SCOTLAND*
DENMARK	*HOLLAND*	*SOVIET UNION*
ENGLAND	*HUNGARY*	*SPAIN*
FINLAND	*IRELAND*	*SWEDEN*
	ITALY	*SWITZERLAND*
	NORWAY	*YUGOSLAVIA*

Each country of Europe with its distinctive foods deserves a separate chapter. But this book cannot be that big and so we have grouped them together.

Geographically close as they are, it was inevitable that these countries would share their customs and foods. What is more natural than for France, geographically located in the heart of Europe, to draw from almost every type of European cuisine to vary and supplement her own?

France includes a variety of types of cookery—from the haute cuisine of famous restaurants to the peasant cookery and interesting regional dishes. Probably the heart of French cooking is the superb knowledge of seasonings and sauces that make the simplest dishes into masterpieces.

Italy has fed her people and her visitors well and happily for hundreds of years. Her pastas, vegetables, and fruits are bountiful and superb. Visitors to this warm and vital country come away with satisfying memories of tender, tantalizing pizzas, exciting chicken and fish dishes, and fruits that defy description.

Greece, too, produces excellent fruits and, of course, olives and olive oil. Among the Greek dishes are fish stews and lentil soups and the famous lemon-flavored chicken soup.

The visitor to Belgium fares well at the table since Belgium's food is hearty but imaginative. Belgian vegetables are noted for their tenderness and flavor.

From Hungary come wonderful stews and also superb desserts in the diverse forms of tortes, soufflés, pastries, and cakes. Masters in the art of seasoning, Hungarian cooks use paprika generously, and very often dill or caraway seeds to give an unexpected but delightful flavor.

When a country has a deep interest in and appreciation of food as much more than just body sustenance, it is immediately apparent in the food itself. Such a country is Austria—with its sturdy, nourishing soups and stews, its rich and delicious tortes and pastries, its cosmopolitan flavor that recognizes the dishes adopted from neighboring countries but given Austria's own special touch.

Another mid-European country whose food reflects its close neighbors is Czechoslovakia. Yet here, too, there is a definite individual touch. Knedliky, or dumplings, pork, goose, and many kinds of sausages are used in many ways. Traditional, too, are their yeast rolls and cakes, gingerbread, and cookies. Anyone who has ever been in a true Czech kitchen at Christmas-baking time never forgets the tastes and aromas that delight body and spirit.

Polish cookery has profited by adding to its own national foodstuffs such as sausages, hams, fish, and vegetables many new foods brought into the country by visitors and newcomers from all parts of the world. Today, meals in many countries are enriched by Poland's hams and dried mushrooms and jams and preserves.

Gracing the northern tip of Europe, the Scandinavian countries of Norway, Denmark, and Finland are famous for their fish, game, and dairy products, and their food reflects the use of these fresh and wholesome products.

Perhaps best known of the many delectable Swiss foods is its national dish, the fondue. Divided as it is by mountain ranges, Switzerland has sharply defined customs, accents, and cookery within its borders. Its food is hearty and good and, fortunately for people who cannot go there, Switzerland sends all over the world its fine chocolates, cheeses, wines, and liquors.

Who could think of European cookery and its delights without remembering Sweden's smorgasbord, Holland's cheese and chocolate, Spain's gazpacho and wonderful wines, and Portugal's many intriguing fish dishes?

Each district of Germany has its own specialties—Bavaria's famous dumplings and white sausages, Ulm's sugar bread, Frankfurt's cheese and fine asparagus, the Rhineland's sauerbraten, and Westphalia's hams.

From the vast country of Russia comes a wide variety of foods and food customs. Typical throughout, however, is the use of sour cream and such seasonings as dill, sorrel, and nettles. Russia is famous for its soups, too—probably the best known is the beet soup, borsch.

As might be expected from the different customs and people of England, Scotland, Wales, and Ireland, cookery in Great Britain means many different things. At its best, it is England's roast beef and Yorkshire pudding, the famous Irish stew, and Scotland's beef, Highland honey, and wonderful scones and shortbreads. Probably most typical of all of England's food customs is afternoon tea—a ritual that takes place in homes and offices at four o'clock and a custom that should surely be adopted by every country for its general benefits to mind and body.

Out of the vast richness of European food lore and cookery we bring you a choice selection of recipes. Try them—and travel on waves of delectable tastes to the fascinating lands that gave them to us.

Austria

In gay old Vienna Austrians would dine elegantly on a soufflé main dish like this.

SCHÖNBRUNNER LUNCH
(Cheese Puff with Vegetables, Ham, and Mushrooms)

1 10-oz. pkg. frozen cauliflower	¾ teasp. salt
1 10-oz. pkg. frozen peas	⅛ teasp. pepper
Butter or margarine	⅛ teasp. powdered nutmeg
½ lb. fresh mushrooms, quartered	¼ cup all-purpose flour
5 eggs, separated	Grated Parmesan cheese
½ cup commercial sour cream	¼ lb. cooked ham, diced

About 1 hr. and 30 min. before serving:
1. Cook cauliflower with peas; drain. In 1 to 2 tablesp. butter in skillet, sauté mushrooms until golden; set aside.
2. Beat ⅓ cup butter until creamy; beat in egg yolks, one at a time, sour cream, salt, pepper, nutmeg. Gradually beat in the flour, 2 tablesp. cheese. Start heating oven to 350°F.
3. Beat egg whites stiff; fold in sour-cream mixture until smooth. Butter 10″ x 6″ x 2″ baking dish; spread half of soufflé mixture on bottom; top with half of cauliflower, peas, mushrooms, and ham; sprinkle with 3 tablesp. cheese. Pour on rest of soufflé mixture.
4. Arrange rest of vegetables and ham down top center of dish; sprinkle with 3 tablesp. cheese, dot with 1 tablesp. butter. Bake 35 min., or until golden. Makes 4 servings.

For dinner try this glamorously prepared veal, a favorite meat of the Austrians.

WIENER SCHNITZEL

6 boneless anchovies
6 thin lemon slices
Bottled capers
Sweet-dill-pickle strips
Fresh horse-radish (optional)
¼ cup flour
1 teasp. salt
½ teasp. pepper

1½ lb. veal steak, cut into 6 pieces,
  then pounded to ⅛" thickness
2 eggs, beaten
¾ cup pkgd. dried bread crumbs
½ cup butter or margarine
3 tablesp. lemon juice
3 tablesp. snipped parsley

1. Roll each anchovy into circle with hollow center; set on lemon slice; fill center with capers. Thinly slice dill-pickle strips. With knife, shred a little horse-radish. Refrigerate all.
2. Mix flour, salt, pepper. Dip veal in it, then in eggs, then crumbs.
3. Slowly heat large skillet; in it, melt half of butter. In hot butter, brown veal quickly on all sides, a few pieces at a time. Over low heat, cook veal slowly about 15 min., or until tender; remove veal to heated platter.
4. In same skillet, brown remaining butter; stir in lemon juice and parsley; pour over veal. Top each piece with lemon slice, pickle on one side of lemon, horse-radish on other. Makes 4 to 6 servings.

One of the most famous of tortes, from the home of tortes.

LINZERTORTE

¾ cup butter or margarine
¾ cup granulated sugar
2 eggs
¼ teasp. salt
2 teasp. grated lemon rind
¼ teasp. powdered cinnamon

⅛ teasp. powdered cloves
7 oz. (about 1½ cups) shelled
  almonds, finely ground
2 cups sifted all-purpose flour
Raspberry jam
1 egg, beaten

Make one or two days before:
1. In large bowl, with electric mixer at medium speed, beat butter with sugar until creamy; gradually beat in eggs, salt, lemon rind, cinnamon, and cloves.
2. Fold in almonds and flour until well blended. Wrap in wax paper and refrigerate several hours, or until well chilled.
3. Use about ¾ of this dough to press on bottom of 9" layer-cake pan, so that sides are slightly higher than center. In center of dough spread ½ cup raspberry jam. Start heating oven to 350°F.
4. On floured pastry board roll out rest of dough about ¼" thick. With pastry wheel cut out 6 strips, ¾" wide; place them, lattice-

fashion, over raspberry jam. Cut rest of dough into 1″ strips and lay around top edge of torte. (Instead of strips you may cut out small motifs with a cookie cutter and place them around edge, overlapping slightly.)

5. Brush dough with beaten egg. Bake 40 to 45 min., or until golden. Cool on rack, turn out on cake plate, wrap. Serve, as dessert, cut into 8 to 12 wedges.

A light, lovely, lilting dessert omelet like the city whose name it bears—Vienna.

WIENER OMELETTEN
(*Viennese Pancakes*)

⅔ cup sifted all-purpose flour
¼ cup water
⅓ cup milk
1 egg
Butter or margarine
1 8-oz. pkg. cream cheese

6 tablesp. granulated sugar
2 eggs, separated
1 teasp. grated lemon rind
¼ cup dark seedless raisins
Canned roasted, diced almonds
3 tablesp. brown sugar

About 1 hr. before serving:
1. Combine flour, ⅛ teasp. salt, water, milk, 1 egg; with large fork or wire whip beat until smooth. Use to bake 6 thin pancakes in buttered small skillet, then lay them, side by side, on wax paper. Start heating oven to 350°F.
2. In small bowl, with electric mixer at medium speed, beat cream cheese with granulated sugar; then add 2 egg yolks, lemon rind, ⅛ teasp. salt, raisins, and ¼ cup almonds.
3. Now, over each pancake, spread about 1 tablesp. of this mixture. Roll up and place, side by side, in buttered 10″ x 6″ x 2″ baking dish.
4. Beat egg whites until stiff; fold into remaining cream-cheese mixture, then pour over pancakes. Sprinkle with brown sugar and 2 tablesp. roasted almonds. Bake about 30 min., or until golden. Makes 6 servings.

Absolutely delectable, a favorite at coffeehouses with coffee, topped with whipped cream.

APRICOT-CHEESE PASTRY HEARTS

1 cup sifted all-purpose flour
⅛ teasp. salt
½ cup butter or margarine

½ 8-oz. pkg. cream cheese
Apricot or raspberry preserves
1 egg, beaten

Day before, if desired, make this Cheese Pastry:
1. Into medium bowl sift all-purpose flour and salt; add butter or margarine and cream cheese, in small pieces.

2. With pastry blender or two knives, scissor-fashion, cut butter and cheese into flour mixture until all is *well* blended. Shape into a ball, wrap in wax paper, saran, or foil, then refrigerate.

Early on the day, or about 2 hr. before serving:

1. Lightly grease two cookie sheets. Start heating oven to 400°F.
2. On floured surface, roll out cheese dough ⅛" thick. Then, with 3" x 2¾" heart-shaped cookie cutter, cut out hearts. Remove trimmings; reroll and cut out once or twice again.
3. Next, in center of each of half of pastry hearts, place 1 scant teasp. of preserves. Now brush their edges with beaten egg, cover each with another cut-out heart, then, with fork, lightly press edges together.
4. Arrange on cookie sheet. Brush top of each with beaten egg; sprinkle with granulated sugar, if desired. Bake 10 to 12 min., or until golden; cool on rack. Makes about 24.

Belgium

The world over knows the fame of Belgian endive as a beautiful salad green. But have you ever cooked it, the Belgian way?

FRIEDA'S HAM AND ENDIVES AU GRATIN

6 to 8 Belgian endives, roots
  trimmed
½ cup butter or margarine
⅓ cup lemon juice
Salt
¼ cup all-purpose flour

Dash cayenne pepper
2 cups milk
¾ cup grated natural Swiss cheese
6 to 8 thin slices boiled ham
Paprika

1. In large skillet, arrange endives in ¼ cup melted butter, lemon juice, 2 tablesp. water; sprinkle with ¼ teasp. salt. Simmer, covered, 30 min. (Add a little water if needed.)
2. Meanwhile, start heating oven to 450°F. In saucepan, melt ¼ cup butter; remove from heat. Stir in flour, cayenne, milk; bring to boil, stirring; reduce heat; add ½ cup grated cheese. Simmer over low heat till thickened and cheese is melted.
3. Drain tender endives; wrap each with a ham slice, leaving ends uncovered. Arrange in baking dish; cover with sauce; top with ¼ cup grated cheese, paprika. Bake 15 min. Makes 3 or 4 servings.

Europe

ENDIVES MONTMORENCY

Butter or margarine
2 whole chicken breasts, halved
⅓ cup lemon juice
4 Belgian endives, roots trimmed
1 tablesp. flour

½ cup grated natural Swiss cheese
½ cup fresh bread crumbs
2 tablesp. bottled capers
¼ teasp. celery seeds
2 tablesp. snipped parsley

1. In ½ cup water and 2 tablesp. butter, in large skillet, slowly simmer chicken, covered, 45 min., or till tender; drain; reserve broth.
2. Meanwhile, in 2 tablesp. melted butter, combined with lemon juice, in large skillet, slowly simmer endives, covered, 30 min., or till tender; drain.
3. In saucepan, melt 1 tablesp. butter; remove from heat; stir in flour, reserved broth (about ¾ cup). Bring to boil, stirring; simmer till thickened; add cheese.
4. Now start heating oven to 350°F. Toss bread crumbs with 3 tablesp. melted butter; set aside.
5. Remove bones from chicken breasts; arrange in a buttered 10″ x 6″ x 2″ baking dish; top each with an endive, then with capers, celery seeds. Pour sauce over all; top with bread crumbs. Bake 20 min. Sprinkle with parsley. Makes 4 servings.

Another Belgian classic—a long-simmering casserole of beef stew that's moistened with beer and is fragrant with herbs and onions.

CARBONNADES DE BOEUF
(Casserole of Beef)

¼ cup salad oil
2 lb. beef round, in 1″ cubes
2 medium onions, peeled, thinly
  sliced
¼ cup flour
1½ cups hot water
1 cup beer
1 clove garlic, peeled, minced
1 bay leaf

2 teasp. salt
½ teasp. sugar
1½ teasp. vinegar
⅛ teasp. powdered nutmeg
Sprig of parsley
¼ teasp. dried orégano
6 to 8 2″ bread squares, generously
  spread with prepared mustard

About 2½ hr. before serving:
1. Start heating oven to 325°F. In large skillet heat 2 tablesp. salad oil; add beef round, a few pieces at a time, browning them quickly on all sides, then removing.
2. Add 2 tablesp. salad oil and onions, then brown them well. Stir in the flour, then hot water, beer, minced garlic, bay leaf, salt, sugar, vinegar, nutmeg, parsley, and orégano.
3. Return meat to the skillet, bring the whole to a boil, then

8

turn into a 2- to 2½-qt. casserole. Cover; then bake about 2 hr., or until beef is fork-tender.

About 20 min. before meat is done:
Remove casserole from oven. Skim all fat from surface of casserole, then top with mustard-spread bread squares. Spoon a little of the gravy over the bread, then return uncovered casserole to 350°F. oven, until baking time is up and bread is brown and crisp. Makes 4 or 5 servings.

Fish and shellfish abound in Belgium, and a visit to the local fish market is a never-to-be forgotten sight.

SAVORY EGGS MEULEMEESTER

6 hard-cooked eggs, shelled
½ lb. fresh shrimp, cooked, shelled, deveined
1 tablesp. flour
1½ teasp. prepared mustard
1 teasp. seasoned salt
⅓ cup milk
1 cup light cream
¼ cup snipped parsley
¾ cup grated natural Swiss cheese

About 40 min. before serving:
1. Start heating oven to 425°F. Slice eggs, then arrange them and shrimp in bottom of 10″ x 6″ x 2″ baking dish.
2. Combine flour, mustard, seasoned salt, milk, and cream and bring to a boil, while stirring; then stir in parsley and cheese. Pour over eggs and bake 15 to 20 min. Makes 4 servings.

Belgian vegetables are famous for their flavor and tenderness—they literally melt in your mouth! And by the way, did you ever eat cucumbers, cooked?

BELGIAN CUCUMBER

4 medium cucumbers
1 cup yoghurt
½ cup mayonnaise
½ teasp. salt
1 egg yolk
Snipped fresh dill

About 20 min. before serving:
1. Wash and pare cucumbers; cut into 1¼″ chunks. Cook in boiling salted water 10 min., or until tender-crisp.
2. Meanwhile, beat together yoghurt, mayonnaise, salt, and egg yolk. Bring almost to a boil. Drain cucumbers, heap on serving dish. Top with sauce. Serve, sprinkled with dill. Makes about 6 servings.

Europe

FLEMISH CARROTS

2 tablesp. butter	¾ teasp. sugar
5 to 6 medium carrots, pared, cut into thin 2″ sticks	⅓ cup light cream
	2 egg yolks
¾ to 1 teasp. salt	1 to 2 teasp. lemon juice

About 20 min. before serving:
In saucepan melt butter; in it sauté carrots about 5 min. Stir in salt, sugar, and ½ cup water. Simmer, covered, 10 to 15 min., or until carrots are tender. Beat together cream and egg yolks. Remove carrots from heat (do not drain); stir in cream mixture and lemon juice. Makes 4 servings.

This Belgian specialty resembles ours, with its layers of custard, whipped cream, and blueberries in a delightfully delicate crust.

BLUEBERRY CREAM TARTS

Sifted all-purpose flour	2 eggs, beaten
Salt	1 tablesp. brandy
Granulated sugar	1 teasp. grated lemon rind
¼ cup butter or margarine	½ to ¾ cup heavy cream
1 egg yolk	1 10-oz. pkg. frozen blueberries,
1 cup milk	thawed, drained

Make early on the day:
1. Start heating oven to 425°F. Into bowl sift 1 cup flour, ¼ teasp. salt, and 1 tablesp. sugar. With pastry blender or 2 knives, scissor-fashion, cut in butter until like coarse corn meal. Beat together egg yolk and 1½ tablesp. water. Add to flour mixture, form into a soft ball.
2. Roll out the pastry on a floured board. Use to line 8 muffin cups, 2¾″ across top (or 9″ pie plate), rerolling dough as necessary. Prick well; bake 10 to 12 min., or until golden. Cool on rack.
3. In top of double boiler combine ¼ cup flour, ⅓ cup sugar, ¼ teasp. salt; stir in milk and eggs, then cook over boiling water, while stirring, until thickened. Let this custard cool slightly, then stir in brandy and lemon rind. Cover surface with wax paper and refrigerate.

Just before serving:
Spread custard on bottom of crust. Whip cream until stiff (½ cup for tarts, ¾ cup for pie); spread some over custard, next place blueberries over cream; garnish with rest of cream. Makes 8 tarts.

Czechoslovakia

Soup, a favorite beginning to a Czechoslovakian meal, is usually served with some tasty addition. Here it's tender-crisp cauliflowerets, that float on top.

KVĚTÁKOVÁ POLÉVKA
(Cauliflower Soup)

3 tablesp. butter or margarine
3 tablesp. all-purpose flour
⅛ teasp. nutmeg
3⅔ cups canned chicken broth
1 cup water

3 cups small cauliflowerets
1 egg yolk
3 tablesp. heavy cream
Snipped parsley

About 45 min. before serving:
1. In medium saucepan melt butter or margarine; blend in flour and nutmeg. Slowly stir in chicken broth and water, then bring to a boil, while stirring. Now add cauliflowerets; then simmer soup, covered, about 25 min., or until cauliflowerets are tender.
2. In small bowl mix egg yolk with cream, stirring until blended; add to soup, then bring just to boiling point, while stirring constantly. Serve in small bowls, sprinkled with parsley. Makes about 6 servings.

Another triumph! Veal-and-Pork Goulash, cooked with tangy sauerkraut and caraway seeds, then tossed and topped with sour cream.

SZÉKELY GOULYAS
(Veal-and-Pork Goulash with Sauerkraut)

1 lb. veal shoulder, in 1½″ cubes
1 lb. pork shoulder, in 1½″ cubes
2 tablesp. salad oil
2 tablesp. caraway seeds

1 1-lb.-11-oz. can and 1 14-oz. can
  sauerkraut
1 teasp. salt
1½ cups commercial sour cream
Paprika

About 1 hr. and 45 min. before serving:
1. In Dutch oven sauté veal and pork in salad oil until brown on

all sides. Stir in caraway seeds, sauerkraut, salt; cover tightly; then simmer over low heat about 1½ hr., or until meat is tender.

2. Blend in 1 cup sour cream, then bring to a boil. Heap on serving platter. Spoon on rest of sour cream, here and there over sauerkraut; sprinkle with paprika. Serve with boiled potatoes. Makes about 6 servings.

Czechoslovakians have always had special secrets with their gently priced meats. Here, it's liver balls which cook very briefly in the short-rib soup, just before it's served.

BEEF SOUP WITH LIVER BALLS

2 lb. short ribs, or chuck with bone, in 3 or 4 pieces
2 large onions, peeled, sliced
3 or 4 stalks celery, sliced
Salt
Pepper
2 qt. water
2 carrots, pared, halved
2 fresh tomatoes, chopped
3 or 4 sprigs parsley

1 cup ground beef liver (about ½ lb.)
1 cup pkgd. dried bread crumbs
3 tablesp. all-purpose flour
2 eggs
¼ cup snipped parsley
⅛ teasp. powdered marjoram
⅛ teasp. mace
1 clove garlic, peeled, minced

1. Wash short ribs; place in large kettle; add onions and celery (include tops), 4 teasp. salt, ¾ teasp. pepper, and water. Cover; bring to boil; then skim off scum. Reduce heat so meat just simmers; then cook 1½ hr.

2. Now add carrots, tomatoes, and parsley; cook 1 hr., or until meat is tender.

3. Meanwhile, make Liver Balls as follows: Combine liver with crumbs, flour, eggs, parsley, 1 teasp. salt, ⅛ teasp. pepper, marjoram, mace, and garlic; let stand until soup is done; then shape into balls about size of golf balls.

4. Remove meat, bone, and carrots from soup; cut meat and carrots into bite-size pieces; return to soup.

5. Then bring soup to boil; drop in liver balls; cover; cook 10 min.; serve. Makes 4 to 6 servings.

Are Kolačky more fun to make or to eat? We're going to let you and your family decide. But Czechoslovakians would reply "It's a tie."

MARY'S KOLAČKY
(*Prune-filled Cookies*)

THE DOUGH:

1½ cups milk
1 cup butter or margarine
¾ cup granulated sugar
1 teasp. salt
1 pkg. active dry, or cake, yeast

¼ cup warm water
2 eggs, beaten
1 teasp. grated lemon rind
6 cups sifted all-purpose flour

PRUNE FILLING:

1 lb. prunes (2⅓ cups)
2 cups water
¼ cup granulated sugar

¼ teasp. powdered allspice
½ teasp. grated lemon rind
2 tablesp. lemon juice

1. In good-sized saucepan, heat milk just to boiling point; stir in butter, ¾ cup sugar, salt; cool till lukewarm.
2. Sprinkle or crumble yeast on water; stir until dissolved. Add to lukewarm milk with eggs, lemon rind, and flour; beat until smooth.
3. Place dough in greased bowl; cover with towel and let rise in warm place (80°F. to 85°F.) until double in bulk. Punch down and let rise again until double.
4. Meanwhile, make Prune Filling as follows: In saucepan combine prunes, water, sugar, allspice, lemon rind and juice; cook, as label directs, till prunes are tender. Pit prunes; return to their syrup; with fork beat till like smooth paste.
5. Turn yeast dough onto floured board and knead lightly for about 1 min. Roll out a portion of dough ½″ thick.
6. To make *round buns* cut rolled-out dough into 2½″ rounds; place on greased cookie sheet; with thumb make indentation in center of each round; then place a teaspoonful of prune filling in indentation.
7. To make *filled bun squares,* cut rolled-out dough into 4″ squares; place teaspoonful of prune filling in center of each. Moisten corners with water, bring opposite corners to center, overlapping corners and pressing gently together.
8. Place Kolačky on greased cookie sheet. Repeat cutting and filling with rest of dough. Then cover buns with wax paper and let rise in warm place until double in bulk. Brush lightly with cream (or egg yolk, beaten with a little cream).
9. Bake Kolačky at 375°F. 15 to 20 min., or until golden-brown. If desired, sprinkle top with a dusting of confectioners' sugar. Makes about 48.

Denmark

Milk is used most generously in Danish cookery—even in their famous Frikadeller, which they serve with hot or cold potato salad, a hot vegetable, and pickled beets.

FRIKADELLER
(Meat Balls, King-Size)

¾ lb. round beef, ground 4 times
¼ lb. shoulder pork, ground 4 times
⅔ cup milk
½ cup all-purpose flour

1 egg
1 medium onion, peeled, grated
1¼ teasp. salt
½ teasp. pepper
¼ cup butter or margarine

1. In bowl, combine all ingredients except butter, stirring well till light, airy, and smooth.
2. Next, to form each meat ball, dip a tablespoon in and out of the hot butter in a large skillet, over medium heat. Then dip spoon into meat mixture, round off top on side of bowl, and let slide into hot butter. Repeat 12 to 14 times.
3. Now brown meat balls on both sides, turning once; then cook, covered, 5 min. Makes 12 to 14 meat balls or 4 to 6 servings.

One of the less heralded, but no less delicious dishes of Denmark is their stuffed pork with apples and prunes.

STEGT SVINEKAM MED AEBLER OG SVESKER
(Roasted Pork Loin with Apples and Prunes)

5- to 6-lb. loin of pork
2 teasp. salt
1 teasp. granulated sugar
¼ teasp. pepper

1 qt. pared, cored apples, in ¼"-thick slices
1 cup pitted prunes
1 cup water
Brown Gravy, p. 15

1. Start heating oven to 325°F. With sharp knife, partially separate meat from ribs of pork loin.
2. Mix salt, sugar, and pepper; sprinkle some on all cut surfaces of pork. Then stuff pork with apple slices and prunes.
3. Tie string around loin, securing apple-prune mixture with it. Sprinkle outside of loin with remaining seasoning mixture.
4. Stand stuffed loin, on rib ends, in shallow roasting pan. Roast for 1 hr.; then pour on water, and roast 1½ hr. longer, or till very tender, basting often.

5. When roast is done, place on heated large platter; keep warm. Then make Brown Gravy, below; serve with pork.

BROWN GRAVY: Into saucepan, pour drippings from loin of pork; skim off fat. Bring drippings to boil; then stir in a paste made from 1 tablesp. flour, 1½ tablesp. cold water; bring to boil. Next, stir in 1 cup light cream and enough bottled sauce for gravy to make light brown. Season with 1 teasp. salt, ⅛ teasp. pepper, 1 tablesp. currant jelly; bring to boil. Makes about 2 cups.

The fame of Danish open sandwiches is widespread—often three or four apiece are eaten daily in Danish homes, for luncheon or a late evening snack. You can create equally appetizing ones of your own!

SMØRREBRØD
(*Open Sandwiches*)

BREAD: Dark rye bread is likely to be used. If white bread is chosen, it is usually toasted. But as long as the bread is thinly sliced, you may use any kind you wish—white, plain or toasted; light or dark rye; pumpernickel; or French.

SPREAD: Butter, cold but spreadable, is the usual spread, and it should generously cover the entire slice of bread. Sometimes other ingredients are blended with the butter; for example, a little dry mustard for a ham sandwich, grated horse-radish for roast beef, snipped dill or parsley for fish. Thick mayonnaise, plain or with a hint of curry, is also used as a spread, especially for lobster or other fish.

TOP AND GARNISH: The top and garnish go hand in hand and should complement each other in flavor, texture, and color. Perhaps the most popular Danish open sandwich is that made with as many as 100 or even 150 tiny, delicately flavored Danish June shrimp, arranged very closely together in precise, orderly rows, or heaped, pyramid-fashion, on a slice of buttered dark rye bread or white toast. A crisp lettuce leaf is the garnish. Incidentally, shelling these tiny shrimp is a time-consuming process and to have someone shell shrimp for you is a sign of very special affection. Those listed below are a few of the favorites.

Hard-cooked-egg slices, tomato slices, and onion rings on lettuce.

Thin, unpared cucumber slices, sardines, and chopped radishes.

Liver paste, cucumber salad, and fresh dill sprig.

Thin tongue slices, white asparagus spear, mayonnaise, and stuffed-olive slices.

Roast-beef slices, water-cress sprigs, sautéed mushroom slices, and grated fresh horse-radish.

Danish blue-cheese slice, crisp raw Belgian endive leaf, mayonnaise, and thin radish slices.

Tiny shrimp, piled on crisp lettuce leaf.

Hard-cooked-egg slices, smoked-eel strips, and fresh dill sprigs.

Hard-cooked-egg slices and caviar on lettuce leaf.

Thin smoked-salmon slice, soft scrambled egg, and snipped chives on lettuce.

Boiled-ham slice, crisp apple slices, and vegetable salad.

Thin salami slices with onion rings.

Muenster-cheese slice, tomato slice, mayonnaise, and fresh dill sprig.

Here's a step-by-step, easy-to-make version of the world-renowned Danish pastry, to serve any time with a cup of coffee.

DANISH PASTRY

Sifted all-purpose flour	¾ teasp. powdered cardamom
1½ cups butter or margarine	Almond-Paste Filling, or Nut or
2 pkg. active dry, or cakes, yeast	Jam Filling, p. 17
¼ cup warm water	Beaten egg
¾ cup milk, at room temperature	Chopped nuts or coarse crystal
1 egg	sugar
¼ cup granulated sugar	Confectioners' sugar
1 teasp. salt	

Early on day before serving:

1. With pastry blender or 2 knives, scissor-fashion, cut ⅓ cup flour into butter until blended. Place on wax paper and shape into a 12″ x 6″ rectangle. Refrigerate until well chilled.

2. Meanwhile, sprinkle yeast onto warm water to dissolve. In large bowl beat together milk and egg, then stir in yeast. Sift together 4 cups flour, sugar, salt, and cardamom. Stir into yeast mixture, then knead the dough on floured board until smooth.

3. Roll dough out into a 14″ square. Place chilled butter-flour rectangle on one half of dough, leaving 1″ border. Fold other half of dough over it, then press edges together.

4. Roll dough out into a rectangle about ½″ thick. Fold one third of dough over center third, then fold remaining third over top, making three layers. Wrap in wax paper; refrigerate ½ hr.

5. Turn dough so one of open ends faces front. Roll again into a rectangle, ½″ thick. Fold, chill, turn, roll again; repeat once more. Wrap dough in wax paper and refrigerate 2 to 3 hr.

6. Now roll out dough into a rectangle, ¼″ thick, then cut into shapes of envelopes, combs, or crescents and fill as on p. 17. Place on cookie sheets; brush with beaten egg. Sprinkle with chopped nuts or coarse crystal sugar. Refrigerate pastries until ready to bake.

About ½ hr. before serving:

Start heating oven to 450°F. Bake pastries 5 min.; then reduce heat to 350°F. and bake them 8 to 10 min., or until golden and puffy. Remove to racks to cool. If desired, brush with icing, made by blending confectioners' sugar with a little water. Makes about 30 pastries.

To shape envelopes: Cut dough into 4″ squares. Spread each with filling, then fold 4 corners in toward center and press down edges.

To shape combs: Cut dough into lengthwise strips, 4″ wide. Spread filling down center of each strip; fold long side of it over to opposite side; press edges together. Cut into pieces, 4″ long. With scissors make about 4 slashes halfway through width of each pastry; curve pastries so slashes spread apart slightly.

To shape crescents: Cut dough into lengthwise strips, 4″ wide. Cut each strip crosswise into triangles, about 4″ wide at the base, these bases alternating on sides of strip. Place filling on each base, then roll up, curving the ends to make crescent.

ALMOND-PASTE FILLING: Combine 1 8-oz. can almond paste with ¼ cup milk or cream, stirring until smooth.

NUT FILLING: Combine 1 cup chopped or ground pecans or walnuts with ½ cup light-brown sugar, 1 egg, and ¼ teasp. cinnamon.

JAM FILLING: Use raspberry, strawberry, or apricot jam.

P.S. Any leftover Danish pastries may be wrapped in foil and reheated in a 400°F. oven for about 10 min.

This luscious fruited poundcake is in Danish tradition, having been handed down from grandmother to mother to daughter.

EMMY'S PLUMKAGE
(Plum Cake)

1 cup butter or margarine
1 cup granulated sugar
5 egg yolks
3 cups sifted cake flour
2 tablesp. grated lemon rind
2 tablesp. lemon juice

1½ cups raisins
¾ cup chopped unblanched almonds
1 4-oz. jar diced preserved citron
5 egg whites

Make several days before serving, as follows:
1. Start heating oven to 350°F. Grease 10″ x 5″ x 3″ aluminum loaf pan, then line bottom with wax paper.
2. In large bowl, with electric mixer at high speed, cream butter or margarine with sugar till light and fluffy. Add egg yolks, one at a time, beating well.
3. Stir in cake flour, one cup at a time, then lemon rind, lemon juice, raisins, almonds, and citron.
4. Beat egg whites till stiff, but not dry; fold into cake batter; pour batter into loaf pan. Bake 1½ hr., or until cake tester, inserted in center, comes out clean.

5. Remove cake from oven; let stand 10 min.; remove from pan, peel off paper, cool on wire rack. Then wrap cake in foil and store. The cake improves with standing a day or two.

You'll find this cone-shaped tower of almond cakes a handsome dessert centerpiece for your holiday buffet, to be relished with fruit, nuts, and coffee.

KRANSEKAGE
(*Almond Cookies*)

3 lb. canned almond paste   **Decorating Icing, below**
4 egg whites, unbeaten

Prepare a week ahead, or day before, if desired:
1. Start heating oven to 300°F. Grease cookie sheets.
2. In large, heavy saucepan, with wooden spoon, mix almond paste with unbeaten egg whites till well blended. Then, over low heat, heat about 2 to 3 min., or till lukewarm and smooth, while kneading with spoon.
3. Turn into bowl; then, with palms of hands, from some of almond-paste mixture, form a cone-shaped top for the tower, 3" high, 1¼" wide; set, top side up, on cookie sheet.
4. On confectioners'-sugar-covered surface, with palms of hands, roll remaining almond-paste mixture into 12 pencil-shaped rolls, all ½" thick, and in these lengths: 5, 6, 7, 8, 10, 12, 14, 16, 18, 20, 22, and 24 inches.
5. Now, on cookie sheets, shape each roll into a ring, pinching ends together. Then, starting at base of each ring, gently press ring between thumb and forefinger as you move upward, so it tapers off into a sharp crease at top.
6. Then measure, and, if necessary, reshape rings into these diameters: 2, 2½, 3, 3½, 4, 4½, 5, 5½, 6, 6½, 7, and 7½ inches.
7. Bake the rings 20 to 25 min., or till light-golden, then remove and cool on sheets.
8. Then, with decorating tube No. 4 in paper cone, and Decorating Icing, make zigzag lines around each ring, from outside to inside; also decorate cone-shaped top. When dry, store in tight container.

Before serving time:
On large serving plate, in center of table or buffet, pile up rings, one on the other, having broadest (7½") ring on bottom and graduating up to narrowest one. Top with cone-shaped piece. Garnish, at base, with pine boughs, figures, or candy, chocolate, nuts. In serving, give each guest one of smaller rings, or a piece of a large one. Makes 8 servings.

Decorating Icing: Into 2 egg whites, in bowl, gradually stir about 4 cups confectioners' sugar, till mixture is smooth and spreadable; cover with wax paper.

England

Breakfast is the English meal par excellence. It's hearty, and most often includes toast and an intriguing marmalade.

BREAKFAST MARMALADE

2 large oranges
2 grapefruit
2 lemons

1 qt. water
12 cups granulated sugar

1. Wash oranges, grapefruit, and lemons. Cut each into 6 to 8 wedges, then cut crosswise into thin slices. Combine fruit slices in large kettle; add water, then stir until well blended; let stand in refrigerator or a cool place for 2 or 3 days.
2. Now cook fruit, over low heat, 30 min. Stir in sugar, bring to a boil, while stirring, then cook 15 to 20 min., skimming foam from surface occasionally.
3. Pour into hot, sterilized jelly glasses or jars, then seal each with a thin layer of paraffin. Cover, then store in a cool place. Makes about 4 qt.

Here's a light, lovely oxtail soup, perfect as an introduction to a meal.

OXTAIL SOUP

3 tablesp. salad oil
1 medium oxtail, cut into joints
½ cup sliced leeks
1 large onion, peeled, chopped
½ cup chopped celery
1 bay leaf
¼ teasp. whole dried thyme
4 whole cloves

1 teasp. whole peppercorns
3 teasp. salt
2 medium carrots, pared
½ teasp. cornstarch
2 tablesp. sherry
⅛ teasp. pepper
2 tablesp. snipped parsley

Day before:
1. In salad oil, in medium Dutch oven, brown oxtail, on all sides, for 10 min. Now add leeks, onion, and celery to brown with meat. Turn occasionally until *well* browned—about 10 min. Add 1½ qt. water, bay leaf, thyme, cloves, peppercorns, salt.

2. Simmer, covered, 1 hr. 15 min., then add carrots and simmer 30 min.

3. Strain soup; let cool, then refrigerate. Remove meat from bones, trim off fat, dice meat and carrots, wrap in foil, refrigerate.

About 10 min. before serving:
Skim fat from soup; pour soup into medium saucepan. Blend cornstarch with sherry, add to soup with meat, carrots, and pepper, then bring to boil. Serve in cups, sprinkled with parsley. Makes about 8 servings.

This recipe originated in one of the famous English clubs and we say three cheers, for it is a truly elegant way to serve a leg of lamb. The flavor of the filling-topping can't be surpassed.

ENGLISH LEG OF LAMB NELSON

1 6-lb. leg of lamb	**Purée Soubise Nelson (below)**
Shortening	**Packaged dried bread crumbs**
Salt	**Grated Parmesan cheese**

About 3 hr. before serving:
1. Start heating oven to 325°F. Trim lamb of most of its fat; rub surface with shortening and salt; arrange it in 13" x 9" x 2" glass baking dish. Insert roast-meat thermometer into center of roast, halfway down, without touching bone.

2. Roast lamb about 2½ hr., or until meat thermometer reaches 175°F. Meanwhile make up Purée Soubise Nelson.

3. When meat thermometer reads 175°F., remove roast from oven and turn temperature up to 400°F. Carve lamb, as usual, into ⅓" slices, but don't cut them off the bone. Spoon off all drippings.

4. Spoon some of Purée Soubise Nelson between the slices; then completely cover top and sides of roast with rest of purée. Sprinkle with bread crumbs and Parmesan cheese, dot with shortening. Return to 400°F. oven for 30 min., or until golden.

5. Serve from baking dish, cut into slices, with purée spooned over them. Makes about 10 servings. Good with broccoli or green peas.

PURÉE SOUBISE NELSON: In large skillet, over low heat, melt ¼ cup butter or margarine; blend in 2½ cups chopped onions and 2½ cups raw baking potatoes, pared, diced; then cook, covered, until soft, stirring occasionally—about ½ hr.

Meanwhile make this white sauce: In small saucepan, melt 2 tablesp. butter or margarine; blend in 3 tablesp. all-purpose flour, then add 1 cup light cream, while stirring; bring to a boil and cook a few minutes until thickened. Turn into medium bowl.

Now mash onion mixture until a smooth purée. Stir into white sauce with 1 egg, ¼ cup grated Parmesan cheese, 1½ teasp. salt, ¼ teasp. pepper, and 1½ teasp. crumbled rosemary; blend well. Use as stuffing for English Leg of Lamb Nelson, p. 20.

Europeans have always been partial to variety meats, especially as served in England's Beefsteak-and-Kidney Pie. And there's no doubt it's a delicious, nutritious dish.

BEEFSTEAK-AND-KIDNEY PIE

2½ lb. boned chuck, 3″ thick, trimmed of fat
1 beef kidney
Salt
All-purpose flour
¼ teasp. pepper
⅛ teasp. cayenne

1 large onion, peeled, chopped
¾ cup canned condensed beef broth, undiluted
½ cup shortening
2 to 3 tablesp. water
1 beaten egg

About 3 hr. before serving:
1. Cut chuck into 2″ strips, then cut crosswise into ¼″-thick slices. Flatten slices with a rolling pin. Remove fat from kidney, then cut kidney into small pieces and blend with 1 teasp. salt.
2. Combine ⅓ cup flour, 1 teasp. salt, and the pepper and cayenne. Dip meat slices in flour mixture; then roll up, with 1 or 2 pieces of kidney inside each slice. Place, alternately with onion, in 1½-qt. casserole dish, mounding it slightly. Pour on beef broth. Start heating oven to 400°F.
3. In medium bowl place 1½ cups sifted flour. With pastry blender or 2 knives, scissor-fashion, cut in shortening until like coarse corn meal. Stir in water, then toss quickly together, forming a smooth ball.
4. Roll out pastry ¼″ thick. Cut out a circle, 1″ larger than top of casserole. Cut off this extra inch all around circle. Wet rim of casserole and lay 1″ strip all around top edge. Wet strip lightly, then top with remaining circle. Cut out a little hole in center to allow steam to escape.
5. Use trimmings of dough to cut out diamond-shaped leaves, marking center and side veins with a knife. Arrange around top edge of pie and in center. Brush with beaten egg.
6. Bake 20 min., then lower oven heat to 350°F. and bake 2 hr., or until top is golden-brown and meat is tender. Makes 6 to 8 servings.

Here's a fun recipe (with a Yorkshire Pudding base) that origi-nated in England and is now also well accepted in Australia from one end of the country to the other.

TOAD · IN · THE · HOLE

1¼ cups sifted all-purpose flour
1 teasp. salt
1½ cups milk

2 eggs
1½ lb. sausage links

About 40 min. before serving:
1. Into bowl sift flour and salt; gradually beat in milk, then add eggs, while beating until smooth. Start heating oven to 425°F.
2. In hot skillet fry sausages until brown on all sides; then re-move from drippings and cut in half crosswise.
3. Into 12" x 8" x 2" baking dish pour 2 tablesp. sizzling-hot sausage drippings. Arrange sausage pieces over bottom of dish, then, over them, pour batter. Bake 25 min., or until puffy and golden. Serve at once for brunch or as luncheon main dish. Makes about 6 servings.

In most of England, Yorkshire Pudding is served with roast beef as a main course. But in Yorkshire it is traditionally served with gravy before the roast. In the North it is also sometimes served as dessert with syrup.

YORKSHIRE PUDDING

½ cup plus 2 tablesp. sifted all-purpose flour
½ teasp. salt

2 eggs
1 cup milk
Roast-beef drippings

Just before putting roast beef in oven: Into medium bowl sift flour with salt. Make a well in center of it, then drop in eggs and pour in milk. Beat, with large fork, until smooth. Let stand at room temperature.

When roast beef is done: Remove roast from oven and keep warm. Increase oven heat to 450°F. Pour 3 to 4 tablesp. beef drippings from roasting pan into 9" x 9" x 2" pan. Set in oven until drippings are sizzling hot; then pour batter over them. Bake 20 to 25 min., or until puffy and golden. Cut into squares and serve immediately with roast beef. Makes 4 to 6 servings.

22

Czechoslovakia's Prune-Filled Cookies (Koláčky), page 13
Russia's Easter Bread (Kulich), page 86
Yugoslavia's Raisin-and-Nut Coffeecake (Potica), page 108

Custard is a part of many English menus, particularly when combined with cake as in their Trifle or Tipsy Cake—a sherry-soaked cake.

TRIFLE

1 pkg. regular vanilla pudding and pie filling mix
2½ cups milk
1 7" pkgd. spongecake layer
1 cup sherry

⅓ cup raspberry jam
8 almond macaroons (optional)
1 cup heavy cream, whipped
Glacéed cherries
Slivered almonds

Early on the day:
Make up vanilla pudding as label directs, using 2½ cups milk. Lay wax paper on its surface, then refrigerate until chilled.

About 45 min. before serving:
1. Cut spongecake into quarters, then split each quarter crosswise. Place one slice, cut side up, in each of 8 nappy dishes. Sprinkle evenly with sherry and let soak ½ hr.
2. Spread raspberry jam over cakes, then if desired crumble macaroons over them. Now pour custard sauce over cakes.
3. Garnish top with whipped cream, then decorate with cherries and almonds. Makes 8 servings.

England's "cup of tea" is world famous. Unfortunately, not so well known are these teacakes, chockful of currants.

ENGLISH TEACAKES

1¾ cups sifted all-purpose flour
1½ teasp. double-acting baking powder
¼ teasp. salt
¼ cup soft shortening
¼ cup soft butter or margarine
¾ cup granulated sugar

1 egg
3 tablesp. milk
½ cup chopped citron
½ cup currants or raisins
1 egg white, slightly beaten
Granulated sugar

1. Sift together flour, baking powder, and salt.
2. Mix until creamy shortening, butter or margarine, ¾ cup sugar, and egg. Add milk, citron, currants, and flour mixture; mix well; refrigerate until an easily handled dough.
3. Start heating oven to 400°F. Roll dough into balls the size of walnuts. Dip tops in egg white, then sugar.
4. Place, sugared side up, 2" apart, on greased cookie sheets. Bake 12 to 15 min., or till golden. Cool, then store, tightly covered. Makes about 3 doz.

Finland

Nowhere is summer anticipated with greater zest than in Finland, where it often ends months of cold. So, naturally, that's when Summer Soup gets star billing.

KESAEKEITTO
(*Summer Soup*)

2½ teasp. salt
1 cup sliced raw carrots
1 cup pared, diced raw potatoes
1 lb. fresh peas, shelled
1 cup raw cauliflowerets

¼ lb. fresh spinach, chopped
2 tablesp. flour
3 cups milk
¼ teasp. pepper
Snipped parsley

About 35 min. before serving:
1. In large saucepan place 3 cups water and salt, then bring to a boil. Now add carrots and potatoes; simmer, covered, 10 min.
2. Add peas, cauliflowerets, and spinach and simmer, covered, 10 min. Blend flour with small amount of milk until smooth, add to vegetables with remaining milk, pepper; simmer 5 min.
3. Serve in soup bowls or tureen, sprinkled with snipped parsley. Makes 6 to 8 servings.

The list of fish and the ways to serve Finland's wealth of seafood are almost endless. This is only one of the best.

UUNISSA PAISTETTU HAUKI
(*Baked Stuffed Pike*)

1 2-lb. dressed pike
Salt
Pepper
Butter or margarine
1 small onion, peeled, chopped
1 10-oz. pkg. frozen chopped
  spinach

1 cup cooked rice
1 egg, beaten
1 teasp. seasoned salt
¼ cup lemon juice
⅓ cup pkgd. dried bread crumbs

About 1½ hr. before serving:
1. Sprinkle cavity and outside of fish with salt and pepper. In small skillet melt 2 tablesp. butter or margarine; in it sauté onion until golden. Cook spinach as label directs; drain. Start heating oven to 350°F.
2. In medium bowl combine rice, spinach, sautéed onion, egg,

and seasoned salt. Use to fill cavity of pike, then close opening with toothpicks.
3. Sprinkle fish on all sides with lemon juice, then coat with bread crumbs. In oven, in large, shallow baking dish, melt 3 tablesp. butter; in it lay fish; dot with 3 tablesp. butter or margarine; pour in ¼ cup water.
4. Bake fish 1 hr., or until it is easily flaked with a fork, but is still moist, basting it occasionally with liquid in baking dish, while baking. At table slit fish down either side of backbone to loosen fillets. Makes 6 servings.

The mushrooms that grow wild in Finland's forests are served fresh in summer, and dried in winter. This casserole version goes so well with chicken or fish.

SIENIMUREKE
(Baked Mushrooms)

3 tablesp. butter or margarine	¾ cup light cream
2 small onions, peeled, chopped	2 teasp. salt
2 eggs	¼ teasp. pepper
⅔ cup pkgd. dried bread crumbs	1 lb. fresh mushrooms, coarsely
¾ cup milk	chopped

About 1½ hr. before serving:
1. Start heating oven to 350°F. In medium skillet melt butter or margarine; in it sauté onions until golden.
2. Meanwhile, in 1½-qt. casserole beat eggs, then mix in bread crumbs, milk, cream, salt, and pepper until crumbs have absorbed liquid. Now carefully blend in mushrooms and sautéed onions.
3. Bake 60 to 70 min., or until golden and set. Delicious as a vegetable with broiled chicken or fish. Makes 6 servings.

Only in summertime are cucumbers, tomatoes, lettuce, and radishes plentiful. A freshness of the season is unmistakable in this salad—tangy with dill and sour cream.

KURKKUSALAATTI
(Garden-Crisp Cucumber Salad)

4 medium cucumbers	¼ cup salad oil
Salt	½ teasp. sugar
1 cup commercial sour cream	2 tablesp. snipped fresh dill
1½ tablesp. vinegar	¼ teasp. pepper

Early on the day or 2 hr. before serving:
1. Wash, but do not pare cucumbers. Slice them very thin; place

in bowl with 1 tablesp. salt; mix thoroughly, then refrigerate about 1 hr.

2. Drain *all* water from cucumbers, then, to them, add sour cream, vinegar, salad oil, sugar, dill, 1½ teasp. salt, and pepper, mixing until well blended. Transfer to salad bowl, then refrigerate until serving time. Makes 6 servings.

Big luscious strawberries like those used to cap this Strawberry Snow are dear to Finns and travelers alike.

MANSIKKALUMI
(Strawberry Snow)

2 cups fresh strawberries, washed and cut up	2 egg whites
Granulated sugar	¾ cup heavy cream
	6 whole strawberries

About 15 min. before serving:

1. In medium bowl crush strawberries, then stir in ¼ cup sugar. Beat egg whites until they form soft peaks; then gradually add ¼ cup sugar while beating until stiff.

2. Beat cream until thick. Reserve about ⅓ cup, then fold rest of it, together with beaten egg whites, into strawberries.

3. Spoon into 6 sherbet glasses; top each with a dab of reserved cream; garnish each with a strawberry. Makes 6 servings.

All Scandinavian countries are deft in making melt-in-your-mouth cookies. These double-almond sticks are one of Finland's specials.

SUOMALAISET PUIKOT
(Finnish Sticks)

¾ cup butter or margarine	1 egg, beaten
Granulated sugar	⅓ cup finely chopped, blanched almonds
¾ teasp. almond extract	
2 cups sifted all-purpose flour	

Make one or several days ahead as follows:

1. Start heating oven to 350°F. In small bowl, with electric mixer at medium speed, beat butter with ⅓ cup granulated sugar until creamy. Then beat in almond extract and flour until well blended.

2. On lightly floured board form dough into finger-thick rolls. Cut each roll into 2″ sticks. Arrange them on cookie sheet, then brush with egg and sprinkle with almonds and a little sugar.

3. Bake 15 to 20 min., or until golden. Remove to rack to cool. Store in container. Makes about 4 doz. sticks.

France

We're indebted to the cuisine of Burgundy for this ingenious method of cookery called à la bourguignonne. It's a romantic union of braised beef, onions, and mushrooms in a red wine sauce.

BOEUF À LA BOURGUIGNONNE

5 lb. chuck beef, trimmed of all
    fat, in 2″ cubes
All-purpose flour
Butter or margarine
¼ teasp. pepper
¼ cup cognac
1 2-oz. jar extract-of-meat paste
½ lb. sliced bacon, diced
4 garlic cloves, peeled, minced
2 carrots, pared, coarsely chopped

2 leeks, coarsely chopped
2 cups coarsely chopped onions
Snipped parsley
2 bay leaves
1 teasp. dried thyme
2½ cups Burgundy *
2 lb. small white onions, peeled
Sugar
2 lb. fresh mushrooms
2 teasp. lemon juice

Day before:

1. Roll beef cubes in ⅓ cup flour. In ¼ cup hot butter, in large Dutch oven, brown meat *well* on all sides; sprinkle on pepper; pour on cognac; then ignite with a match. When flame dies out, stir in extract-of-meat paste.

2. Start heating oven to 350°F. To beef, add bacon, garlic, carrots, leeks, chopped onions, 1 tablesp. snipped parsley, bay leaves, thyme, 2 cups Burgundy. Bake, covered, 2 to 2½ hr., or till beef is fork-tender.

3. When meat is fork-tender, remove from Dutch oven. Then put all vegetables and liquid through a coarse strainer or food mill, mashing vegetables as you strain. Return strained liquid and meat to Dutch oven; refrigerate.

About 45 min. before serving:

1. Start reheating meat mixture in Dutch oven over low heat on top of range. Now, in 2 tablesp. hot butter in skillet, brown whole onions well on all sides; add 1 teasp. sugar, ½ cup Burgundy; cook, covered, 15 to 20 min., or till onions are tender,

* One cup sherry may replace 1 cup of the Burgundy.

adding ¼ cup water if needed; add to meat, with liquid and
1 tablesp. sugar.
2. Meanwhile, in 2 tablesp. butter, sauté half of the mushroom
caps till golden on one side; sprinkle with 1 teasp. lemon juice;
turn to brown other side; add to meat mixture. Repeat sautéing
rest of mushrooms; keep warm, uncovered.

To serve:
Pour meat mixture from Dutch oven into 4-qt. casserole or serving dish; garnish with remaining mushroom caps and snipped
parsley. Makes 12 servings.

*A homey French family soup of beef and chicken. They serve
it all together in a soup tureen. Or the soup part may be the
first course, along with crusty rolls; then a platter of the meat
and vegetables comes next.*

POT AU FEU
(*French Meat-and-Vegetable Soup*)

3 lb. soup bones (including 2 or 3 marrow bones)	2 beef-bouillon cubes
2 lb. boned beef chuck	½ teasp. seasoned pepper
1 2-lb. broiler-fryer, cut up	2 medium onions, peeled, cut in half
2 large bay leaves	2 medium carrots, pared, cut in thirds
1 medium onion, peeled	2 parsnips, pared, halved length-wise
6 whole cloves	1 wedge cabbage (about ½ lb.)
1 teasp. whole peppercorns	1 white turnip, pared, quartered
2 tablesp. salt	2 medium leeks, halved length-wise
Several parsley sprigs	Snipped parsley
½ teasp. dried thyme	
1 teasp. seasoned salt	
1 teasp. monosodium glutamate	

Day before:
1. In large kettle place soup bones, chuck, and chicken giblets;
add 3 qt. cold water, bring to a boil, then, with spoon, skim surface till it's clear of any floating particles.
2. Attach bay leaves onto onion with whole cloves; add to broth
with peppercorns, salt, parsley, thyme and simmer, covered, 2 hr.
Then add chicken and simmer ½ hr. Remove kettle from heat,
discard onion, giblets, and soup bones, except marrow bones.
Remove marrow bones, meat, and chicken, strain broth, rinse
kettle; then return broth, meat, chicken, and marrow bones to
kettle; refrigerate.

About 1 hr. and 10 min. before serving:
1. Remove fat from surface of broth.
2. Now add seasoned salt, monosodium glutamate, bouillon
cubes, seasoned pepper, onions, carrots, parsnips, cabbage wedge,

turnip, and leeks; bring to a boil, then simmer, covered, 30 min., or until all vegetables have become fork-tender.
3. Transfer vegetables and chicken to a large soup tureen; cut chuck into serving pieces, then add, along with broth, to tureen. Sprinkle with snipped parsley. Serve in open soup plates with fork, knife, and spoon. If desired, spread marrow on toasted French bread. Makes 6 servings with leftovers for the next day.

This nobly satisfying French classic unites veal, mushrooms, and little onions in a white velvet sauce—whisked to perfection.

BLANQUETTE DE VEAU

2 lb. boned veal or lamb shoulder
4 whole cloves
1 small onion, peeled
1 qt. boiling water
5 medium carrots, scraped, quartered
1 bay leaf
⅛ teasp. dried thyme
2 parsley sprigs
½ cup thinly sliced celery
4 peppercorns
1 tablesp. salt
Butter or margarine

15 small white onions (1 lb.), peeled
½ lb. small fresh mushrooms, washed
½ cup reserved veal stock
¼ cup all-purpose flour
3 cups reserved veal stock
2 egg yolks
2 tablesp. lemon juice
1 tablesp. snipped parsley or fresh dill
Hot fluffy rice or mashed potatoes

About 2½ hr. before serving:
1. Remove membrane and fat from veal; then cut veal into 1¼″ pieces. Simmer veal with clove-studded onion, boiling water, carrots, bay leaf, thyme, parsley sprigs, sliced celery, peppercorns, and salt, in deep saucepan, covered, for 1 hr., or until veal is tender.
2. Drain stock from veal and reserve—there should be 3½ cups. Discard onion, bay leaf, peppercorns, and parsley.
3. Thirty minutes before veal is done, melt ¼ cup butter or margarine in large, heavy skillet; add 15 onions; simmer, tightly covered, over low heat 30 min., or until tender. Then add to drained, cooked veal.
4. Now, in same skillet, cook mushrooms in ½ cup veal stock, uncovered, for 15 min.; then add veal and onions.
5. Next, in same saucepan in which veal cooked, melt 2 tablesp. butter or margarine; stir in flour until smooth. Slowly stir in 3 cups veal stock. Cook over medium heat, stirring, until mixture thickens and comes to boil.
6. With wire whip beat egg yolks slightly with lemon juice. Slowly stir in some of hot sauce. Then slowly stir this into rest of sauce.
7. Add hot sauce to veal with snipped parsley. Heat—do not

boil. Arrange a ring of fluffy rice or mashed potatoes in large, heated, deep platter or casserole. Heap veal in center. Sprinkle with additional parsley if desired. Makes 6 servings.

P.S. May be made day before, refrigerated, then reheated over very low heat.

Surprise "him" with a French dinner that starts off with jellied madrilène, followed by these beef fillets which you serve on French bread toast, topped with mushrooms in wine.

TOURNEDOS MEDICI
(Beef Tenderloin and Mushrooms in Wine)

4½ tablesp. butter or margarine	6 medium fresh mushrooms
2 1"-thick slices French bread	½ teasp. seasoned salt
2 ¾"-thick beef tenderloins	¼ cup port wine
	Snipped parsley

1. In small skillet melt 1½ tablesp. butter or margarine. In it brown French bread slices on both sides; then arrange them on heated platter.
2. To butter left in skillet add 2 tablesp. butter; in it sauté beef tenderloins about 2 to 3 min. per side, or until of desired rareness. Then remove tenderloins and arrange on French bread.
3. To butter left in skillet, add 1 tablesp. more butter, then mushrooms, thinly sliced; sprinkle with seasoned salt; then sauté until golden.
4. Now add port wine; stir well; then cook 1 min. Arrange mushroom slices between tenderloins. Then spoon sauce over both tenderloins and mushrooms. Garnish with parsley. Makes 2 servings.

This de-luxe version of the French sauerkraut boiled dinner will be especially welcome on one of those wintry nights.

CHOUCROUTE À L'ALSACIENNE

2 onions	9 cups drained canned sauerkraut
8 whole cloves	(2 1-lb.-13-oz. cans plus 1 1-lb.-
2 or 3 slices fat salt pork	4-oz. can)
2 pared carrots	1 tablesp. lard or shortening
1 2-lb. piece bacon	3 chicken-bouillon cubes, dis-
1 2-lb. smoked boneless shoulder	solved in 3 cups boiling water
butt	1½ cups white wine
10 whole peppercorns	8 medium potatoes, pared
8 juniper berries (optional)	1 lb. frankfurters

1. Stud each onion with 4 cloves. In large kettle, arrange onions,

salt pork, carrots, bacon, shoulder butt. Tie peppercorns and juniper berries together in small piece of cheesecloth; place in kettle. Cover all with sauerkraut; drop in lard. Pour bouillon and wine over all.

2. Bring mixture to boil; then cook, covered, over low heat 2 to 3 hr., or until shoulder butt is fork-tender.

3. Meanwhile, cook potatoes until tender—about 45 min. Heat frankfurters in water, just below boiling point, 5 to 8 min.

4. To serve sauerkraut, remove cheesecloth bag from kettle; discard. Remove bacon, butt; cut each into 8 slices. Drain sauerkraut; arrange on large platter with meat slices and frankfurters on top. Slice carrots; use to garnish platter. Pass potatoes separately. Also, if desired, pass liquid from kettle. Makes 8 servings.

Try these sautéed apples the next time you're having pork. Their tart-sweetness makes them a nice foil.

POMMES SAUTÉES
(*Apples Sauté*)

3 tablesp. butter or margarine	4 cups chopped unpared red apples

In skillet, melt butter; add apples and sauté until pink and soft, 5 to 10 min., stirring occasionally. Makes 4 to 6 servings.

The French family's casseroles work miracles with braised meats and stews. Here, a loin of pork, when partly roasted, is laid over a bed of seasoned raw potato slices, then returned to the oven where both bake to delectable tenderness.

RÔTI DE PORC À LA BOULANGÈRE
(*Roast Loin of Pork à la Boulangère*)

1 5-lb. pork loin, center cut	1 tablesp. seasoned salt
1 clove garlic, peeled, cut	⅛ teasp. pepper
1 teasp. salt	½ cup boiling water
10 cups thinly sliced potatoes	3 tablesp. melted butter or margarine
1 cup coarsely chopped onion	
2 teasp. snipped parsley	Snipped parsley

1. Start heating oven to 425°F. Trim loin free of all but thin layer of fat.

2. Rub pork with cut garlic and salt. Place pork, fat side up, on rack in shallow open roasting pan (or large shallow earthenware casserole).

3. Insert roast-meat thermometer through fat side of pork into center (don't let it touch bone).

4. Roast pork 1 hr. at 425°F. Then reduce oven temperature to 400°F.; remove pork and rack from roasting pan; pour off all fat.
5. In roasting pan, toss potatoes with onion, 2 teasp. snipped parsley, seasoned salt, pepper; pour in boiling water; lay pork on top; then brush potatoes with butter.
6. Roast all about 1 hr., or to 185°F. on roast-meat thermometer.
7. On heated platter, arrange roast; serve potatoes in vegetable dish, sprinkled with parsley. (If casserole was used, serve pork and potatoes from it.) Nice with Pommes Sautées, p. 31. Makes 6 servings.

More than one great chef has built his reputation on fish fillets poached in white-wine sauce. You can, too, if you follow these directions to the letter.

FILETS DE POISSON DUGLÉRÉ
(Superb Poached Fish with Tomato)

1½ lb. fish fillets *
1 teasp. salt
⅛ teasp. pepper
1 clove garlic, peeled (optional)
1 tablesp. butter or margarine
1 medium onion, peeled, minced
2 shallots, peeled, minced
¾ cup well-drained canned tomatoes

Snipped parsley
¼ cup white wine or ¼ cup water plus ½ teasp. lemon juice
¼ cup light cream
1 tablesp. soft butter or margarine
1 teasp. flour
Snipped parsley

1. Set out large skillet (about 10″) with cover. Tear or cut circle of wax paper to fit skillet; tear small hole in center; set aside. Sprinkle fish with salt and pepper. Stick toothpick in garlic.
2. In 10″ skillet, melt 1 tablesp. butter; add onion, shallots, garlic; top with fish, tomatoes, then 1 tablesp. snipped parsley; pour in wine. On fish, lay paper circle.
3. Bring to boil; cover, cook over high heat 5 to 10 min., or until fish is easily flaked with fork *but still moist.* Remove cover, paper, garlic.
4. Pour cream around fish. Mix 1 tablesp. butter with flour; stir into cream; move skillet in circular motion to combine and thicken sauce. Spoon some sauce onto fish; sprinkle with parsley. Serve from skillet.

PLATTER STYLE: Make as in steps 1, 2, and 3; then to broil-and-serve platter or shallow casserole, gently remove fish, with tomatoes on top. Into skillet, pour cream mixed with 1 egg yolk, then butter-flour mixture. Cook over medium heat, stirring, till thickened; season if needed. Pour sauce over fish; if desired, broil until golden.

* Use bass, cod, flounder, haddock, pompano, perch, or sole.

To assure delicacy of flavor and tenderness in veal kidneys do them this French way, sautéing them quickly, while tossing, just until all red color is gone.

ROGNONS DE VEAU FLAMBÉS
(Veal Kidneys Aflame)

4 veal kidneys	⅛ teasp. freshly ground black
4 large mushrooms	pepper
2 tablesp. sweet (unsalted) butter	⅛ teasp. dry mustard
2 tablesp. brandy	2 tablesp. heavy cream
½ teasp. salt	

1. Slice kidneys ¼″ thick; then with scissors, snip out white fat and discard it.
2. Slice mushrooms. Next, in skillet, melt butter; in it sauté kidneys quickly, while tossing, just until all red color is gone; then remove kidneys from skillet.
3. Now, in same skillet, sauté mushrooms about 5 min.; then remove them. Then cook down liquid left in skillet until almost evaporated.
4. Meanwhile, in small saucepan, gently warm brandy.
5. Return kidneys to skillet; pour warm brandy over them, then with match carefully light brandy. Let flame burn out; then stir in sautéed mushrooms, salt, pepper, and mustard.
6. When kidney mixture is well mixed, remove it to heated platter. Into skillet pour heavy cream, and heat. Pour cream over kidneys; serve. Makes 4 servings.

The French cuisine without potatoes is unthinkable. And a traditional favorite you'll enjoy is their Potato Pie with its flaky lining and top, that's served hot with cold meat, or cold, the next day with salad.

PÂTÉ DE POMMES DE TERRE
(Potato Pie)

2¼ cups sifted all-purpose flour	2 teasp. salt
1¼ teasp. salt	⅛ teasp. pepper
1 tablesp. sugar	1 large onion, peeled, thinly
½ cup shortening	sliced
¼ cup butter or margarine	1 tablesp. snipped parsley
About 3½ tablesp. water	2 tablesp. butter or margarine
7 cups pared potatoes, thinly	Milk
sliced (6 medium)	1 cup heavy cream

1. Start heating oven to 375°F.
2. Into medium bowl, sift flour, 1¼ teasp. salt, sugar.
3. With 2 knives or pastry blender, cut in shortening until mix-

ture is as fine as corn meal; then, cut in ¼ cup butter until particles are pea-size.

4. Sprinkle water, a little at a time, over mixture, mixing thoroughly with a fork; when mixture forms dough that leaves sides of bowl clean, pick it up and press gently into smooth ball; wrap in wax paper and set aside.

5. Toss potatoes with 2 teasp. salt, pepper, onion, and parsley.

6. Roll out one half of pastry so it is about 1½″ larger and same shape as 1½-qt. shallow baking dish; fit pastry into dish; fill with potato mixture; top with 2 tablesp. butter; then trim pastry even with edge of dish.

7. Roll out rest of pastry; lay over potatoes. Trim it so it extends 1″ beyond edge of dish; fold it under bottom crust; press firmly together in stand-up rim; make rope or fluted edge; cut few slits in top. Brush with a little milk.

8. Bake 1 to 1¼ hr., or until potatoes are tender when tested with knife. Remove from oven; make small hole in crust; pour in cream (a baster works well). Let stand few minutes; then serve. Makes 6 to 8 servings.

For 3 or 4 servings: For pastry use: 1½ cups sifted all-purpose flour, 1 teasp. salt, 2 teasp. sugar, ⅓ cup shortening, 3 tablesp. butter, about 2½ tablesp. water. For filling, use half of ingredients used above. Make as directed, using 8″ pie plate; bake at 350°F. 1 to 1¼ hr.

Here's a soup—a Mediterranean fish soup—that's one of the unique food specialties of France. If you like fish, you'll love Bouillabaisse—a meal in itself.

BOUILLABAISSE

1 1-lb. live lobster (or 1 6-oz. can lobster meat)
1 lb. fresh shrimp
2 lb. haddock, cut into 2″ pieces
2 doz. small hard-shell clams
Liquid from steaming clams, plus boiling water to make 4 cups
1 cup drained canned or thawed frozen King-crab meat
½ cup salad oil or olive oil
1 large clove garlic, peeled, minced
1 teasp. dried thyme
½ teasp. saffron
2 bay leaves
1 tablesp. salt
½ teasp. fennel seeds (optional)
Speck cayenne pepper
1 medium onion, chopped
1 leek, sliced
6 tomatoes, peeled, cut up
1 cup dry white wine
Snipped parsley
Cubes French bread, toasted

1. Order lobster cleaned and split, with claws cracked and removed from body; snip lobster, through shell, into 2″ pieces. Shell and devein uncooked shrimp.

2. Remove bones from haddock. Open clams by steaming in

small amount of water; remove top shells. Place haddock bones in kettle with clam liquid and water. Cook, covered, 10 min.; strain and reserve stock. Look over crab meat for membrane to discard.

3. In Dutch oven, heat salad oil. Meanwhile, in small bowl, combine garlic, thyme, saffron, bay leaves, salt, fennel seeds, cayenne, onion, and leek.

4. In Dutch oven, layer haddock, lobster, shrimp, clams, crab meat, and tomatoes, sprinkling each layer with garlic mixture and wine.

5. Simmer 10 min., *carefully* stirring occasionally with fork. Add reserved fish stock and simmer, uncovered, 20 min.

6. Serve bouillabaisse, sprinkled with parsley, right from Dutch oven or in heated casserole or tureen. Arrange French bread in basket. Provide small dishes for shells. Guests dunk French bread cubes into their plates of bouillabaisse. Makes 10 to 12 servings.

In France, scallops are usually sold in the shells, these shells making attractive individual serving dishes. We can use ramekins or the like.

COQUILLES SAINT-JACQUES
(Scallops, Baked in Shells)

¾ cup water
¼ cup sauterne
½ teasp. salt
Few grains cayenne
1 pt. sea scallops
2 tablesp. butter or margarine
1 small onion, peeled, minced

2 tablesp. flour
½ clove garlic, peeled, minced
1 teasp. snipped parsley
1 egg yolk, well beaten
¾ cup buttered tiny fresh bread crumbs
2 tablesp. grated Parmesan cheese

1. Start heating oven to 425°F. In skillet, combine water, wine, salt, cayenne; in it simmer scallops 5 min.; drain, reserve liquid. Coarsely chop scallops (or try snipping them with kitchen shears).

2. In hot butter in same skillet, sauté onion until tender; stir in flour well; stir in reserved liquid and cook until thickened. Add garlic and parsley, and, stirring constantly, cook 5 min.

3. Now, gradually stir some of sauce into beaten egg yolk; then, into remaining sauce, gradually stir egg yolk mixture. Add scallops; heat gently.

4. Into 5 buttered 6" pie plates or into scallop shells spoon scallop mixture. Top with crumbs and cheese; bake until brown—about 5 min. Makes 5 servings.

For salad, the French like to serve tender-crisp green beans tossed with a bit of fresh tomato, hard-cooked egg, onions, and a skillfully seasoned vinaigrette dressing.

SALADE AUX HARICOTS
(Green-Bean Salad)

1 lb. green beans	1 onion, peeled, chopped
3 tablesp. salad oil	2 tablesp. chopped pickles
2 teasp. vinegar	2 tablesp. snipped parsley
⅛ teasp. pepper	2 teasp. bottled capers, chopped
¾ teasp. salt	1 hard-cooked egg, shelled,
½ teasp. prepared mustard	chopped
1 small tomato, chopped	

1. Wash, trim, then halve green beans crosswise. Cook until tender-crisp; drain, cool.
2. Combine salad oil, vinegar, pepper, salt, mustard. Then add tomato, onion, pickles, parsley, capers, egg.
3. Toss beans with dressing; refrigerate. Delicious with cold meat or chicken. Makes 4 servings.

Sometimes called "Burnt Cream," this chilled French custard is topped with brown sugar, which you caramelize under the broiler. Served with a wreath of cut-up fresh fruits—it's really fabulous.

CRÈME BRÛLÉE AUX FRUITS
(Crème Brûlée with Fruits)

3 cups heavy cream	½ cup brown sugar, sifted
6 egg yolks	2 to 3 cups strawberries or cut-up
6 tablesp. granulated sugar	pineapple or peaches or a mix-
1 teasp. vanilla extract	ture of all 3

Day before:
1. In bottom of double boiler, heat cream till scalded. In double-boiler top, beat egg yolks with granulated sugar. Slowly stir cream into yolks.
2. Cook mixture over hot, not boiling, water until it coats spoon. Add vanilla. Refrigerate in 1- to 1½-qt. ovenware casserole or flat baking dish.

Just before serving:
1. Over custard, sprinkle brown sugar.
2. Set custard dish in pan; surround with ice cubes. Broil custard till sugar caramelizes—about 1 min.
3. Breaking brown-sugar crust by tapping with spoon, serve at once over fruits, in nappy dishes or sherbet glasses. Or arrange Crème Brûlée in center of large chop plate with fruits arranged around it. Guests help themselves. Makes 6 servings.

Dessert? Chocolate Mousse. Light! Superb! Some brandy, coffee, eggs, whip, whip, chill—mousse.

MOUSSE AU CHOCOLAT
(Chocolate Mousse)

6 sq. semisweet chocolate
3 tablesp. water
2 tablesp. instant coffee
5 egg whites

¼ cup granulated sugar
5 egg yolks
1 tablesp. brandy

Early on the day:
1. In double boiler, melt over hot, *not boiling*, water, the chocolate, water, and coffee, stirring occasionally. Cool slightly.
2. Meanwhile, in large bowl beat egg whites until frothy; then gradually add sugar, while beating stiff.
3. Into chocolate mixture, blend yolks, one at a time, then brandy. Then fold into egg whites.
4. Spoon into sherbet glasses; refrigerate at least 4 hr. Makes 6 servings.

Baba au Rhum may have seemed to call for a bit of cookery courage. But, in truth, it's just a rich yeast-citron or currant dough which, after baking, absorbs the fragrant rum sauce in which it steeps.

BABA AU RHUM

2 pkg. active dry, or cakes, yeast
½ cup warm water
4 cups sifted all-purpose flour
6 eggs, beaten
⅔ cup melted butter or margarine

¼ cup granulated sugar
1 teasp. salt
⅔ cup currants or cut-up citron
Rum Sauce, p. 38
Apricot Glaze, p. 38 (optional)

Make at least 6 hr. before serving:
1. Grease a 4"-deep 10" tube pan or a 4-qt. mold. Sprinkle yeast onto warm water in measuring cup; let stand 5 min. Meanwhile, measure flour into a large bowl.
2. Stir up yeast, combine with beaten eggs, pour onto flour, mix together, then beat thoroughly about 1 min. Let stand, covered, 30 min.
3. Now gradually add butter, one fourth at a time, working it in with spoon or fork. Dough will ooze butter, but don't worry. Stir in sugar, salt, and citron or currants. Knead dough smooth in bowl with blending fork or wooden spoon.
4. Turn dough into tube pan or mold and spread until even. Let rise in warm place (80°F. to 85°F.) until tripled in bulk and almost to top of pan.

5. Meanwhile, start heating oven to 375°F. Bake Baba 40 to 45 min., or until a rich golden-brown. Remove to rack, cool. Set on platter; spoon on Rum Sauce, let stand 2 hr., occasionally spooning on sauce from platter.

6. Just before serving, spread with Apricot Glaze. Serve, cut in 1″ slices. Makes about 28 servings.

RUM SAUCE: In a small saucepan, simmer 1½ cups granulated sugar, 2 cups water, 4 thin orange slices, and 4 thin lemon slices for about 5 min.; allow to cool. Add ½ to 1 cup white rum as desired.

APRICOT GLAZE: Press ⅓ cup apricot jam through strainer and combine it with 1 tablesp. lemon juice.

To make a small Baba or individual Babas: Grease a 3½″-deep 9″ tube pan or 18 2½″ cups of muffin pans. Proceed as directed for larger Baba, halving all ingredients. Bake the 9″ Baba at 375°F. for about 35 min., or the individual Babas at 375°F. 15 to 18 min. When cool, spoon half recipe for Rum Sauce over Baba, then glaze (if desired) with Apricot Glaze.

Fruit Tart is spectacular but not difficult—just rows of radiant fruit on a custard-topped quick puff pastry.

TARTE AUX FRUITS
(*Fruit Tart*)

2 cups sifted all-purpose flour	1½ cups milk
¼ teasp. salt	½ cup heavy cream
1 cup butter, in small pieces	1 1-lb.-4-oz. can pineapple slices
1 8-oz. pkg. cream cheese, in small pieces	1 17-oz. can cling-peach slices
1 beaten egg	1 pt. fresh strawberries, hulled
1 pkg. vanilla-pudding and pie-filling mix	¼ cup granulated sugar

Day before:
In large bowl blend flour with salt. With fingers rub in butter till crumbly, then rub in cream cheese thoroughly until smooth and free of streaks. Form into a ball, wrap in wax paper, refrigerate.

Early on day:
1. Start heating oven to 425°F. Lightly flour a cookie sheet. Cut off about ⅔ of chilled pastry dough; roll it out on cookie sheet into a 15″ x 13″ rectangle. Brush edges with beaten egg.

2. On floured board roll out rest of pastry dough ⅛″ thick. With pastry wheel cut into 1″-wide strips. Use part of these strips to outline top edges of rectangle, placing strips end to end. Brush with egg.

3. With rest of strips form 4 to 6 two-looped "bows," then place

at corners of rectangle and on long edges; brush with egg. With fork prick bottom of pastry well. Bake about 12 min., or until golden. Then cool on sheet.

4. Prepare vanilla-pudding mix as label directs, using only 1½ cups milk. Lay wax paper on its surface; refrigerate.

About 30 min. before serving:

1. Whip cream until stiff. Beat vanilla pudding until creamy; fold in whipped cream; spread evenly over bottom of pastry.

2. Drain pineapple and peaches, reserving ½ cup juice. Cut pineapple slices into quarters, strawberries into lengthwise slices.

3. In small saucepan simmer ½ cup reserved fruit juice with sugar 10 to 15 min., or until slightly thickened. Meanwhile, arrange strawberries, pineapple, and peaches alternately over custard, overlapping slightly. Use syrup to brush on fruit. Serve, cut into 12 squares.

P.S. You may substitute fresh fruit in season for canned fruit. Sprinkle with confectioners' sugar, instead of brushing with sugar syrup.

This is how your "banquet" should end. Made of crushed pralines, and whipped into a cool cloud, it's a velvet masterpiece!

SOUFFLÉ PRALINÉ
(Praline Soufflé)

1½ cups granulated sugar	1 cup milk
½ teasp. cream of tartar	4 egg whites
½ cup cold water	3 cups heavy cream
1 cup blanched whole almonds	Decorating bag
2 env. unflavored gelatine	Tube no. 30
⅔ cup boiling water	¼ cup heavy cream
2 tablesp. rum	Small bunches green grapes
4 egg yolks	Tangerines

Day before, or early on the day:

1. Prepare praline mixture as follows: In saucepan combine sugar, cream of tartar, cold water, and almonds. Cook, without stirring, until a dark molasses color, shaking pan occasionally.

2. Meanwhile, butter a cookie sheet well. When praline mixture is cooked, pour out at once onto cookie sheet. Let cool and harden at room temperature.

3. Now run spatula under praline to loosen it from cookie sheet; break some of it into electric-blender container; turn on high speed until powdered, then turn into bowl; repeat until all praline is powdered. (Or pound praline fine by placing it in folded wax paper and pounding with a hammer.)

4. Now fold a 30″ length of foil, 12″ wide, in half lengthwise, then wrap around outside of 1½-qt. china soufflé dish, so a collar, at least 3″ high, stands above rim; fasten with cellophane tape.

5. Place gelatine in large mixing bowl; add boiling water, then beat with egg beater until light and frothy. With same beater, beat in rum, egg yolks, milk, and 3 cups powdered praline.
6. Beat egg whites until stiff, but not dry; fold into praline mixture along with 3 cups cream, whipped. Carefully turn into prepared soufflé dish. Refrigerate until just before serving—at least 3 hr. or longer.

Just before serving:
1. Remove foil band from soufflé dish.
2. In decorating bag, with tube no. 30, and ¼ cup heavy cream, whipped, press out small half moons all around top outer edge of soufflé.
3. Gently press remaining powdered praline all around sides of soufflé.
4. Garnish with green grapes and sectioned tangerines. Makes 12 servings.

As soon as these delicate almond cookies come out of the oven, the French quickly bend each one over a rolling pin, so it takes on the shape of a curved tile (tuile).

FRENCH TUILES
(Rolled Cookies, Like Tiles On A Roof)

¾ cup (5 or 6) egg whites, unbeaten
1⅔ cups granulated sugar
¼ teasp. salt
¾ cup lukewarm melted butter or margarine

¼ cup lukewarm melted shortening
1 cup sifted all-purpose flour
¾ cup finely chopped blanched almonds

1. Start heating oven to 350°F. Beat egg whites with sugar and salt until sugar is dissolved, mixture thick. Add melted butter and shortening; beat well. Add flour and almonds; mix well.
2. Drop by level tablespoonfuls, 5″ apart, onto ungreased cookie sheets. Bake 8 to 10 min., or until done.
3. Let cookies stand ½ min.; then quickly and gently remove, one at a time, and mold into half circle over rolling pin. Makes about 5 doz.
NOTE: Bake only a few cookies at a time. If they harden before you can mold them, soften them in oven. These keep a week or so.

Germany

Most people consider sauerbraten and red cabbage the most typical of German dishes. They boast of an intriguing sweet-sour flavor.

SAUERBRATEN

1½ cups vinegar
½ cup sweet red wine
1 cup water
2 tablesp. granulated sugar
1 teasp. whole peppercorns
4 bay leaves
3 onions
18 whole cloves
1 teasp. mustard seeds
Salt

4 lb. rump or chuck beef
2 tablesp. flour
⅛ teasp. pepper
¼ cup shortening
1 onion, peeled, sliced
½ teasp. mustard seeds
⅓ cup gingersnap crumbs
½ cup commercial sour cream
  (optional)

1. Two to four days before serving, combine vinegar, wine, water, sugar, ½ teasp. peppercorns, bay leaves, 3 onions, peeled and sliced, 12 cloves, 1 teasp. mustard seeds, 2 teasp. salt in a large bowl.
2. Set the beef in this pickling mixture or marinade, then let stand, covered, in refrigerator 2 to 4 days, turning meat each day. (If you like a sour sauerbraten, let meat stand 4 days.)
3. At the end of the pickling process, remove beef and dry it *well* on paper towels. (Save marinade until gravy time.) Combine flour, 1½ teasp. salt, and pepper; then coat meat on all sides with it.
4. Brown meat *well* on all sides in hot shortening in Dutch oven. This will take 15 to 20 min.
5. Now add ¾ cup reserved marinade, 1 onion, peeled, sliced, ½ teasp. mustard seeds, 6 cloves, ½ teasp. whole peppercorns. Cover tightly; simmer slowly 3½ to 4 hr., or until tender, adding ¼ cup marinade, if needed.
6. When done, remove pot roast to hot platter, slicing it beforehand, if desired; keep warm.
7. Strain drippings from Dutch oven into small bowl; let stand about 2 min. to settle. Remove all fat from surface, then return to Dutch oven.
8. Into drippings stir gingersnap crumbs. Slowly stir in 1 cup strained reserved marinade. Cook, stirring, until thickened.
9. Stir in sour cream; heat, but *do not boil*. Season if needed; then spoon some gravy over meat; pass rest. Makes 8 to 10 servings.

Veal in all forms is a most popular dish. Here it's combined with potato dumplings, also dear to the German heart.

KALBSNIERENBRATEN MIT KARTOFFEL-KLOESSEN
(Rolled Stuffed Veal Roast with Potato Dumplings)

1 boned breast of veal, stuffed with 2 veal kidneys, rolled, then tied (about 3½ lb.)	All-purpose flour
	2 teasp. paprika
	2 bay leaves
4 teasp. seasoned salt	6 whole cloves
2 teasp. onion salt	1 teasp. dried rosemary
Shortening	1 teasp. dried basil
1 medium carrot, pared, cut in half	Fried Onion Rings, below
	Potato Dumplings, below
1 large onion, peeled	

About 2½ hr. before serving:

1. Rub veal with seasoned salt and onion salt. In large Dutch oven heat 3 tablesp. shortening; in it brown veal, carrot, and onion on all sides, then remove them from Dutch oven. Then, into remaining drippings, stir 3 tablesp. flour and paprika and brown lightly.

2. Now add bay leaves, cloves, rosemary, basil, and 4 cups water and bring to a boil, while stirring constantly. Return veal, carrot, and onion to Dutch oven, then cook, covered, 2 hr., or until veal is fork-tender.

3. Meanwhile make Fried Onion Rings. Also, about 1 hr. before veal is done, start Potato Dumplings.

4. When veal is done, remove string, then cut it into ½″ slices and arrange along center of heated large serving platter. With slotted spoon remove dumplings from kettle, arrange beside veal with onion rings over them. Strain gravy; spoon part over meat, pass rest. Makes 6 servings.

FRIED ONION RINGS: Cut 1 medium onion, peeled, into thin rings; flour well; then sauté in salad oil, in medium skillet, until golden. Drain on paper towel; keep warm.

POTATO DUMPLINGS:

2 lb. white potatoes	⅛ teasp. nutmeg
Salt	Butter or margarine
1½ cups sifted all-purpose flour	2 slices white bread, cut into small cubes
2 eggs, beaten	
½ teasp. pepper	

About 1 hr. before serving:

1. Cook potatoes in their jackets, in plenty of boiling salted water, until tender. Drain, then let cool slightly.

2. Peel potatoes, then force through a potato ricer. In large

bowl combine potatoes, flour, eggs, 1½ teasp. salt, pepper, and nutmeg until *well* blended.

3. In skillet melt 2 tablesp. butter; in it sauté bread cubes until golden. Shape potato mixture into about 2″ balls, wrapping a few bread cubes into center of each.

4. Drop dumplings into plenty of boiling salted water. Then cook, uncovered, 10 to 15 min., or until done. With slotted spoon transfer to platter. Makes about 17 dumplings.

P.S. Steps 1 through 3 may be done ahead of time and dumplings refrigerated until ready to cook.

This substantial meat pie is popular in Germany, as well as in Switzerland, where they feast on it hot or cold.

FLEISCHPASTETE
(*Meat Pie*)

¾ cup butter or margarine	¼ teasp. pepper
2 cups sifted all-purpose flour	2 teasp. Worcestershire
½ lb. ground pork	½ teasp. dried basil
½ lb. ground veal	1 tablesp. Madeira or brandy
1 small onion, peeled, chopped	2 eggs, separated
¼ cup snipped parsley	½ lb. cooked ham slices
¾ teasp. salt	1 egg, beaten

About 1 hr. and 45 min. before serving:

1. With pastry blender or two knives, scissor-fashion, cut butter into flour until like coarse corn meal; add 3 tablesp. water; toss quickly together, forming a smooth ball. Roll out part of this pastry to line 9″ pie plate; then trim pastry even with edge. Start heating oven to 375°F.

2. Thoroughly combine pork, veal, onion, parsley, salt, pepper, Worcestershire, basil, Madeira, and egg yolks. Beat egg whites until stiff; fold into meat mixture. Arrange half of ham on bottom of pie shell; on it place meat mixture, mounding it slightly, then rest of ham slices. Brush edge of pastry with beaten egg.

3. Roll part of remaining pastry into a 10″ circle. Use to top pie; press edges of bottom and top crust together; brush with egg. Roll out rest of pastry; with pastry wheel cut into several ¾″-wide strips. Lay, lattice-fashion, on top of crust and all around edge; brush with egg. Bake 60 min., or until golden, and meat is done. Serve, cut into 12 to 16 wedges, for lunch or at a buffet supper.

P.S. This pie is delicious served cold, too!

Europe

German menus are full of dumplings, potato pancakes, and well-made breads—all deservedly so.

POTATO PANCAKES

5 tablesp. flour	1 egg, unbeaten
1½ lb. pared, raw white potatoes	1 teasp. salt
1 small onion, peeled, grated	⅛ teasp. pepper

Shortly before serving time, measure flour into bowl. Then grate potatoes, on *very* fine grater, into it; stir in rest of ingredients. Grease medium skillet lightly. Place over medium heat. Drop potato mixture, by heaping tablespoons, into *hot* skillet. Fry until crisp and golden-brown on underside. Turn; brown on other side, adding more shortening as needed. Drain on paper towels.

Serve with sauerbraten and red cabbage, or with pot roast or shortribs. Makes about 16 pancakes.

Many have a special affection for the hearty potato salad of the Germans. Served hot, it's "wonderfully good."

WARMER KARTOFFELSALAT
(Hot Potato Salad)

2 lb. medium white potatoes	2 teasp. granulated sugar
8 slices lean bacon	3 beef-bouillon cubes
1 large onion, peeled, chopped	½ cup water
⅓ cup vinegar	2 to 3 tablesp. salad oil
1½ teasp. salt	Snipped parsley
¼ teasp. pepper	

About 45 min. before serving:
1. Cook potatoes in plenty of boiling salted water until just tender—15 to 20 min. Drain, let stand a few minutes or until cool enough to handle, then peel, cut into ¼" thick slices and place in a salad bowl.
2. In skillet fry bacon until crisp; remove, crumble, then add to potatoes. To fat in skillet add onion and cook until transparent. Next add vinegar, salt, pepper, sugar, bouillon cubes, and water.
3. Bring to a boil, while stirring and dissolving bouillon cubes. Pour, with salad oil, over potatoes; toss together carefully. Sprinkle with parsley. Makes 4 to 6 servings.

ROTKOHL MIT ÄPFEL
(*Red Cabbage with Apples*)

1 2½-lb. red cabbage, shredded	¼ cup vinegar
¾ cup boiling water	1½ teasp. flour
3 large cooking apples, pared, cored, sliced	¼ cup brown sugar, packed
	2 teasp. salt
3 tablesp. melted butter or margarine	Dash pepper

1. Put shredded cabbage in kettle. Add water; cook, covered, 10 min.
2. Add apples; cook, covered, 10 min., or until tender.
3. Combine butter, vinegar, flour, sugar, salt, pepper; add to cabbage-apple mixture. Makes 4 to 6 servings.

Frankfurters (from Frankfurt, Germany), sauerkraut, Westphalian ham, potato pancakes, and these wonderful thick soft pretzels are all German specialties.

KÜMMEL KRINGEL
(*Caraway Pretzels*)

¼ cup butter or margarine	¼ cup warm water
1¾ cups milk, scalded	1 egg, unbeaten
5 cups sifted all-purpose flour	1 tablesp. caraway seeds
1 teasp. salt	1 tablesp. flour
1 tablesp. sugar	1 egg, slightly beaten
1 pkg. active dry, or cake, yeast	2 to 3 tablesp. caraway seeds

About 3 hr. before serving:
1. Melt butter in scalded milk in large bowl; let milk cool to lukewarm. Sift together 5 cups flour, salt, and sugar. Sprinkle or crumble yeast onto warm water; stir until dissolved.
2. With electric mixer at medium speed, mix unbeaten egg and dissolved yeast with lukewarm milk. Next, mix in flour mixture, a little at a time, then 1 tablesp. caraway seeds; beat until well blended.
3. Sprinkle about 1 tablesp. flour over dough. Then cover with clean towel, and let rise in warm place (80°F. to 85°F.) until doubled. Meanwhile, grease two large cookie sheets.
4. When dough is doubled, turn onto lightly floured surface; knead until smooth. Now, with palms of hands, roll dough into 12″ roll; then cut it into twelve pieces of equal size.
5. With palms of hands, roll one dough piece into a long roll 26″ x ½″. With one end of roll in each hand, cross ends twice, about 3″ down; then tuck these ends under the curve in front of you, to complete a pretzel shape. Repeat with rest of dough pieces.

6. Then lay two pretzels in large skillet, three fourths full of boiling water. Let them sink, then rise to the surface of the water. Then lift out with slotted pancake turner; place on greased cookie sheet, and gently press into original shape. Repeat with rest of pretzels.

7. Now, brush top surface of all pretzels with slightly beaten egg; then sprinkle lightly with 2 to 3 tablesp. caraway seeds.

8. While pretzels rise in a warm place until doubled, start heating oven to 400°F. Bake pretzels 15 to 20 min., or until a nice brown. Remove to cake racks where they will keep warm.

9. Serve pretzels warm, with butter, cheese, jam, or a crisp salad. Makes 12.

Similar to our poundcake, yet different. This delectable "plain cake" is as basic to the German menu as a little black dress is to the Parisian wardrobe.

NAPFKUCHEN
(*German Bundt Cake*)

Butter or margarine	2 teasp. double-acting baking
Blanched almonds	powder
1 cup granulated sugar	¼ teasp. salt
1 cup confectioners' sugar	1 teasp. vanilla extract
4 eggs, separated	Grated rind 1 lemon
3 cups sifted cake flour	1 cup milk

Make 1 or 2 days ahead as follows:

1. Start heating oven to 325°F. Grease well 10″ heavy cast aluminum bundt-cake pan. Put dabs of butter into creases of pan. Place an almond into each.

2. In large bowl, with electric mixer at medium speed, beat 1 cup butter until creamy. Sift together granulated sugar and confectioners' sugar; beat into butter until smooth. Next add egg yolks, one at a time, and beat until very light and fluffy—about 10 min.

3. Meanwhile, sift together flour, baking powder, and salt three times. Into butter mixture beat vanilla extract and grated lemon rind.

4. Now beat in flour mixture and milk alternately, starting and ending with flour. Beat egg whites until stiff; carefully fold into batter. Turn batter into prepared pan, then bake 1 hr. 15 min., or until cake tester, inserted in center, comes out clean.

5. Cool in pan 15 min., then turn out on rack; cool; wrap; store. Serve, cut into wedges.

Christmas cookies in Germany are a tasty store in themselves—
pfeffernüsse, anise drops, lebkuchen, and these delightful leckerli.

LECKERLI

2 cups sifted cake flour	1 egg
¼ teasp. salt	1 cup ground blanched almonds
¼ teasp. nutmeg	1½ teasp. grated lemon rind
¾ cup granulated sugar	⅓ cup finely cut mixed candied
¼ cup honey	lemon and orange peel

Make two to four weeks before serving:
1. Sift together flour, salt, and nutmeg.
2. In medium bowl combine sugar, honey, unbeaten egg, almonds, lemon rind, and candied peels.
3. Now gradually add flour mixture, stirring until well blended. Wrap dough in wax paper or saran; refrigerate at least 1 hr., or till easy to roll.
4. Meanwhile, grease 2 cookie sheets. Start heating oven to 350°F.
5. When dough is chilled, on lightly floured pastry cloth, roll it ⅛" thick. Cut into 2" rounds and/or 3" x 1½" rectangles. Arrange on cookie sheets.
6. Bake 10 to 12 min., or until done; cool on cake racks. Store, tightly covered, for two to four weeks before serving. They keep well. Makes about 5 doz.

Stollen, lavished with raisins, candied fruits, and almonds, is the traditional Christmas bread in all parts of Germany.

CHRISTMAS STOLLEN

1 cup milk	1 cup seedless raisins
Granulated sugar	2 eggs, well beaten
½ teasp. salt	¾ cup softened butter or mar-
1 pkg. active dry, or cake, yeast	garine
¼ cup warm water	¼ teasp. nutmeg
5 cups sifted all-purpose flour	¼ cup melted butter or mar-
½ cup finely cut citron	garine
½ cup finely cut candied cherries	½ teasp. powdered cinnamon
1 cup slivered blanched almonds	Confectioners' sugar
Grated rind 1 lemon	

Early on the day:
1. In very large saucepan scald milk; add ½ cup granulated sugar and salt; cool till lukewarm. Meanwhile, sprinkle or crumble yeast onto water; stir until dissolved.
2. Add yeast to lukewarm milk with 1 cup flour; with egg beater, beat to remove lumps. Cover with clean towel; let rise in warm place (80°F. to 85°F.) until doubled—about 2 hr.

3. Now stir in citron, cherries, almonds, lemon rind, raisins, eggs, softened butter or margarine, nutmeg, then 3 cups flour.

4. On lightly floured surface, knead 1 cup flour into dough until dough is smooth and elastic. Then roll into a large 18″ x 12″ oval, about ½″ thick. Brush with some of melted butter; sprinkle with combined cinnamon and 2 tablesp. granulated sugar.

5. Now make lengthwise crease down center of dough; fold over. Remove to large greased cookie sheet. Push into shape of crescent; then, with palm of hand, press down along crease to shape. Brush with rest of melted butter.

6. Cover dough with wax paper, then with towel; let rise in warm place until nearly doubled. Meanwhile start heating oven to 350°F.

7. When doubled, bake stollen 45 to 50 min., or until golden. Cool, then sprinkle with confectioners' sugar. Keeps well, wrapped and refrigerated, or freezer-wrapped and frozen.

P.S. If preferred, dough may be shaped into 2 stollens, rather than 1 large one.

This is very much a "special" cake, some recipes for it using as many as 11 eggs.

HASELNUSSTORTE
(Hazelnut Torte)

Butter or margarine
Spring-form pan, 9″ x 3″
1½ cups granulated sugar
8 eggs
1 teasp. vanilla extract

1¾ cups sifted cake flour
2½ cups whole shelled hazelnuts
2 cups heavy cream
2 cups sifted confectioners' sugar
3 tablesp. water

Early on the day:

1. Butter spring-form pan; cut wax paper 1″ larger than the bottom. Then use paper to line bottom and part of sides. Butter wax paper, than flour paper and sides.

2. In small skillet melt ½ cup butter; set aside. Start heating oven to 350°F.

3. In 3-qt. bowl combine 1¼ cups granulated sugar, eggs, vanilla. On work surface, set bowl either into large pot, with plenty of hot tap water around it, or over a round 5-qt. Dutch oven, filled about halfway with hot tap water. Beat, with portable mixer at high speed, until mixture fills bowl and is very fluffy—about 20 min.; *now remove from water.*

4. Then, alternately sift in cake flour and add melted butter, beating at low speed until blended. Turn into spring-form pan. Bake 45 min., or until cake tester comes out clean.

5. Let cool in pan 10 min.; then loosen cake around edges and invert on rack; remove pan, then wax paper; let cake cool. Leave oven temperature at 350°F.

6. Place hazelnuts in shallow baking pan. Bake them about 20 min. Remove all of loose skin by rubbing the nuts between two towels or fingers, then grind nuts medium fine.

Thirty minutes before serving:

1. Cut cake into 3 even crosswise layers. In large bowl, whip cream until slightly thick; gradually add ¼ cup granulated sugar, beat stiff; into this fold 2 cups ground hazelnuts.

2. Spread half of this mixture on bottom layer of cake; cover with second layer; spread rest of mixture over it, cover with third layer.

3. Combine confectioners' sugar with water, stir smooth. Spoon over top and sides of cake, then spread with spatula. Sprinkle top and sides with rest of nuts. Makes about 16 servings. Refrigerate any leftover Hazelnut Torte; it will keep well in refrigerator for a few days.

Greece

Sometimes the Greeks serve this magnificent main dish as a hot or cold appetizer, cut into squares.

PASTITSU
(Baked Beef and Macaroni)

1 cup uncooked macaroni, in 1½" pieces, or 1½ cups uncooked ziti	1 tablesp. snipped parsley
1½ qt. boiling water	2 tablesp. flour
Salt	1½ cups milk
¼ cup salad oil	1 cup grated sharp process cheese
½ cup minced onion	2 eggs
½ lb. chuck beef, ground once	¼ teasp. bottled thick meat sauce
⅛ teasp. pepper	2 tablesp. pkgd. dried bread crumbs

1. Start heating oven to 375°F. Also cook macaroni in boiling water with 1 tablesp. salt for 10 min., or till almost tender. Drain; then set aside.

2. In skillet, heat 2 tablesp. salad oil. In it, sauté onion until golden. Then add chuck and brown lightly. Next stir in ½ teasp. salt, pepper, and parsley; set aside.

3. In small saucepan over low heat, heat 2 tablesp. salad oil; then stir in flour. Slowly stir in 1 cup milk. Then cook, stirring, till smooth and thickened; remove from heat.

4. Next blend in ½ cup grated cheese; ½ teasp. salt; 1 egg yolk, slightly beaten; and bottled meat sauce.

5. Now, to meat mixture, add macaroni, ¼ cup grated cheese, and mixture of 1 egg white and 1 egg, beaten with ½ cup milk.

6. Sprinkle bread crumbs over bottom of 9" x 5" x 3" loaf pan. Pour in meat mixture; then sprinkle with ¼ cup grated cheese; next, pour on cheese sauce.

7. Bake meat dish 35 min.; then remove from oven. To serve as hot main dish, let Pastitsu stand for 15 min., and then cut into squares. Or cool baked dish, refrigerate until needed, then serve as main dish in squares. Makes 6 servings.

Although raisins and chestnuts are often used to stuff the Greek's Easter Lamb, this version is preferred in the Dodecanese Islands.

ARNI YEMESTO
(Stuffed Lamb)

1 cup uncooked regular or processed white rice	1 4-lb. cushion shoulder lamb roast
½ cup hot butter or margarine	½ teasp. salt
1 lb. chuck beef, ground once	¼ teasp. pepper
½ lb. calf liver, ground once	¼ cup butter or margarine
1 large onion, peeled, grated	⅓ cup lemon juice
2 teasp. salt	6 fringed leek stalks
¾ teasp. pepper	1 large onion, in rings
1 teasp. powdered cinnamon	1 7¾-oz. bottle green olives
2 tablesp. snipped mint leaves	9 or 10 lemon wedges
1 cup light or dark raisins	Fresh dill

1. Start heating oven to 325°F. Cook rice as label directs. Meanwhile, in ½ cup butter or margarine, heated in large skillet, sauté beef, calf liver, and grated onion till onion is golden.

2. Remove from heat; add 2 teasp. salt, ¾ teasp. pepper, cinnamon, mint, raisins, and cooked rice.

3. Rub pocket of lamb shoulder with ½ teasp. salt, ¼ teasp. pepper; fill with meat and rice stuffing; skewer in place.

4. Place lamb in shallow roasting pan; dot with ¼ cup butter; sprinkle with lemon juice. Roast, basting often, for 2 to 2½ hr., or to 182°F. on meat thermometer.

5. Place rest of stuffing in baking dish; cover with sheet of foil. Bake along with lamb, last half hour of roasting.

6. When lamb is done, arrange it on heated large platter with extra stuffing heaped near pocket in lamb.

7. If desired, garnish with leek stalks; onion in rings, green olives, lemon wedges, and fresh dill. Makes 6 servings.

A dish loved all over the Balkans, Turkey, and the Middle East. This is a delicious Greek version.

MOUSSAKA
(Baked Eggplant)

3 tablesp. butter or margarine
1 large onion, peeled, minced
1 teasp. salt
½ teasp. pepper
1½ lb. lamb, ground once *
1 clove garlic, peeled, minced
1 cup canned tomato purée
½ cup cold water

¼ teasp. nutmeg
½ cup salad oil
1 cup flour
1 teasp. salt
½ teasp. pepper
2 medium eggplants, pared and sliced lengthwise into ½″ slices
½ cup grated Parmesan cheese

1. In butter, in skillet, over medium heat, cook onion with 1 teasp. salt and ½ teasp. pepper for 5 min., or till golden. Add ground lamb and garlic; cook 10 min., or until browned.
2. Add tomato purée, cold water, and nutmeg; cook 15 min.
3. Start heating oven to 350°F.
4. In large skillet, start heating salad oil. Mix flour with 1 teasp. salt and ½ teasp. pepper; use to coat eggplant slices. Fry eggplant in hot oil until it is light-brown.
5. Place about half of eggplant slices in 13″ x 9″ x 2″ baking dish; spread with half of meat sauce; repeat layers. Sprinkle top with Parmesan cheese. Bake 30 min.
6. Serve hot, cut into squares, with hot green limas. Makes 6 servings.

* Or use 1 lb. beef and ½ lb. very lean pork, ground once.

To the Greek people, dessert is usually fruit. Rich pastries (the majority topped off with a rich, rich syrup) are reserved for special occasions.

AMYGDALOPITA
(Almond Pie)

1 4½-oz. can blanched almonds, ground
1 teasp. double-acting baking powder
1 tablesp. flour

1½ tablesp. fine graham-cracker crumbs
1 cup butter or margarine
1 cup granulated sugar
3 eggs
½ cup cold water

1. Start heating oven to 375°F. In bowl combine ground almonds, baking powder, flour, and graham-cracker crumbs.
2. In small bowl, with electric mixer at medium speed, mix butter or margarine with ½ cup sugar till light and fluffy; gradually add almond mixture, mixing well.

3. Now add eggs, one at a time, beating well after each addition. Pour into 9″ pie plate.
4. Bake 25 to 30 min., or until cake tester, inserted in center, comes out clean.
5. Meanwhile, in saucepan, combine ½ cup granulated sugar with the cold water; simmer until reduced to ½ cup; then pour this syrup over hot baked pie.
6. Cool pie thoroughly. Serve in wedges. Makes 6 servings.

Holland

On a cold day in Holland you might find yourself eating a bowl of Erwtensoep, also lovingly called "Snert."

ERWTENSOEP
(Pea Soup)

1 lb. quick-cooking green split peas	2 lb. spareribs, cut into 2 rib pieces *
3 qt. water	2 medium-thick leeks
1½ tablesp. salt	1 medium onion, peeled
½ teasp. pepper	1 cup celery, in slices ½″ thick
¼ teasp. powdered allspice	1 lb. smoked sausage
¼ teasp. powdered marjoram	¼ cup butter or margarine
1 beef-bouillon cube	3 to 4 slices white bread
	Snipped parsley

About 3 hr. before serving:
1. In large kettle place peas and water. Let come to a boil, then simmer, covered, 1¼ hr.
2. Add salt, pepper, allspice, marjoram, bouillon cube, and spareribs, trimmed of excess fat. Stir well, then bring to a boil and simmer, covered, 45 min.
3. Meanwhile, halve leeks lengthwise, then wash and cut into slices 1″ thick. Cut onion into thin rings. Add these, with celery and sausage, to soup; bring to a boil; let simmer, covered, 30 min., or until spareribs are tender.
4. Meanwhile, in medium skillet, heat butter or margarine; in it toast bread, cut into small cubes, until brown and crisp. Heap in small bowl.
5. Serve in one of these two ways: Remove spareribs and sausage from soup; keep warm. Transfer soup to tureen or soup bowls; sprinkle with parsley; serve as first course with bread cubes. Follow with main course of spareribs and sausage, cut into 2″ pieces,

* In Holland, pigs' feet replace the spareribs.

along with a favorite potato dish and a green vegetable, like broccoli, cabbage, or beans. Or remove meat from spareribs, cut up if needed; add to soup with peeled sausage in thin slices. Serve as main-dish soup with the croutons and a tossed crisp salad. Follow with a hearty dessert. Makes 6 to 8 servings.

The Dutch like six meals a day and hearty fare to boot. Yet this light, lovely wine whip is a specialty at dessert.

WINE·LEMON WHIP

4 eggs, separated	¾ cup dry white wine
½ cup granulated sugar	Grated rind ½ lemon
¼ cup lemon juice	

Day before or early on the day:
1. Refrigerate the egg whites. In small bowl, with electric mixer at medium speed, beat egg yolks with sugar until thick and fluffy; add lemon juice and wine, blending well; then stir in lemon rind.
2. Turn into double boiler. Cook over boiling water, beating constantly, with fork or wire whip, until thickened; refrigerate.

Just before serving:
Beat egg whites until stiff; fold into egg-lemon mixture; beat up with egg beater until smooth. Turn into pretty glass dish. Makes 8 servings.

The Dutch enjoy a good cup of cocoa; their chocolates are exported everywhere. Naturally their chocolate cake would be a chocolate cake to end all chocolate cakes.

CHOCOLADETAART
(Dutch Chocolate Torte)

8 sq. unsweetened chocolate (8 oz.)	2 cups sifted cake flour
½ cup hot water	½ teasp. salt
1½ cups butter or margarine	2 teasp. double-acting baking powder
½ cup granulated sugar	½ cup milk
½ cup light-brown sugar	2 egg whites
2 eggs	Confectioners' sugar
1 teasp. vanilla extract	

Early on the day, or day before:
1. In double boiler melt 3 sq. chocolate; then add water and stir until smooth. Cool slightly. Start heating oven to 350°F.
2. In large bowl, with electric mixer at medium speed, beat ½ cup butter with granulated and brown sugars until creamy. Beat in eggs, one at a time, then vanilla and melted chocolate.

3. Sift flour with salt and baking powder. Add, alternately with milk, to chocolate mixture, beating until well blended. Pour into 2 greased 8″ layer-cake pans. Bake about 20 min., or until cake springs back from sides of pan. Cool 5 to 10 min., then turn out on rack to cool completely.

Two to three hours before serving:
1. Make up this Chocolate Frosting: In double boiler melt 4 sq. chocolate; set aside to cool.
2. Meanwhile beat egg whites until stiff, but not dry. Gradually beat in 1½ cups confectioners' sugar, beating until thick.
3. In another bowl beat 1 cup butter until creamy. Slowly beat in egg-white mixture, then melted chocolate, beating until thoroughly blended.
4. Use this frosting to fill and frost the 2 layers. With vegetable parer and 1 sq. unsweetened chocolate make chocolate curls; use to sprinkle on top of cake. Also, if desired, lay a paper doily on top of cake (or cut one out with scissors), then over doily sprinkle some confectioners' sugar; carefully remove doily, leaving its pattern.
5. Refrigerate cake to allow frosting to firm up. Serve, cut into 12 to 16 wedges.

Ginger cookies made in fascinatingly shaped, decorative, carved wooden molds. Lacking them, you can roll out the spicy dough with a patterned rolling pin, or slice and bake it.

SPECULAAS
(Dutch St. Nicholas Cookies)

1 cup dark-brown sugar	⅛ teasp. double-acting baking
3 tablesp. milk	powder
3 cups sifted all-purpose flour	⅛ teasp. salt
1½ teasp. powdered cloves	1¼ cups butter or margarine
1½ teasp. powdered cinnamon	¼ cup canned slivered blanched
¾ teasp. powdered ginger	almonds
¾ teasp. powdered nutmeg	

Prepare dough the day before:
1. In small bowl, combine brown sugar and milk; stir till smooth.
2. Into large bowl, sift flour with cloves, cinnamon, ginger, nutmeg, double-acting baking powder, and salt. With pastry blender, or two knives in scissor-fashion, cut in butter or margarine, until like corn meal.
3. Add brown-sugar mixture, almonds; mix well. Wrap in foil, saran, or wax paper, and refrigerate until needed.

If using large wooden mold:
1. Brush carvings in mold well with a small brush; do not wash; then dust every nook and cranny well with flour.
2. Start heating oven to 350°F. Lightly grease cookie sheet. Press

enough dough into mold to fill it *completely;* then, with small knife, cut around edge of pattern, removing trimmings.

3. Invert cookie sheet over mold, then turn both together until mold is on top; tap it lightly, till dough slips out on sheet. Bake 20 to 30 min., or till light-brown. Cool on sheet, then wrap carefully in foil or saran until needed.

If using small wooden molds: Prepare dough day before, as on p. 54; then follow steps 1 and 2 under "If using large wooden mold." Now invert filled mold on floured surface and tap to release cookie. Place, pattern side up, on cookie sheet. Repeat. Then bake at 350°F. 15 min., or until light-brown; remove to wire cake rack; cool. These keep well, stored in a tight container.

If using patterned rolling pin: Prepare dough day before, as on p. 54. On lightly floured surface, roll out some of dough ¼" thick, then stamp it with a patterned rolling pin. Cut out cookies; arrange on lightly greased cookie sheets. Repeat. Bake at 350°F. 15 min., or till golden; remove to rack; cool. These keep well in tight container. Makes about 98.

If slice-and-bake kind: Prepare dough day before as on p. 54; refrigerate 1 hr.; then shape, on lightly floured surface, into 2 rolls about 10" x 1½". Wrap each roll in foil, saran, or wax paper; refrigerate them. At baking time, on lightly floured surface, cut each roll into ¼" rounds; place on lightly greased cookie sheets; bake at 350°F. 15 min. Remove to racks; cool. Keep well in tight container. Makes about 80.

Do as they do in Holland. Give this ever-so-luscious almond-filled cookie letter as a family gift at Christmas.

BANKETLETTER
(Almond-Filled Puff Paste)

1 cup sifted cake flour
½ teasp. salt
½ cup butter or margarine
2½ tablesp. ice water

1¼ lb. (2 cups) canned almond
   paste
½ cup granulated sugar
1 egg, well beaten
¼ teasp. lemon extract

Make two or three days ahead:

1. Into bowl sift flour, salt. With pastry blender, or two knives, scissor-fashion, cut in butter till particles are like peas. Gradually, with fork, work in ice water to make dough; refrigerate 1 hr.

2. Meanwhile, in bowl, mix canned almond paste, granulated sugar, egg, well beaten, lemon extract. Start heating oven to 425°F. Lightly grease large cookie sheet.

3. On lightly floured surface, roll pastry into 12" square; then cut into 3 strips, each 4" wide.

4. Shape almond-paste mixture into 3 equal rolls, 12" x ¾". Place

a roll on each pastry strip; fold pastry around it; press seams and ends firmly.

5. Then, on cookie sheet, use the three rolls to shape a *large* family initial. Place rolls seam side down; brush ends with beaten egg before joining.

6. Bake 20 to 25 min., or till light-golden. Remove from oven; let cool on sheet. With help of spatula, slide initial into foil-lined box; then gift-wrap. Makes 1 *large* initial.

SMALL BANKETLETTERS: Make as above with these changes: In step 3, cut 12" sq. into 6 equal strips; halve crosswise. In step 4, shape almond paste into 12 rolls, each 6" x ½". Makes 4 initials.

P.S. Rijsttafel—so popular in Holland, can be found in our Indonesian section, see p. 135.

Hungary

Hungarians love good food. Uniquely tempting is this ragout, tastily seasoned with their favorite sweet paprika.

ÖKÖRFAROK RAGÚ
(*Hungarian Oxtail Ragout*)

1 carrot, diced	1 teasp. paprika
2 large onions, chopped	1 clove garlic, minced
8 whole peppercorns	1 cup canned tomato purée
⅛ teasp. poultry seasoning	4 cups diagonally-sliced pared
2 cups Burgundy wine	carrots
2 oxtails, cut up	1 8-oz. package wide noodles
3 tablesp. shortening	2 tablesp. butter or margarine
3 tablesp. flour	2 tablesp. poppy seeds

Early on day before serving:

1. In bowl mix diced carrot, next 4 ingredients, and 1 teasp. salt as a marinade. Add oxtails; refrigerate 3 hr.

2. Now remove oxtails from marinade; dry on paper towels; then, in hot shortening, in Dutch oven, brown them well.

3. Stir in flour, paprika, then marinade, garlic, tomato purée, 3 cups water, 1 tablesp. salt. Simmer, covered, 2 to 2½ hr., or until oxtails are fork-tender. Cool, then refrigerate.

About 1 hr. before serving:

Skim fat from oxtail mixture; add sliced carrots; simmer, covered, 40 min., or till carrots are fork-tender. Cook noodles; drain; add butter, seeds. On heated platter heap noodles; spoon on oxtails, carrots, some gravy; pass rest of gravy. Makes 6 servings.

If you had any thought that Hungarian food began and ended with goulash, hurry and have a taste of this chicken paprika, oven-style, and the sirloin steaklets, caper-sour-cream-braised.

RÁNTOTT CSIRKE
(Oven-Fried Chicken)

¼ cup butter or margarine	1 tablesp. paprika
¼ cup all-purpose flour	½ teasp. onion salt
1 2- to 2½-lb. broiler-fryer, cut up	2 tablesp. lemon juice
2 eggs	1 cup pkgd. dried bread crumbs
1½ teasp. salt	

About 1 hr. before serving:
1. Start heating oven to 350°F. In 13" x 9" x 2" baking dish in oven, melt butter.
2. Meanwhile, in flour in paper bag, shake chicken pieces, one at a time, until coated; set aside.
3. In bowl, using fork, beat eggs with salt, paprika, onion salt, and lemon juice until well blended.
4. Dip floured chicken pieces, one at a time, in egg mixture, then in crumbs, turning to coat evenly. Then, in melted butter in baking dish, arrange chicken, skin side down.
5. Bake about 45 min., or until fork-tender, turning once. Makes 4 servings.

ESZTERHÁZY ROSTÉLYOS
(Braised Sirloin Eszterházy)

6 carrots, pared	3 tablesp. flour
8 to 12 celery stalks	6 whole peppercorns
6 sirloin steaks, about ½ lb. each, ¼" thick	1 tablesp. paprika
	1 can condensed beef bouillon, undiluted
1 tablesp. salt	
1 teasp. pepper	6 bottled capers
3 tablesp. butter or margarine	1 lemon, thinly sliced
6 onions, peeled, sliced	1½ cups commercial sour cream

About 2 hr. before serving:
1. Cut carrots and celery in long, thin strips. Lay meat on board; then, with rim of saucer, pound in salt and pepper on both sides.
2. In hot butter in large skillet, brown meat on both sides. Remove from skillet, and set aside.
3. In butter left from browning meat, sauté carrots, celery, and onions about 15 min., stirring occasionally. Stir in flour, then peppercorns, paprika, beef bouillon. Return meat to skillet; cover; simmer 30 min., or till vegetables and meat are tender.
4. Add capers, lemon. Cook, uncovered, about 15 min., or until liquid is reduced by about one third.

5. Dilute sour cream with about 1 cup of liquid in skillet; then stir it into mixture in skillet. Heat thoroughly, but do not boil. Makes 6 servings.

Hungarian vegetables are rarely served plain. They're usually sauced with sour cream, sweet cream, or milk, then skillfully seasoned, with a touch of dill, parsley, chives, etc., as well.

TEJFÖLÖS TÖKFŐZELÉK
(Squash with Dill)

2½ lb. yellow squash *	1 teasp. vinegar or lemon juice
2 teasp. salt	Sprig fresh, or 1 teasp. dried,
2 tablesp. butter or margarine	dill
1 small onion, peeled, minced	2 teasp. flour
¼ teasp. paprika	¼ cup hot water
¼ teasp. sugar	3 tablesp. commercial sour cream

1. Pare squash; cut in half lengthwise (if mature, rather than young and tender, remove seeds); then halve crosswise into pieces about 3″ long.
2. Now place these pieces flat on board and cut into thin strips; place in bowl; sprinkle with salt. Let stand about 1 hr. Lift out of bowl and dry on paper towels.
3. Melt butter in skillet; add onion and cook until tender; add squash, paprika, sugar, vinegar, and snipped fresh dill. Cover and cook 10 to 12 min., or until tender.
4. Sprinkle flour over top of squash; gently stir, then cook 2 to 3 min. Pour in water and cook about 1 min. Gently stir in sour cream. Serve at once or chill and serve. Makes 4 servings.

* If preferred, squash may be grated on coarsest grater, before salting, and then proceeding as in step 2.

These cream-cheese crescents, with their cinnamon-nut centers are a heavenly delight—warm and fresh from their baking.

KIFLI
(Cream-Cheese Pastry)

1 cup soft sweet butter	1 cup chopped California wal-
½ lb. soft cream cheese	nuts
¼ teasp. salt	½ cup granulated sugar
2 cups sifted all-purpose flour	1 tablesp. cinnamon

Day before:
Mix butter, cheese, and salt until creamy. Mix in flour. Shape into 14 balls. Refrigerate overnight.

Bake next day as follows:
1. Start heating oven to 350°F. On lightly floured, cloth-covered board, roll each cream-cheese ball to 6" circle. Cut each circle into quarters.
2. Mix nuts, sugar, cinnamon; drop a rounded teaspoonful of this nut mixture on each quarter of butter-cheese. Pinch edges of dough together, enclosing filling; then form into crescents.
3. Place crescents on ungreased cookie sheet. Bake 12 min., or till light-brown. Best served soon after baking. Makes about 5 doz.

The sour cream filling in this flaky, flavorsome pie reveals a delicate blend of lemon, cinnamon, cloves, and raisins.

TEJFELES PITÉ
(Sour-Cream Pie)

1 unbaked 9" pie shell	¼ teasp. salt
3 eggs, separated	1 cup seedless raisins, chopped
¾ cup granulated sugar	1 teasp. grated lemon rind
½ teasp. powdered cinnamon	1 cup commercial sour cream
¼ teasp. powdered cloves	

Make several hours before serving:
1. Prepare unbaked pie shell. Start heating oven to 425°F.
2. Beat egg whites until stiff but not dry.
3. Without washing beater, beat egg yolks until thick and lemon-colored; beat in sugar, cinnamon, cloves, salt. Fold in raisins, lemon rind, ½ cup sour cream, and stiffly beaten whites. Pour into unbaked pie shell.
4. Bake 15 min.; then reduce oven temperature to 350°F.; bake 30 min. longer, or until a silver knife, inserted into center of pie, comes out clean.
5. Let pie cool to room temperature. Top each serving with a dab of remaining sour cream.

Another of those melt-in-your-mouth pastry desserts for which Hungary is famous—this time topped with fresh peach slices and pastry strips before it bakes.

ŐSZI BARACK TÉSZTA
(Peachcake)

3 cups sifted all-purpose flour	About 8 peaches, peeled, halved
⅔ cup granulated sugar	⅓ to ½ cup granulated sugar
1¼ cups butter	1 whole egg, beaten
5 egg yolks	

1. Start heating oven to 450°F. Sift flour into large bowl; add

⅔ cup sugar; drop in butter; with pastry blender or 2 knives, scissor-fashion, work in butter until mixture is very crumbly.
2. Drop in egg yolks; then work in yolks, first with wooden spoon, then with hands, until mixture forms ball. Divide dough in half.
3. On floured board, roll one half of dough into 12″ x 10″ rectangle; with pancake turner, slip dough onto cookie sheet. Or roll dough over rolling pin; then unroll on cookie sheet. (Because dough is soft, it may break. Patch by pressing bit of unrolled dough over hole.)
4. Now, with hands, roll rest of dough into thin round strips. Place just enough strips around edges of rectangle to form border all around.
5. Arrange peach halves, close together, on dough, inside border; sprinkle with ⅓ to ½ cup sugar.
6. Then attractively arrange remaining dough strips on top of peaches, pressing ends gently to border to hold in place. Brush entire top of cake with beaten egg.
7. Bake Peachcake at 450°F. 10 min.; reduce heat to 375°F. and bake 25 min. longer, or until peaches are tender and cake is golden-brown. Makes 15 servings.

Ireland

In some parts of Ireland, celery and tomatoes are added to this famous white stew. Either way, it's truly a great dish.

IRISH STEW

2 lb. lamb shoulder, in 2″ cubes	4 medium onions, peeled, quartered
1 tablesp. salt	
½ teasp. pepper	3 medium carrots, pared, cut into thirds
Water	
6 medium potatoes, pared, halved	1 tablesp. flour
	Snipped parsley

About 1 hr. and 40 min. before serving:
1. Place lamb, salt, and pepper in large kettle or Dutch oven. Add 1¾ cups water; bring to a boil, then simmer, covered, 1 hr. Skim excess fat from surface.
2. Now add potatoes, onions, and carrots. Cook, covered, about ½ hr., or until meat and vegetables are tender.
3. Beat together flour and ¼ cup water; stir into stew, then bring to a boil. Serve as main dish, sprinkled with parsley. Makes 6 servings.

Delicious Irish Soda Bread and Scones were always standard fare in Ireland. Even today yeast is not used when the bread is home-made.

IRISH SODA BREAD

4 cups sifted all-purpose flour
¼ cup granulated sugar
1 teasp. salt
1 teasp. double-acting baking powder
2 tablesp. caraway seeds

¼ cup butter or margarine
2 cups light or dark raisins
1⅓ cups buttermilk
1 egg, unbeaten
1 teasp. baking soda
1 egg yolk, or a little cream

1. Start heating oven to 350°F. Grease 2-qt. casserole.
2. Into mixing bowl, sift flour, sugar, salt, baking powder; stir in caraway seeds. With pastry blender or 2 knives, scissor-fashion, cut in butter till like coarse corn meal; stir in raisins.
3. Combine buttermilk, egg, soda; stir into flour mixture till just moistened. Turn dough onto lightly floured surface; knead lightly till smooth; shape into ball. Place in casserole.
4. With sharp knife, make 4″ cross, ¼″ deep, in center of ball. Brush with yolk, beaten with fork.
5. Bake bread about 1 hr. 20 min., or until cake tester, inserted in center, comes out clean.
6. Cool bread in baking dish 10 min., then turn out on rack to finish cooling. Serve in slices. Makes 1 loaf.

You've heard of the Kerry Dancers; now here's a Kerry Cake. Let it add a bit of Irish charm to your meals.

KERRY CAKE
(*Apple Cake*)

¾ cup butter or margarine
½ cup granulated sugar
3 eggs
Grated rind 1 lemon
3 medium apples, pared, cored

1½ cups sifted cake flour
¼ teasp. salt
1½ teasp. double-acting baking powder

Make early on the day, or 1½ hr. before serving:
1. Start heating oven to 375°F. In large bowl, with electric mixer at medium speed, beat butter with sugar until creamy. Then beat in eggs, one at a time.
2. Stir in lemon rind and diced apples. Sift together flour, salt, and baking powder. Fold into butter mixture until well blended.
3. Pour into greased 8″ x 8″ x 2″ baking dish. Bake about 30 min., or until golden, and cake tester, inserted in center, comes out clean. Serve, slightly warm, cut into 9 squares, with or without topping of vanilla ice cream. Or cool, cut, and serve.

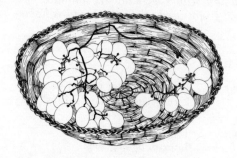

Italy

This delightfully refreshing Italian first course features one or more thin wedges of honeydew, topped with paper-thin slices of prosciutto—a delicately cured Italian-style ham that's available in U.S.A., too.

PROSCIUTTO CON MELLONE
(*Prosciutto with Melon*)

1. Cut chilled cantaloupe in half; remove seeds; pare off rind. Slice each half into thin wedges. Arrange one or more wedges on each salad plate; top with paper-thin slices of prosciutto.
2. Or place a wedge of pared honeydew melon or cantaloupe on each plate, with a few paper-thin slices of prosciutto at the side. Eat with a fork and knife, cutting off a piece of melon, then a piece of ham, and combining the two flavors.

In the northern provinces of Italy, rice is popular—in fact more so than spaghetti. And it's often served, yellow with saffron, as their first main course.

RISOTTO ALLA MARIA
(*Maria's Risotto*)

2 tablesp. butter or margarine	Generous pinch dried saffron
1 small onion, peeled, minced	2 cups chicken broth
¾ cup uncooked regular white rice	2 tablesp. butter or margarine

1. In 2 tablesp. hot butter, in skillet, sauté onion and rice until golden, stirring constantly.
2. Mix saffron with 2 tablesp. chicken broth; set aside.
3. Add remaining broth to rice; bring to boil; then simmer, covered, 20 min.
4. Just before serving, stir in 2 tablesp. butter, and saffron. Makes 3 servings.

For 6 servings: Use 1 medium onion, generous pinch dried saffron, and double other ingredients.

Minestrone is the Italian word for "a big soup." So a soup must be hearty, with plenty of vegetables, etc., to be a minestrone.

MINESTRONE
(*A Big Soup*)

½ lb. shin beef with bone
1¾ qt. water
1 tablesp. salt
¼ teasp. pepper
½ tablesp. olive or salad oil
1 clove garlic, peeled
¼ cup chopped onions
¼ cup snipped parsley

½ cup canned or cooked kidney beans
½ cup green beans or zucchini, cut up
½ cup fresh or frozen peas
1 cup shredded cabbage
½ 8-oz. can tomato sauce
¼ cup spaghetti, in small pieces
Grated Parmesan cheese

1. Simmer beef with water, salt, and pepper, covered, 1 hr. Skim off fat; simmer, covered, 3 hr. Remove meat, bone.
2. In hot oil in skillet, sauté garlic until golden; discard garlic. In same oil, sauté onions and parsley. Add to soup with rest of ingredients except meat, spaghetti, and grated Parmesan. Cook, covered, 30 min.
3. Add spaghetti. Cook 10 min. If desired, add meat, cut into chunks; heat thoroughly. Or reserve meat for another meal. Serve soup sprinkled with Parmesan cheese. Makes 6 servings.

For 12 servings: Double ingredients; make as directed.

Pasta (spaghetti, macaroni, noodles, etc.) popularly precedes the dinner main course in some parts of Italy. Here are two luscious sauces with which to top or sauce it.

SALSA BIANCA ALLE VONGOLE
(*White Clam Sauce*)

½ cup olive or salad oil
½ cup butter or margarine
8 garlic cloves, peeled, minced
2 tablesp. snipped parsley

2 teasp. salt
2 cups clam liquid
2 doz. shucked hard-shell clams

1. In hot oil and butter in skillet, sauté garlic till golden. Add parsley, salt, clam liquid. Simmer, uncovered, 10 min.
2. Add finely snipped clams; simmer 2 min. Pour over hot spaghetti on heated platter. Makes 6 servings.

PESTO GENOVESE
(*Genovese Green Sauce*)

5 or 6 garlic cloves, peeled, minced
¼ cup snipped fresh basil; or 2
   tablesp. dried basil
¼ cup grated Parmesan cheese

2 tablesp. finely chopped California walnuts
½ teasp. salt
6 tablesp. olive or salad oil

1. In mortar (or small bowl) with pestle (or back of spoon), mix garlic, basil, cheese, walnuts, salt; pound mixture to smooth paste. Gradually add oil, working mixture to make smooth *pesto*.
2. On each heated dinner plate, arrange mound of hot noodles (allow ½ lb. for 6 servings); top with pat of butter, then with 1 tablesp. *pesto*. Just before eating, each person tosses noodles with *pesto*. Makes 6 servings.

A production to be sure—but the kind of a meal-in-a-dish that will bring you nothing but ecstatic praise!

LASAGNA AL FORNO

¼ lb. salt pork, diced
¾ lb. chuck beef, ground
1 egg
2 tablesp. pkgd. dried bread
   crumbs
1 tablesp. snipped parsley
Salt
Pepper
2 tablesp. milk
1 clove garlic, peeled, minced
Grated Parmesan cheese
½ lb. boned fresh pork shoulder,
   in one piece

½ lb. boned lamb shoulder, in one
   piece
1 large onion, peeled, minced
1 1-lb.-13-oz. can Italian tomatoes
1 6-oz. can tomato paste
1½ cans water (use tomato-paste
   can as measure)
¼ teasp. dried basil
6 qt. water
1 tablesp. salad or olive oil
1 lb. lasagna (very broad) noodles
1 lb. ricotta or pot cheese
1 lb. mozzarella or Münster
   cheese, sliced

1. In Dutch oven, sauté diced salt pork till crisp. Meanwhile, make meat balls: With fork, lightly stir together chuck, egg, crumbs, parsley, ½ teasp. salt, ⅛ teasp. pepper, milk, garlic, and 1 tablesp. grated Parmesan cheese. Shape into 6 balls.
2. Brown pork shoulder, lamb, and meat balls in pork fat in Dutch oven. Add onion; sauté till browned.
3. Strain tomatoes through coarse strainer into Dutch oven. Add tomato paste, 1½ cans water, 1 tablesp. salt, basil, ¼ teasp. pepper; simmer, covered, for 2 hr.
4. Half an hour before this sauce is done, bring 6 qt. water to boil in large kettle. Add 3 tablesp. salt, salad oil. When water boils rapidly, add lasagna noodles slowly, piece by piece, so boiling doesn't stop. Cook till tender—about 25 min.; don't overcook.

Drain well; quickly separate pieces of lasagna, to prevent sticking.

5. Now start heating oven to 350°F. In bottom of 14" x 10" x 2" baking pan or 2 8" x 8" x 2" baking dishes, place some of sauce. Remove meat balls from sauce; mash. Remove pork and lamb; save for Meat Salad, below.

6. Mix ricotta with about ¼ cup sauce. Now place layers in pan in this order: noodles (laid straight), mozzarella, 1 cup grated Parmesan, ricotta, mashed meat balls, sauce, etc. Repeat till all ingredients are used, ending with noodles, topped with sauce.

7. Bake lasagna 25 min. Let stand about 15 min. to set. Then cut into 2" squares; lift out with broad spatula, and serve. Makes 8 to 10 servings. (If any is left over, reheat for 30 min. in top of double boiler.)

THE BONUS—MEAT SALAD ITALIANO: Chill lamb and pork that were cooked in lasagna sauce; dice meat. Toss meat with 4 cut-up scallions, 2 tablesp. olive or salad oil, 2 tablesp. vinegar, ½ teasp. salt, ⅛ teasp. pepper, 1 cup cooked peas. Arrange on salad greens. Makes 4 servings.

Italians have a knowing way with paper-thin veal cutlets—a savory tomato sauce and two kinds of cheese work wonders.

VEAL PARMIGIANA

Olive or salad oil
3 cloves garlic, peeled, finely minced
1 onion, peeled, minced
1 1-lb.-4-oz. can tomatoes (2½ cups)
1¼ teasp. salt
¼ teasp. pepper
1 8-oz. can tomato sauce
¼ teasp. dried thyme
1 lb. veal cutlet, cut very thin
1 egg
¼ cup pkgd. dried bread crumbs
Grated Parmesan cheese
½ lb. mozzarella or Münster cheese

1. In 3 tablesp. hot oil, in saucepan, sauté garlic and onion till golden. Then add tomatoes, salt, and pepper, breaking up tomatoes with spoon. Simmer, uncovered, 10 min. Then add tomato sauce and thyme and simmer 20 min.

2. While tomato sauce simmers, fix veal. Cut cutlet into 8 slices, each of about 4½" by 2" size. In pie plate beat egg well with fork. Combine bread crumbs and ¼ cup grated Parmesan cheese on piece of wax paper.

3. Dip each piece of veal, first in egg, then in crumbs. Sauté, 3 pieces at a time, in 1 tablesp. hot oil, in skillet. When browned on bottom, loosen crumbs from skillet; turn with broad spatula; sauté till golden-brown underneath. When all veal slices are browned, set, side by side, in 12" x 8" x 2" baking dish.

4. Now start heating oven to 350°F. Slice mozzarella thinly. Pour two thirds of tomato sauce over veal, straining it, if desired. Ar-

range mozzarella slices on top. Spoon on rest of sauce. Sprinkle with ¼ to ⅓ cup grated Parmesan.
5. Bake 30 min., then serve. Makes 4 generous servings.

Marsala wine adds the master touch to this young veal favorite, that all but melts in your mouth!

SCALOPPINE MARSALA
(*Veal Marsala*)

1 lb. *very thin* cutlets from veal leg (1/16″ thick)	¼ cup flour
Salt	3 tablesp. butter or margarine
Pepper	¼ cup Marsala wine
	Snipped parsley

1. Cut *very thin* cutlets into 5″ x 3″ pieces. Sprinkle with salt and pepper; pass them through flour to lightly coat.
2. In hot butter or margarine, in skillet, sauté cutlets about 2 min. on each side, or until golden. Remove to heated platter.
3. To fat left in skillet, add Marsala wine. Cook 1 min., stirring to loosen browned bits.
4. Pour sauce from skillet over veal; garnish with snipped parsley. Nice with broiled mushrooms and tomatoes. Makes 4 servings.

For 2 servings: Halve ingredients; make as directed.

Another Italian veal dish, which boasts of prosciutto and truffles as a filling, before browning and then simmering briefly to delectable tenderness.

SALTIMBOCCA ALLA ROMANA
(*Veal, Roman-Style*)

1 lb. very thin veal steak	Pinch powdered sage
2 truffles, cut into 8 slices	Snipped parsley
4 thin slices prosciutto	Flour
Butter or margarine	Olive oil
Freshly ground pepper	⅓ cup dry white wine

1. Have meatman flatten veal to ⅛″ thickness, then cut into 8 slices.
2. For each saltimbocca, top 1 piece of veal with 2 slices truffles, a slice of prosciutto, about 1 teasp. melted butter, pinch each of pepper and sage, and 1 teasp. snipped parsley. Top with a second piece of veal, then pinch edges together (or secure with pick), then dip piece in flour to lightly coat both sides. Repeat with other veal slices.
3. Now, in large skillet, heat 1 to 2 tablesp. butter with 1 to 2 tablesp. olive oil. In it sauté saltimbocca until light-brown on

both sides. Then pour in wine and simmer, covered, 10 min., or until veal is tender.

4. Serve, spooning sauce over meat. Makes 4 servings.

Steak with a sauce!—the kind that's colorful with tomatoes, and fragrant with orégano.

BISTECCA ALLA PIZZAIOLA
(Beefsteak with Pizza Sauce)

1 lb. chuck or sirloin steak, 1 to 1¼″ thick
½ 16- to 17-oz. can whole tomatoes, undrained
¼ teasp. dried orégano
½ teasp. snipped parsley

½ clove garlic, peeled, minced
½ tablesp. minced onion
⅛ teasp. salt
Dash pepper
1 tablesp. olive or salad oil

Start heating oven to 350°F. Arrange steak in 10″ x 6″ x 2″ baking dish. Mash tomatoes with spoon; spread evenly over steak. Sprinkle with orégano, parsley, garlic, onion, salt, pepper, oil. Bake, uncovered, 1¾ hr., or until tender. Makes 3 servings.

For 6 servings: Double ingredients, using same amount of pepper.

When this famous Manicotti with Braciole is the main dish at a dinner party, bread sticks, a crisp green bean salad, and fruit compote are likely to follow.

MANICOTTI WITH BRACIOLE

Braciole, p. 68
4 cups sifted all-purpose flour
2 eggs
¾ cup lukewarm water

1 lb. ricotta or creamed cottage cheese
2 egg yolks
1 teasp. salt
1 tablesp. snipped parsley

Day before:
Make Braciole, then refrigerate until needed next day.

Early on the day:
1. Make noodles,* by stirring together well the flour, eggs, and water. On lightly floured board, knead this mixture into a smooth ball (takes about 3 min.), then cut into 3 parts. Roll each part into a very thin sheet, then cut into 6″ squares—14 to 16 squares in all. Let these noodles dry 1 hr.

2. Meanwhile, prepare filling by mixing together ricotta, egg yolks, salt, and parsley. Then, at end of hour, cook noodles, a few at a time, in boiling salted water till tender—about 15 min. Then drain them, and lay each one flat.

* You can buy 6″ noodle squares, if preferred.

3. Now place 2 to 3 tablesp. filling in center of each noodle, from corner to corner, then fold diagonally opposite points to center (it now looks like a pillow). Refrigerate until needed.

About 45 min. before dinner:

1. Start heating oven to 350°F. Heat Braciole, first lifting off fat. Now spoon some of sauce down center of 3 baking dishes, each about 12" long.

2. Then cover sauce with row of Manicotti, and spoon more sauce on top. Bake 30 min. Serve, with rest of sauce and Braciole beef rolls, cut into 1" slices. Makes 14 to 16 Manicotti.

BRACIOLE

1 1-lb.-13-oz. can Italian tomatoes	2 tablesp. bacon drippings
1 6-oz. can tomato paste	2 tablesp. grated Parmesan cheese
1 teasp. dried sweet basil	½ teasp. salt
1½ teasp. salt	⅛ teasp. pepper
3 ¼" thick slices top round (about 2 lb.)	1½ teasp. special herb blend *
	2 tablesp. fat or salad oil
1 clove garlic, peeled, slivered	2 cloves garlic, peeled

Day before:

1. In medium saucepan, combine tomatoes, tomato paste, basil, and 1½ teasp. salt. Let simmer while you fix beef rolls.

2. Cover beef slices with 1 clove slivered garlic, bacon drippings, cheese, ½ teasp. salt, pepper, and herb blend.

3. Then, roll each piece from short side, jelly-roll-fashion, and tie with string. Brown in fat in skillet on all sides, adding whole garlic cloves for extra flavor.

4. Then add meat and drippings to tomato mixture and simmer about 3 hr., uncovered, or until tender.

5. Cool; refrigerate until needed next day for Manicotti, p. 67.

* For special herb blend, toss together ¼ teasp. each dried orégano, rosemary, basil, and marjoram, plus 2 teasp. snipped parsley.

In Southern Italy you'll find Polenta served often—usually topped with tomato sauce and grated cheese. In Northern Italy, however, the mush is often served plain, in place of potatoes.

POLENTA, SOUTHERN-STYLE
(Corn-Meal Mush)

3 cups water	1 cup corn meal
½ teasp. salt	1 tablesp. butter or margarine

Bring water to boil; add salt; then gradually stir in corn meal. Boil 5 min., stirring, until thick. Cook, covered, over boiling water 30 min., stirring occasionally. Stir in butter. Serve, topped with tomato sauce and grated cheese, if desired. Makes 4 servings.

It's not unusual for Italians to have salad twice a day. Here it's tender-crisp cauliflowerets to which they add bits of anchovy, olives, shallots, and capers, just before the oil and vinegar are tossed in.

INSALATA DI CAVOLFIORE
(*Cauliflower Salad*)

½ medium head cauliflower
3 anchovy fillets, cut into small
  pieces
5 ripe olives, pitted, sliced
1½ teasp. minced shallots or
  onion

1½ teasp. bottled capers
Freshly ground pepper
1½ tablesp. olive or salad oil
1½ teasp. wine vinegar

1. Wash, then trim, head of cauliflower; break into small flowerets. Cook in 1″ boiling salted water about 10 min., or until tender-crisp. Drain; refrigerate.
2. In salad bowl, place chilled cauliflower, anchovy fillets, olives, shallots, capers. Sprinkle generously with pepper; pour oil and vinegar over all. Toss well. Refrigerate 30 min.; then serve. Makes 2 servings.

For 4 servings: Use 7 anchovy fillets, doubling all other ingredients. Proceed as directed.

One delicately flavored version of Italy's very popular Easter cheese pie.

TORTA DI RICOTTA
(*Cheese Torte*)

1½ cups sifted all-purpose flour
⅓ cup granulated sugar
1 teasp. double-acting baking
  powder
¼ teasp. salt
¼ cup butter or margarine
About ¼ to ⅓ cup milk

½ teasp. vanilla extract
1 lb. ricotta cheese
1½ cups granulated sugar
¼ teasp. salt
4 eggs
2 teasp. vanilla extract

1. Start heating oven to 350°F.
2. Into large bowl, sift flour, ⅓ cup sugar, baking powder, ¼ teasp. salt. With pastry blender or 2 knives, scissor-fashion, cut butter into flour mixture until like coarse meal.
3. Make well in center of mixture; into it, pour ¼ cup milk, ½ teasp. vanilla. With fork, mix lightly and quickly. Add enough more milk to form dough just moist enough to leave sides of bowl and cling to fork as ball. Turn onto lightly floured surface.
4. Knead slightly, by picking up side of dough farthest away; fold over; with palms, press down, pushing dough away *lightly*.

Turn dough around part way; repeat 5 times, working *gently*.
5. Set aside one fourth of dough. Lightly roll remaining dough from center to edge in all directions, forming circle about 1½" wider all around than inverted 9" pie plate. Line pie plate with pastry, leaving overhang.
6. Make filling: With rotary beater or electric mixer at medium speed, beat cheese, 1½ cups sugar, ¼ teasp. salt, eggs, and 2 teasp. vanilla until very thick and smooth. Turn into pie shell.
7. Roll reserved dough into circle; cut into ½" strips. Attach 4 strips from one edge of pie to other, then 4 more strips, criss-crossing pie. Flute edge.
8. Bake about 45 min., or until nicely browned. Cool on wire rack. Serve slightly warm.

A treat from Italy—often their Christmas delicacy supreme. Bits of pastry that pop into golden nuggets when shallow fried. Then they're honey-coated, tossed with pine nuts, and sprinkled with candy confetti.

STRUFOLI OR PIGNOLATA

4 to 5 cups unsifted all-purpose flour	1 qt. salad oil
2 teasp. double-acting baking powder	6 eggs, beaten
1 teasp. salt	1½-lb. jar honey
3 tablesp. white wine	½ cup pine nuts
	Colored sprinkles
	Candied cherries

Prepare several days or a week ahead:
1. Put 4 cups flour in sifter on pastry board; add baking powder and salt; sift onto board. Make a well in center, then add wine, ¼ cup salad oil, and beaten eggs gradually, blending them in with a fork. Knead dough on board until blended, smooth, and soft. Divide dough in half, keeping one half under damp cloth.
2. On well-floured board, roll unwrapped dough to ¼" thickness; then cut it into strips ½" wide. With palms of hands roll each strip, once over, into a pencil-shaped roll; with floured knife, cut each roll into ¼" pieces.
3. In deep saucepan, heat rest of salad oil to 350°F. on deep-fat-frying thermometer. Then drop in pieces, stirring to brown evenly. Remove with slotted spoon, drain on paper toweling. Repeat with rest of dough; then, after draining, place all the Strufoli in large bowl.
4. Now simmer honey to 250°F. on a candy thermometer, or until a little of the mixture, dropped in cold water, forms a soft ball. Remove from heat; stir in pine nuts; pour over golden nuggets, tossing to coat well.

5. Let stand, covered, for 12 to 24 hr. or up to a week or so.
6. At serving time, heap them in a large serving dish or individual paper cups. Top with colored sprinkles and candied cherries. Then place where everyone can help himself, with paper napkins close by. They are irresistible nibblers for dessert time. Makes about 13 cups.

To Vary: You may omit ¼ cup salad oil. Or add 1 cup chopped walnuts and/or some semisweet-chocolate pieces to the heated honey before pouring it over the Strufoli.

Among Italians this is a favorite light custardy dessert.

ZABAGLIONE
(*A Delicious Wine Whip*)

3 egg yolks
1½ tablesp. granulated sugar

2 half eggshellfuls Italian Marsala

1. In top of double boiler, beat egg yolks, gradually adding sugar and Marsala.
2. Cook over hot, *not boiling,* water, beating vigorously with whip or egg beater until very thick. Serve hot. Makes 2 servings.
NOTE: The half eggshell is used to measure Marsala so that the wine will be in proportion to the amount of egg used.

For 4 servings: Double ingredients; proceed as above.

Norway

One of Norway's two-in-one dinners in which meat and vegetables simmer together until tender. Then they're divided into two courses—a luscious soup, followed by meat and vegetables.

FERSK SUPPE OG KJØTT
(*Two-Course Dinner Dish*)

2 lb. chuck beef, or meaty short
ribs
1 knucklebone
2 qt. water
4 teasp. salt
1 piece whole ginger

½ lb. cabbage, cut in strips
1 leek, sliced
5 carrots, pared
1 parsnip, pared
4 or more medium potatoes
Snipped parsley

Place meat and bone in large kettle with water and salt. Bring to boil; skim surface; add ginger. Cover and let simmer 1½ hr., then add cabbage and leek and cook about 15 min.; then add carrots and parsnip and cook 30 min., or until meat and vegetables are tender. Meanwhile, start boiling potatoes until tender.

When meat and vegetables are tender, remove meat to platter; surround with 4 carrots and potatoes; keep hot. Remove 1½ cups soup broth with as little cabbage as possible. Slice remaining carrot and parsnip and return to soup in kettle; keep hot.

Now make this onion gravy (Löksaus): In small saucepan, stir 1 tablesp. butter with 5 teasp. flour until well mixed. Slowly stir in reserved 1½ cups soup broth; add 2 tablesp. minced onion; simmer 5 min. Add 1 tablesp. vinegar and 2 teasp. sugar. Dinner is now ready!

Serve soup with sprinkling of snipped parsley. Follow it with the meat-and-vegetable main course platter, topped with the onion gravy. Makes 4 servings.

Norwegians live robust, open-air lives and have hearty appetites. Their cooks respond with favorites such as these.

KONGESUPPE
(Royal Soup)

Butter or margarine	Snipped parsley
1 small onion, peeled, minced	2 teasp. seasoned salt
¾ cup finely diced, pared carrots	¼ cup pkgd. dried bread crumbs
5 tablesp. flour	1 egg, beaten
⅛ teasp. cayenne pepper	½ 10-oz. pkg. frozen peas
5 beef-bouillon cubes	3 tablesp. sherry
1 lb. chuck, ground	

About 1 hr. before serving:

1. In large saucepan melt 3 tablesp. butter or margarine; in it sauté onion and carrots until golden-brown. Add flour, cayenne pepper, and bouillon cubes; then add 5½ cups water and bring to a boil, while stirring constantly. Simmer, partially covered, for 15 min.
2. Meanwhile make meat balls: Combine ground chuck, ¼ cup snipped parsley, seasoned salt, bread crumbs, and egg. Form into about 25 balls. In a large skillet, melt 1 tablesp. butter or margarine; in it sauté meat balls until brown on all sides. Add to soup, together with frozen peas and sherry and simmer 5 min.
3. Serve as a main-dish soup in individual bowls, sprinkled with parsley. Makes about 6 servings.

NORSK NØTT BRØD
(*Norwegian Walnut Bread*)

1 cup sifted all-purpose flour
1 teasp. baking soda
1 teasp. salt
½ cup chopped California walnuts

1 cup unsifted whole-wheat flour
¾ cup chopped pitted dates
1 beaten egg
1 cup buttermilk
2 tablesp. salad oil

Make day before, or early on the day, as follows:
1. Start heating oven to 375°F. Into medium bowl sift flour with soda and salt; then add walnuts, whole-wheat flour, and dates.
2. Combine egg, buttermilk, and salad oil; stir into flour mixture until well blended. Spoon into 3 greased, empty 16-oz. cans.
3. Bake 50 min., or until golden and done. With small spatula loosen around edges, then turn out on rack to cool. Serve with butter or cream cheese. Makes 3 small loaves.

The gayest holiday on Norway's calendar is Constitution Day, May 17. Favorites of the day are two desserts that follow.

BLØT KAKE
(*Layer Cake*)

1¼ cups sifted cake flour
2 teasp. double-acting baking powder
6 egg yolks
¾ cup granulated sugar
6 egg whites

3 sq. German sweet cooking chocolate
¾ cup butter or margarine
1¼ cups confectioners' sugar
2 eggs
2 cups heavy cream

Make, then freeze several days ahead, as follows:
1. Start heating oven to 325°F. Line bottom of 3 9″ layer-cake pans with wax paper. Sift cake flour with baking powder.
2. In small bowl, with electric mixer at high speed, beat egg yolks with granulated sugar till light. In large bowl, beat egg whites stiff; fold in yolks and flour. Pour into pans.
3. Bake 15 min., or till golden. Cool, inverted on racks; remove from pans. Freezer-wrap; freeze.

Early in afternoon on the day:
1. Thaw wrapped cakes at room temperature 1 hr. Meanwhile, with knife, shred chocolate; reserve ¼ cup. Also, in small bowl, with electric mixer at high speed, mix butter with confectioners' sugar; beat in 2 eggs till creamy; refrigerate this butter-cream.
2. On serving plate, place one layer, bottom side up; top with half of butter-cream, then half of shredded chocolate. Set second layer in place; top as before; place third layer.
3. Whip cream; frost cake with some; decorate with rest. Garnish with reserved chocolate; refrigerate till served.

FYRSTE KAKE
(Prince Cake)

1 cup blanched almonds
¾ cup confectioners' sugar
¼ cup egg whites, unbeaten
2 eggs
¾ cup butter or margarine

1½ teasp. almond extract
3 tablesp. granulated sugar
1½ cups sifted all-purpose flour
⅓ cup raspberry jam (optional)

Early on the day:

1. Using very fine blade of food chopper, grind almonds three times. Blend with confectioners' sugar, unbeaten egg whites, 1 egg, ¼ cup butter, and almond extract. Refrigerate this almond paste.

2. In small bowl, with electric mixer at medium speed, mix ½ cup butter with granulated sugar and 1 egg. Fold in flour; refrigerate this dough 15 min.

3. On lightly floured wax paper, roll two thirds of dough into 11" circle, ⅛" thick. Place, dough side down, in 9" layer-cake pan; carefully pull off paper. Fit to pan; patch, if needed, to make even with top.

4. Now, over dough on pan bottom, spread raspberry jam, then almond paste.

5. Roll reserved third of dough into rectangle, ⅛" thick. With pastry wheel, cut six 8" x ¾" strips. Lay three strips, 1¼" apart, over almond paste; lay rest at right angles.

6. Reroll pastry trimmings; cut five 5" x ¾" strips. Place, end to end, against inside edge of pan; with pastry wheel, trim even with top of cake.

7. Bake at 350°F. 45 min.; cool in pan; with spatula, carefully lift out cake. Serve, cut into wedges.

Do as they do in Norway. Serve this cardamom-flavored Christmas bread, with or without butter, for morning or afternoon coffee.

JULEKAKE
(Norwegian Holiday Bread)

½ cup butter or margarine
½ cup milk
1 pkg. active dry, or cake, yeast
½ cup warm water
¼ cup granulated sugar
1 teasp. salt
1 egg, slightly beaten
1 teasp. powdered cardamom
1 cup light or dark raisins

¼ cup diced preserved orange peel
¼ cup diced preserved pineapple
¼ cup snipped candied cherries
3½ to 4 cups sifted all-purpose flour
Egg white, beaten
Confectioners' sugar
Candied cherries
Angelica leaves

Make early on the day, as follows:
1. In saucepan, heat butter with milk until butter is just melted; cool to lukewarm.
2. In 3-qt. mixing bowl, sprinkle yeast onto warm water, then stir until dissolved. Now stir in sugar, salt, egg, cardamom, raisins, orange peel, pineapple, cherries, milk mixture.
3. Gradually stir in flour, beating well after each addition, until a stiff dough. Cover; let rise in a warm place (80°F. to 85°F.) until double—1½ to 2 hr.
4. Turn dough on lightly floured board and knead lightly until no longer sticky. Grease a 2-lb. coffee can well; shape dough into rounded loaf; place in can; let rise until double. (Or divide in half; shape, place in two greased 1-lb. coffee cans. Cover, let rise until double—about 1 hr.)
5. Meanwhile, start heating oven to 350°F. When bread has doubled, brush it with beaten egg white.
6. Then bake 2-lb. loaf 1 hr.; or 1-lb. loaves 30 to 35 min., or until done. Remove from cans at once; cool on racks.
7. Then decorate top with icing made of confectioners' sugar and a little water; garnish with cherries and angelica leaves.

Poland

In Poland everyday fare is traditionally substantial (prompted by a stern winter climate). But it's exciting too—especially when there are fresh mushrooms in sour cream—a national favorite.

PIECZEN HAZARSKA
(Hussar Roast)

⅓ cup butter or margarine
5 to 6 lb. boned bottom round beef
1 cup canned condensed beef broth, undiluted
1 large onion, peeled, quartered
2 teasp. salt

2 cups fresh bread crumbs, packed
3 large onions, peeled, grated
2 teasp. salt
¼ teasp. pepper
¼ cup butter or margarine, melted
2 tablesp. flour

1. In ⅓ cup butter or margarine, in Dutch oven, over medium heat, brown beef well on all sides. Then pour in beef broth.

2. Add the quartered onion and 2 teasp. salt; simmer roast, covered, for 2½ to 3 hr., or until tender, turning now and then.
3. Meanwhile, in bowl, combine bread crumbs, grated onions, 2 teasp. salt, pepper, and ¼ cup melted butter.
4. Remove roast from Dutch oven; untie; with knife, cut ¼"-thick crosswise slices from top of roast to within 1" of bottom.
5. Now place some of bread-crumb mixture between every two slices. Then insert two 3" wooden skewers into each end of the stuffed roast.
6. Skim all fat from drippings in Dutch oven; replace roast in Dutch oven; sprinkle with flour; simmer, covered, for ½ hr.
7. Arrange roast on heated large platter; remove skewers. Nice served with boiled potatoes and Mushrooms with Sour Cream, below. Makes 6 to 8 servings.

GRZYBY W SMIETANIE
(Mushrooms with Sour Cream)

6 tablesp. butter or margarine	1¼ lb. fresh mushrooms, sliced
1 large onion, peeled, chopped	¾ teasp. salt
2 tablesp. flour	¼ teasp. pepper
2 tablesp. milk	¼ teasp. paprika
1½ cups commercial sour cream	

1. In melted butter in large skillet, sauté onion till golden. Sprinkle with flour; add milk and ¾ cup sour cream; while stirring, bring just to a simmer.
2. Then add sliced mushrooms, salt, pepper, and paprika. Simmer, covered, for 5 min., stirring occasionally.
3. Stir in remaining ¾ cup sour cream; heat thoroughly, while stirring constantly. Serve at once. Makes 6 servings.

Rings of Polish sausage, known in U.S.A. as kielbasa, are available most everywhere. Their mild, slightly garlicky flavor has made them very popular.

KIELBASKI DUSZONE W CZERWONEJ KAPUSCIE
(Sausage Smothered in Red Cabbage)

1 small head red cabbage	1 small onion, chopped
1 small apple, pared and diced	⅛ teasp. pepper
Salt	1 tablesp. wine vinegar
1 tablesp. lemon juice	1 kielbasa (Polish sausage)
1 tablesp. butter or margarine	

About 50 min. before serving:
1. Quarter cabbage, then with sharp knife shred it coarsely, discarding tough center; rinse cabbage, then place in kettle along

with diced apple, 2 teasp. salt, lemon juice, and ½ cup water. Bring to a boil, then simmer, covered, about 15 min., stirring occasionally.

2. Meanwhile, in hot butter or margarine, in skillet, sauté onion until golden; then add to cabbage along with 1 teasp. salt, pepper, vinegar, and sausage. Cook, covered, 20 to 30 min., or until sausage is heated through.

3. Spoon cabbage onto heated platter; then top with sausage, cut into pieces. Makes 5 servings.

Portugal

As one would expect, Portuguese cookery highlights fish and shellfish in all sorts of delectable ways. And, of course, their canned sardines are famous the world over.

BACALHAU À GOMES DE SÁ
(*Codfish, Portuguese-Style*)

4 eggs	3 medium yellow onions, peeled, sliced
4 medium potatoes	
3½ teasp. salt	½ cup chopped ripe pitted olives
1½ lb. fresh cod fillets	½ teasp. seasoned salt
½ cup olive oil	⅛ teasp. pepper
2 cloves garlic, peeled, finely chopped	¼ cup dry white wine
	Few sprigs parsley
	2 tablesp. snipped parsley

About 1 hr. and 15 min. before serving:

1. Hard-cook eggs; drain, cool in cold water.

2. Cook potatoes in boiling water with 1 teasp. salt for 20 min., or until just tender. In saucepan, over medium heat, cook cod with 1 cup water and 2 teasp. salt, covered, until tender, about 15 to 20 min.

3. Drain and peel potatoes; cut in half lengthwise, then cut crosswise into ¼"-thick slices. Drain and flake cod, removing bones. Start heating oven to 350°F.

4. In large skillet, heat olive oil; add garlic, onions, and potatoes; brown well over medium heat, turning occasionally, about 10 min. Add olives, seasoned salt, and ¼ teasp. salt.

5. Arrange half of this mixture over bottom of 12" x 8" x 2" baking dish; evenly lay cod over it; sprinkle with ¼ teasp. salt and pepper. Cover with rest of potato mixture. Pour on wine, then bake 15 to 20 min., or until hot.

6. Meanwhile, shell eggs; cut two into 4 wedges each, chop other two coarsely.

7. Before serving, place two egg wedges and a sprig of parsley in each of the four corners of the baking dish. Sprinkle chopped eggs and snipped parsley along center of dish.

8. Serve immediately as a luncheon or dinner dish, preferably with grilled tomato halves, a tossed mixed salad, hot rolls and butter. Makes 4 or 5 servings.

In their liberal use of garlic, oil, onions, and tomatoes, Portuguese dishes seem more closely akin to the Italian table than any other.

FRANGO GUISADO
(*Stewed Chicken*)

2 tablesp. flour	3 tablesp. snipped parsley
2 teasp. salt	3 medium tomatoes
⅛ teasp. pepper	1 teasp. ground coriander seed
1 2½-lb. broiler-fryer, cut up	1½ teasp. seasoned salt
¼ cup olive oil	½ cup hot water
1 large onion, peeled, chopped	1 cup port wine
1 large clove garlic, peeled, crushed	1 medium green pepper, seeded, in 1″ pieces

About 1 hr. and 15 min. before serving:

1. In large paper bag, combine flour with salt and pepper. Add chicken pieces; shake vigorously to coat all pieces well.

2. In large skillet, over medium heat, heat olive oil; add chicken pieces; with two-tined fork, turn chicken pieces occasionally to brown them well on all sides. Remove them from skillet to sheet of wax paper. Now, to remaining drippings in skillet, add chopped onion and crushed garlic. Then sauté until a delicate light-brown.

3. Into same skillet, stir 2 tablesp. snipped parsley; 2 tomatoes, coarsely chopped; ground coriander seed, and seasoned salt. Now add reserved chicken pieces, hot water, and ½ cup port wine; bring to a boil and simmer, covered, over low heat, for about 15 min.

4. Now add green-pepper pieces and simmer 15 min. longer, or until chicken is done and green pepper is tender-crisp. Then pour in ½ cup port wine, blending slightly. Bring to a boil and arrange on heated serving platter.

5. Cut 1 medium tomato into 6 wedges, place here and there on chicken pieces to garnish. Then sprinkle with 1 tablesp. snipped parsley. Makes 4 servings. Serve with fluffy rice or noodles.

Scotland

Scotch broth, as they serve it in Scotland, is a superb two-course meal in itself.

SCOTCH BROTH

3 lb. lamb shoulder, in one piece
Salt
½ teasp. pepper
⅓ cup quick-cooking split peas (yellow or green)
⅓ cup barley
3 qt. water
2 medium carrots
About ½ yellow turnip
2 medium onions, peeled, cut into eighths

1 leek, sliced
2 tablesp. butter or margarine
3 tablesp. flour
½ teasp. dry mustard
1 tablesp. vinegar
1 tablesp. bottled capers
Snipped parsley
Boiled potatoes
Cooked cabbage or broccoli

About 2 hr. and 15 min. before serving:

1. In large kettle place lamb, 2 tablesp. salt, pepper, split peas, and barley. Add water, bring to a boil, then skim surface. Now simmer, covered, 1½ hr. Then skim off fat, if desired.
2. Pare carrots; cut one into ½" cubes; coarsely shred the other; pare turnip, cut half of it into ½" cubes, shred rest to make 2 cups in all. Add to soup with onions and leek. Simmer 30 min., or until meat and vegetables are tender.
3. Meanwhile, make this Caper Sauce: Melt butter in small saucepan. Stir in flour until smooth, then 1½ cups broth from soup, mustard, ½ teasp. salt, vinegar, and capers. Bring to a boil, while stirring, then cook until thickened.
4. Remove meat from soup. Serve soup as a first course, sprinkled with parsley. Slice the meat; arrange with potatoes and cabbage on platter. Serve as main course, passing Caper Sauce. Makes 6 servings.

Europe

Scotland impresses travelers at teatime with its delicious teacakes and breads.

DUNDEE CAKE
(A Light Fruitcake)

1 cup butter or margarine
⅔ cup granulated sugar
4 eggs
2½ cups sifted cake flour
1 teasp. double-acting baking
  powder
½ teasp. salt
1 cup currants
½ cup dark seedless raisins

½ cup finely chopped candied
  citron
1 4½-oz. can blanched almonds,
  coarsely chopped (about 1¼
  cups)
Grated rind 1 lemon
2 tablesp. grated orange rind
2 tablesp. orange or lemon juice

Make one to three days before serving:
1. In large bowl, with electric mixer at medium speed, beat butter and sugar until creamy; then beat in eggs, one at a time, until fluffy. Start heating oven to 325°F.
2. Sift together cake flour, baking powder, and salt; then stir in currants, raisins, citron, almonds, lemon rind, and orange rind. Beat into butter mixture alternately with orange or lemon juice. Pour into greased 10″ x 5″ x 3″ loaf pan.
3. Bake 70 to 80 min., or until cake tester, inserted in center, comes out clean. Cool in pan 10 min., then turn out on rack to cool completely. Wrap in foil to keep fresh. Serve cut into slices.

Scotland is famed for its buttery cookie—shortbread—and its scones, those delicious, slightly sweet biscuits. There's a tradition in Scotland that the first one who crosses the threshold on New Year's Day bearing a gift of shortbread will have good luck.

SCOTCH SHORTBREAD

1 cup butter
½ cup superfine sugar

1½ cups sifted all-purpose flour
½ cup rice flour *

A few days ahead:
1. In medium bowl, with electric mixer at medium speed, beat butter with sugar until creamy. Start heating oven to 300°F.
2. Sift together the two flours, then beat into butter mixture until smooth. With small spatula spread this mixture evenly on bottom of 2 8″ layer-cake pans. With pointed knife make indentations all around edge, then prick top all over with fork.
3. Bake 1 hr., or until light-brown. Cool in pans on racks. Then remove, and when time to serve, cut each into 12 wedges. To store, wrap in foil.

* An equal amount of sifted all-purpose flour may be substituted for the rice flour.

RAISIN SCONES

2⅓ cups sifted cake flour
2½ teasp. double-acting baking
    powder
½ teasp. salt
Granulated sugar

6 tablesp. butter or margarine
½ cup light or dark raisins
5 tablesp. milk or light cream
2 eggs

1. Start heating oven to 450°F. Lightly grease cookie sheet. Into large bowl, sift cake flour, with baking powder, salt, and 2 teasp. sugar.
2. With pastry blender or two knives, used scissor-fashion, cut butter or margarine into flour mixture till it's like corn meal. Blend in raisins and milk or light cream.
3. Separate 1 egg; reserve 1 tablesp. egg white. Beat rest of this egg with another egg; stir into flour mixture.
4. On lightly floured surface, roll out dough ½" thick. Cut into 3" squares; then cut each square into two triangles.
5. Arrange on cookie sheet; brush with reserved egg white, slightly beaten; sprinkle with 2 tablesp. sugar. Bake 10 to 15 min., or till golden. Serve, hot or cold, with butter, jam, or marmalade for a tea or breakfast, or as is for supper. Makes 10.
NOTE: You may substitute ½ cup chopped pitted dates for the light or dark raisins.

Soviet Union

There are several versions of this elegant dish, named for a Russian gourmet, Count Stroganoff. The classic one boasts of mustard in the sauce.

BEEF STROGANOFF

Butter or margarine
1½ tablesp. flour
1 10½ oz. can condensed con-
    sommé, undiluted
½ cup water
1 teasp. prepared mustard
1 to 2 tablesp. canned tomato
    paste (optional)
1 medium onion, peeled, chopped

½ lb. fresh mushrooms, quartered
    (optional)
1½ lb. lean sirloin steak or fillet
    of beef, cut into thin strips, 2"
    long, ½" wide
1½ teasp. salt
½ teasp. pepper
¼ cup commercial sour cream
Boiled potatoes or cooked broad
    noodles

About 40 min. before serving:
1. In saucepan melt 1 tablesp. butter; in it brown flour lightly;

then stir in consommé, water, mustard, and tomato paste. Bring to a boil and cook until thickened. Set aside.

2. In large skillet melt 2 tablesp. butter; in it sauté onion and mushrooms until golden. Next add sirloin and brown, stirring frequently. Stir in salt and pepper, then the sauce. Simmer, covered, about 25 min., or until meat is tender.

3. In small bowl beat together sour cream and part of sauce from skillet. Return to meat in skillet. Heat gently, then serve with small boiled potatoes or buttered noodles. Makes 4 to 6 servings.

P.S. If fillet of beef is used, reduce cooking time to 5 to 8 minutes.

Traditionally a Pirog is a large, well-filled, rectangular envelope of pie crust. The fillings vary from meat, to fish, mushrooms, cabbage, or carrots. In Russia they bring it to the table on a wooden board, covered with a napkin, and serve a slice as an accompaniment to soup.

MIASO PIROG
(*Meat Pie*)

2 cups sifted all-purpose flour	2 medium onions, peeled, chopped
½ teasp. double-acting baking powder	½ lb. fresh mushrooms, sliced
½ teasp. salt	1½ lb. lean chuck, ground once
Butter or margarine	½ cup snipped parsley
1 egg, beaten	½ teasp. pepper
1¼ cups commercial sour cream	1 tablesp. salt
	3 hard-cooked eggs, shelled, sliced

About 1 hr. and 40 min. before serving:

1. Sift flour, baking powder, and ½ teasp. salt. With pastry blender, or 2 knives, scissor-fashion, cut 6 tablesp. butter into flour mixture until like coarse corn meal. Beat together egg and ¼ cup sour cream. Add to flour mixture and toss quickly together, forming a smooth ball. Wrap in wax paper and refrigerate until chilled.

2. In large skillet melt 2 tablesp. butter; in it sauté onions and mushrooms until golden. Next add chuck and sauté about 10 min., turning frequently. Remove from heat. Stir in parsley, pepper, 1 tablesp. salt, and 1 cup sour cream. Set aside. Start heating oven to 375°F.

3. Roll out two thirds of pastry; use to line a 10″ fluted pie plate, 2″ deep, then trim pastry even with edge. Pour half of meat mixture on bottom of pie plate; over it arrange egg slices. Pour on rest of meat mixture, mounding it slightly.

4. Roll out rest of dough, a little larger than pie plate. Use to top pie, then turn edge of top crust under, making scalloped edge. Cut out little circle in center of top crust to let steam escape.

5. Bake 50 min. to 1 hr., or until golden-brown. Serve, cut into 8 to 12 wedges, with a tossed mixed salad.

P.S. Pie may be made up early on the day, or day before, then refrigerated until it is time to bake it.

RIBA PIROG
(*Fish Pie*)

Pastry (see step 1 in Meat Pie, p. 82)
2 tablesp. butter or margarine
1½ lb. haddock fillets
½ cup snipped parsley
1 tablesp. snipped dill
2 teasp. salt
¼ teasp. pepper
Dash nutmeg
1 cup commercial sour cream
½ lb. smoked salmon, thinly sliced

About 1 hr. and 40 min. before serving:

1. Make up pastry, then refrigerate until chilled. In large skillet melt butter; in it sauté haddock fillets until golden. Remove from heat, then stir in parsley, dill, salt, pepper, nutmeg, and sour cream. Set aside. Start heating oven to 375°F.

2. Roll out two thirds of pastry; use to line a 10″ fluted pie plate, 2″ deep; then trim pastry even with edge. Arrange half of salmon slices on bottom of pie plate. Over them spread fish mixture. Top with rest of salmon slices. Now proceed as in steps 4 and 5 of Meat Pie, p. 82. Makes 8 to 12 servings.

P.S. Pie may be made up early on the day, or day before, then refrigerated until it is time to bake it.

GURITCHA Y RIS PIROG
(*Chicken-and-Rice Pie*)

1 3-lb. broiler-fryer
1 onion, peeled, sliced
1 stalk celery, cut up
1 clove garlic, peeled
10 whole peppercorns
4 whole cloves
2 bay leaves
1 qt. water
Pastry (see step 1 in Meat Pie, p. 82)
1½ tablesp. flour
¾ cup heavy cream
¼ cup snipped parsley
1 tablesp. lemon juice
⅛ teasp. nutmeg
½ lb. fresh mushrooms, sliced
2 tablesp. butter or margarine
1½ cups cooked rice
4 hard-cooked eggs, shelled, sliced

About 2½ hr. before serving:

1. In large kettle place chicken, onion, celery, garlic, peppercorns, cloves, bay leaves, 1 tablesp. salt, and water. Bring to a boil, then cook, covered, 45 min., or until chicken is just tender. Meanwhile, make up pastry, then refrigerate until chilled.

2. Strain broth from chicken, then remove skin and bones. Cut chicken meat into small pieces. In small saucepan beat together flour and cream; add 1 cup chicken broth. Bring to boil, while stirring, then cook until thickened; set aside. Start heating oven to 375°F.

3. Combine chicken meat with parsley, lemon juice, nutmeg, and 1½ teasp. salt. Sauté mushrooms, in butter in skillet, until golden; set aside.

4. Roll out two thirds of pastry; use to line a 10″ fluted pie plate, 2″ deep; then trim pastry even with edge.

5. Spread half of rice over bottom of pie plate. On it spread half of sliced eggs, then half of chicken mixture. Top with mushrooms, rest of eggs, then rest of chicken mixture and rice. Pour on sauce. Now proceed as in steps 4 and 5 of Meat Pie, pp. 82–83. Makes 8 to 12 servings.

P.S. Pie may be made up early on the day or day before, then refrigerated until it is time to bake it.

One of the interesting features of Russian cooking is a generous use of sour cream. They find the piquant flavor appealing (you will too), and use it whenever possible.

ZAVIANI BYTKY
(Veal Rolls)

8 veal cutlets, 5″ x 2½″ x ¼″	¼ teasp. pepper
¼ lb. beef round, ground	1 tablesp. minced onion
¼ lb. lean pork, ground	3 tablesp. snipped parsley
2 tablesp. pkgd. dried bread crumbs	3 tablesp. butter or margarine
	1 4-oz. can sliced mushrooms
¼ cup light cream	½ pt. commercial sour cream
1 egg	1 teasp. sugar
1½ teasp. salt	1 teasp. Worcestershire

1. Trim fat and connective tissue from cutlets. Mix well beef, pork, crumbs, light cream, egg, 1 teasp. salt, pepper, onion, parsley.

2. Then spoon 2 rounded tablesp. of meat mixture onto one end of each cutlet. Roll each cutlet from filled end; skewer.

3. Now, in skillet, heat butter; in it, brown veal well. Add undrained mushrooms, sour cream; simmer, covered, ¾ hr., or till tender.

4. Remove skewers from rolls; arrange on heated platter. Season gravy with ½ teasp. salt, sugar, Worcestershire; pour over rolls. Serve with mashed potatoes or fluffy rice. Makes 4 servings.

Russia's Chicken Kiev—chicken cutlets stuffed with butter—are international favorites. Here's another, that shows their touch with chicken.

FARSHIROVANAYA GURITCHA
(*Stuffed Boneless Chicken*)

1 3½- to 4-lb. roasting chicken	Seasoned salt
Breasts of 2 broiler-fryers, skinned, boned	¼ teasp. pepper
	½ teasp. poultry seasoning
Butter or margarine	1 teasp. dried marjoram
½ lb. fresh mushrooms, sliced	¼ cup heavy cream
1 slice fresh bread, crumbled	1 teasp. cornstarch
1 egg	1 cup canned chicken broth

Early on the day or day before:
1. Ask meatman to separate skin from chicken in one piece, making incision on the back, and separating wings and drumsticks from body at the joints, but leaving them in the skin.
2. Remove meat from all but wings and drumsticks; pass, with chicken breasts, through coarse blade of food chopper.
3. In medium skillet melt 2 tablesp. butter or margarine; in it lightly brown mushrooms. Add them to ground chicken together with bread, egg, 2 teasp. seasoned salt, pepper, poultry seasoning, marjoram, and cream, stirring until well blended.
4. Spoon chicken mixture onto inside of chicken skin and sew together with kitchen thread, in shape to resemble body of chicken. Tuck wings under, then sprinkle chicken with 1 teasp. seasoned salt and brush with 2 tablesp. melted butter or margarine. Place in medium baking pan, cover with foil and refrigerate.

About 1 hr. and 20 min. before serving:
Start heating oven to 350°F. Stir cornstarch with chicken broth until smooth, then pour into baking pan around chicken. Bake chicken 1 hr. and 15 min., or until firm and golden, basting it occasionally. Serve hot, cut into slices, with gravy spooned over them. Nice with fluffy rice for lunch or dinner. Delicious cold too, served with a tossed mixed salad. Makes 6 to 8 servings.

Europe

In old Russia, Paskha, a pyramid-shaped treat of pot cheese, and Kulich, a cylindrical-shaped yeast bread, stood on the tables at Eastertime.

PASKHA
(*Easter Cheese "Cake"*)

1 lb. pot cheese or dry cottage
   cheese
½ cup butter or margarine
½ cup granulated sugar
1 egg yolk
½ cup commercial sour cream

½ cup shelled almonds, chopped
½ cup mixed glacéed fruit
1 teasp. vanilla extract
Heavy cream
Glacéed cherries

Day before:
1. Pass cheese through a fine sieve. In large bowl, with electric mixer at medium speed, beat butter with sugar until fluffy. Then beat in egg yolk, cheese, sour cream, almonds, glacéed fruit, and vanilla extract. Now carefully blend in ½ cup heavy cream, whipped.
2. Line a sieve or colander with cheesecloth. Spoon in cheese mixture, then fold ends of cheesecloth over top. Set in larger bowl to catch any drippings; refrigerate.

Just before serving:
Unfold ends of cheesecloth, invert cheese mixture on serving dish; remove cheesecloth. Decorate with a little whipped cream, then some glacéed cherries. Makes 8 to 10 dessert servings.

KULICH
(*Russian Easter Bread*)

2 pkg. active dry, or cakes, yeast
½ cup warm water
½ cup milk, scalded
¾ cup granulated sugar
¾ cup melted butter or margarine
1 teasp. vanilla extract
¼ teasp. powdered cardamom
1 teasp. salt
2 tablesp. grated lemon rind

3 eggs, beaten
¾ cup canned, toasted, slivered
   almonds
¾ cup mixed glacéed fruit
6 cups sifted all-purpose flour
1 cup sifted confectioners' sugar
5 teasp. lemon juice
Glacéed cherries

Day before serving:
1. Sprinkle yeast onto warm water to dissolve. In large bowl combine milk, granulated sugar, butter or margarine, vanilla extract, cardamom, salt, rind; when lukewarm add yeast, eggs, stirring until well blended. Add almonds (reserving about 2 tablesp. for later use), and glacéed fruit.

    Holland's St. Nicholas Cookies (Speculaas), page 54

2. Now gradually beat in flour, then turn onto a floured board and knead until smooth and satiny.

3. Place in greased bowl, cover with towel and let rise in warm place (80°F. to 85°F.) until doubled, about 2 hr. Punch down dough, divide in half, then place each half in a well-greased 1½-qt. casserole, or a 3-lb. shortening can. Cover and let rise in warm place until doubled.

4. Start heating oven to 350°F. Bake loaves 35 to 40 min., or until golden. Remove to rack, let cool; remove from casseroles.

5. Combine confectioners' sugar and lemon juice, blending until smooth. Spoon over tops of Kulich, sprinkle with reserved almonds, then decorate with glacéed cherries. Cover with wax paper until serving time. If desired, freeze one for later use. Nice for Easter breakfast, cut into wedges. Makes 2 loaves.

Spain

This famous iced soup-salad of Spain has a multitude of variations, each one more refreshing than the next.

GAZPACHO
(*Andalusian Cold Soup*)

6 medium tomatoes, peeled, minced	3 tablesp. vinegar
2 medium cucumbers, seeded, minced	4 teasp. salt
	¼ teasp. pepper
1 medium onion, peeled, minced	⅛ teasp. cayenne
1 4-oz. can pimentos, drained, minced	1 to 1½ cups canned tomato juice
	Ice cubes
1 to 2 cloves garlic, peeled, minced	Snipped parsley
¼ cup olive oil	Pitted ripe olives, sliced (optional)
	Toasted bread cubes (optional)

Several hours before serving:

1. In large bowl combine tomatoes, cucumbers, onion, pimentos, and garlic. Then stir in olive oil, vinegar, salt, pepper, cayenne, and tomato juice, blending well. Cover and refrigerate until well chilled.

2. Serve in soup bowls, with an ice cube in center of each, and sprinkled with parsley. If desired, sprinkle with olive slices and bread cubes. Makes about 8 servings.

Europe

The Spanish custom of dining late makes a nice once-in-a-while change of pace. Why not cap some evening out with this late-hour supper—quickly baked fish and a serve-it-cold dessert, both from Spain.

PESCADO ESPAÑOL
(Baked Fish, Spanish-Style)

6 2″ slices sea bass (3 lb.)
1¼ teasp. salt
⅜ teasp. pepper
¼ teasp. red pepper
¼ teasp. nutmeg
1 tablesp. olive oil
1 large onion, peeled, thinly sliced
1½ tablesp. chopped pimento

6 fillets of anchovy
6 thick slices peeled tomatoes
3 tablesp. snipped chives
1 cup thinly sliced fresh mushrooms
¼ cup white wine
½ cup melted butter or margarine
1 cup fresh bread crumbs

Early in day:
1. Wipe fish with damp cloth; dry. Sprinkle with mixture of salt, pepper, red pepper, and nutmeg.
2. Put olive oil in 12″ x 8″ x 2″ baking dish; top with onion, then pimento.
3. Now arrange seasoned fish slices, side by side, on top of onion slices. Next, place one anchovy fillet on each fish slice. Then cover each with a tomato slice and sprinkle with snipped chives. Next, scatter mushroom slices over all; then pour on wine.
4. Now tightly cover dish with foil and refrigerate.

About 1 hr. before serving:
1. Start heating oven to 450°F. Then place covered fish dish in oven and bake 25 to 30 min.
2. Meanwhile, combine melted butter and bread crumbs. Then uncover fish dish and sprinkle top of fish with buttered bread crumbs.
3. Bake, uncovered, until well browned—5 to 10 min.
4. Serve fish, piping hot, with crusty bread sticks or fluffy rice, seasoned with onion and paprika. Makes 6 servings.

MANZANAS EN DULCE
(Honeyed Apples)

½ cup chopped dried figs
⅓ cup chopped blanched almonds
½ cup water
1 cup honey

1 teasp. melted butter or margarine
6 medium apples

Early in day:
1. Start heating oven to 325°F. In small bowl, combine figs and almonds.

2. In another small bowl, stir together water, honey, and butter.

3. Now twist stems out of apples. Then, starting at blossom end, pare apples about a third of way down; also remove cores partway down.

4. Fill apples with almond filling; arrange in 12″ x 8″ x 2″ baking dish; pour on water-and-honey mixture. Bake, basting often with honey syrup, until tender but shapely—about 1¼ hr. Refrigerate until served. Makes 6 servings.

Our Spanish friends love colorful, spicy fare. Paella, their national dish, is dinner-on-a-platter—a succulent blend of chicken, shrimp, clams, saffron, and rice as the main stars.

PAELLA

¼ cup olive or salad oil
1 3-lb. broiler-fryer, cut up
2 large onions, peeled, sliced
2 cloves garlic, peeled, minced
1 1-lb.-12-oz. can whole tomatoes
1 teasp. salt
½ teasp. dried saffron
¼ cup boiling water
1 cup uncooked regular white rice

½ teasp. dried orégano
2 teasp. salt
1 lb. shelled, deveined raw shrimp
1 doz. soft-shell clams in shell, scrubbed well
1 10-oz. pkg. frozen peas
1 4-oz. can pimentos, cut into strips

1. In Dutch oven heat olive oil. In it sauté cut-up chicken until golden.

2. Now add onions and garlic and sauté until tender.

3. Add tomatoes, 1 teasp. salt, cover Dutch oven, and simmer chicken 30 min.

4. Combine saffron and boiling water. Add to chicken with rice, orégano, and 2 teasp. salt.

5. Stir well, cover Dutch oven, then simmer 25 min., stirring occasionally.

6. Now add shrimp and clams, then cover and cook about 10 min., or until shrimp are done and clam shells have opened, stirring rice once or twice.

7. Meanwhile, cook peas as label directs. Then toss, with pimentos, cut into strips.

8. Arrange chicken mixture on large platter; surround with peas. Makes 8 servings.

The artichoke is beloved throughout the Mediterranean region, and like most of their vegetables, often served cold with olive-oil dressing. Hot or cold artichokes and olive oil go together like hand in glove.

ALCACHOFAS GRANADINA
(*Artichokes, Granada-Style*)

3 tablesp. olive oil
1 medium onion, peeled, chopped
2 medium carrots, pared, coarsely grated
2 teasp. flour
1 teasp. salt
⅛ teasp. pepper

¼ teasp. dried rosemary
1 cup fresh or canned chicken broth
2 9-oz. pkg. frozen artichoke hearts, thawed
2 teasp. lemon juice

About 20 min. before serving:
1. In saucepan heat olive oil; in it sauté onion and carrots until tender. Next stir in flour, salt, pepper, rosemary, and chicken broth.
2. Bring to a boil while stirring; then add artichoke hearts and cook, covered, 6 to 8 min., or until artichokes are tender. Stir in lemon juice. Makes 4 to 6 servings.

In this flaky Spanish tart-pie, the mingled flavors of lemon juice, lemon rind, and white wine play leading roles.

TART IBIZA

6 tablesp. butter or margarine
1 cup sifted all-purpose flour
4 eggs, separated
⅓ cup granulated sugar

¼ cup lemon juice
2 teasp. grated lemon rind
⅔ cup dry white wine
1 cup seedless grapes

Early on the day:
1. With pastry blender or two knives, scissor-fashion, cut butter into flour until like coarse corn meal; add 2 tablesp. water and toss quickly together, forming a smooth ball. Use to line 9″ pie plate, making fluted edge; prick well. Bake at 375°F. 20 min., or until golden.
2. Meanwhile, in top of double boiler, combine egg yolks, sugar, lemon juice and rind, wine. Cook, over boiling water, while stirring, till thickened. Into this fold egg whites, beaten stiff. Spoon into baked pie shell; bake at 375°F. 15 min., or until golden.
3. Cool on rack. Garnish with grapes, then refrigerate until needed. Serve, cut into 8 wedges.

Whether the dessert is an elaborate pastry or simply fruta del tiempo (fruit of the season), a flan (custard), or queso (cheese), invariably it will be followed by Spanish brandy, a fine sherry, or anise liqueur.

AMOR FRÍO*
("Spanish Cream" with Oranges)

1 env. unflavored gelatine
½ cup granulated sugar
¼ teasp. salt
Powdered cinnamon
4 eggs, separated
2 cups milk

2 large oranges, sectioned, cut in half crosswise
¼ cup dry sherry
1 tablesp. lemon juice
½ cup heavy cream, whipped
Chopped nuts
1 orange, thinly sliced (optional)

Early on the day:
1. In top of double boiler, thoroughly combine gelatine, sugar, salt, ⅛ teasp. cinnamon, and egg yolks. Add milk, then cook over boiling water, while stirring, until thickened. Refrigerate until mixture mounds when dropped from spoon. Meanwhile, let oranges stand in sherry, in refrigerator.
2. Next combine egg mixture with lemon juice, oranges in sherry, and whipped cream; now carefully fold in egg whites, beaten stiff. Turn into pretty glass dish and refrigerate until set.

Just before serving:
Sprinkle top of Spanish cream with a little cinnamon and chopped nuts. If desired, garnish with orange slices. Makes 8 servings.

* Amor Frío literally means "cold love."

Sweden

Meat balls—tiny ones—are a must among hot dishes on Sweden's Smorgasbord. But, meat balls, a bit bigger perhaps, are also a popular warm course for everyday dinner.

SWEDEN'S KÖTTBULLAR
(Swedish Meat Balls)

4 tablesp. butter or margarine	¼ teasp. powdered nutmeg
⅓ cup minced onion	1 lb. chuck beef, ground once
1 egg	¼ lb. shoulder pork, ground
½ cup milk	3 tablesp. flour
½ cup fresh bread crumbs	⅛ teasp. pepper
2½ teasp. salt	1 cup water
3 teasp. sugar	¾ cup light cream
½ teasp. powdered allspice	

1. In 2 tablesp. hot butter in large skillet, sauté onion till golden. Meantime, in large mixing bowl, beat egg; add milk and bread crumbs; let stand 5 min. Add 1¼ teasp. salt, 2 teasp. sugar, allspice, nutmeg, meats, and onion. Blend well with fork.
2. In same skillet, heat 2 tablesp. butter. Using two teaspoons, shape the meat mixture into small balls, about ½" to ¾" in diameter. Drop some balls into skillet; brown well all over; remove to warm casserole; repeat until all the meat balls are browned.
3. Into fat left in skillet, stir flour, 1 teasp. sugar, 1¼ teasp. salt, and pepper; slowly add water and cream; stir until thickened. If desired, return meat balls to gravy; heat well. Or serve balls in covered casserole; pass gravy. Makes 6 servings.

To do ahead: Make day ahead; refrigerate. Reheat the meat balls just before serving.

No wonder menfolks like these patties. That delicate tartness which the pickled beets contribute is so welcome!

BIFF À LA LINDSTRÖM
(Beef-and-Beet Patties)

1¼ lb. chuck beef, ground once
1 cup mashed potatoes (about 2 medium)
2 egg yolks
½ cup heavy cream
½ cup diced pickled beets

1 small onion, minced
2 tablesp. chopped capers
1 teasp. salt
¼ teasp. white pepper
2 to 3 tablesp. butter or margarine
Parsley

1. With fork, combine chuck, potatoes, and egg yolks. Slowly stir in cream.
2. Then add beets, onion, capers, salt, and pepper. Shape beef-and-beet mixture into 12 thin patties, 3″ in diameter.
3. In melted butter, in skillet, sauté patties until a nice brown on both sides.
4. Arrange on heated platter; garnish with parsley; serve at once. Makes 6 servings.

Day-in-and-day-out cookery in Sweden is both distinctive and delicious. Treasured dishes have often been handed down from generation to generation.

KALOPS
(Swedish Braised Short Ribs)

1 tablesp. butter or margarine
3 lb. short ribs, cut into 2″ pieces
1 medium onion, peeled, sliced
1½ teasp. salt
¼ teasp. white pepper

2 teasp. granulated sugar
½ teasp. whole allspice
2 bay leaves
1 tablesp. flour
2 tablesp. heavy cream

About 2½ hr. before serving:
1. Heat Dutch oven until very hot; add butter, then short ribs. Cook over high heat until ribs are very well browned on all sides—about 20 min.
2. To ribs in Dutch oven add onion slices; push them down into fat around ribs, then cook a minute or so, or until browned. Now add salt, pepper, 1 teasp. sugar, allspice, bay leaves, and 1 cup water. Cover and simmer 1½ hr., or until meat is very tender.
3. Remove ribs to heated platter and keep warm. Skim about ¼ cup fat from surface of gravy; also remove allspice and bay leaves. Stir ¼ cup water into flour until smooth; slowly add, stirring, to gravy; cook until thickened. Stir in heavy cream, 1 teasp. sugar, and enough water to make gravy as you like it; bring to a boil; then pour over ribs and serve immediately. Makes 5 or 6 servings.

Tender veal rolls with a parsley-butter filling and rich creamy gravy. A cherished dish in Swedish homes.

KALVRULADER
(Parsley-Stuffed Veal Rolls)

2 lb. *thin* veal cutlets
1½ teasp. salt
½ teasp. white pepper
½ cup butter or margarine
1 cup snipped parsley
2 medium carrots, pared, cut into 1″ chunks

2 medium onions, peeled, quartered
1 10-oz. can condensed beef bouillon, undiluted
1 tablesp. all-purpose flour
¾ cup light cream
⅛ teasp. white pepper
2 teasp. granulated sugar

Early in day, or day before, if desired:
1. Have meatman flatten veal to ¼″ thickness. Cut into serving pieces; sprinkle both sides with salt and ½ teasp. pepper.
2. Melt ¼ cup butter; add parsley; spread some on each piece of veal; roll up, tie well with string; refrigerate.

About 1¾ hr. before serving:
1. In ¼ cup hot butter, in Dutch oven, sauté carrots, onions, and veal until meat is well browned.
2. Add water to bouillon to make 2 cups liquid; add to meat and vegetables; simmer, covered, 1 hr., or until meat is fork-tender.
3. Remove veal rolls; snip off string; then arrange on heated platter; keep warm.
4. For gravy: With fork, mash vegetables in liquid in Dutch oven. Into flour, gradually stir cream; then stir briskly into Dutch oven. Add ⅛ teasp. pepper and sugar; cook, stirring, just until heated. Strain; then serve with veal rolls. Makes 6 servings.

A rich, creamy pie, with the hearty flavor of onions and bacon, and a tender, flaky butter crust. Often served with the meat dish at company Sunday dinner in Sweden.

MRS. LINDER'S LÖK PAJ
(Mrs. Linder's Onion Pie)

1¼ cups sifted all-purpose flour
1½ teasp. salt
¼ cup butter or margarine
¼ cup shortening
2½ tablesp. milk
8 bacon slices

2 cups thinly sliced onions
3 eggs
1 cup commercial sour cream
⅛ teasp. white pepper
1½ teasp. snipped chives
½ teasp. caraway seeds

About 1¼ hr. before serving:
1. Start heating oven to 425°F.
2. Into bowl, sift flour and ¾ teasp. salt. With pastry blender or

2 knives, scissor-fashion, cut in butter and half of shortening until mixture is very fine; cut in remaining shortening until particles are the size of peas.

3. Sprinkle milk, about a tablespoonful at a time, over mixture, stirring with fork until dough clings together and cleans the bowl. Shape dough into a smooth ball.

4. On lightly floured surface, roll dough into a 12" circle; fit into 9" pie plate. Fold overhang under, making a stand-up rim; flute edge; with fork, prick pastry well. Bake 10 to 12 min., or until golden; remove. Then reduce oven temperature to 300°F.

5. Meanwhile, sauté bacon until crisp; crumble. In 3 tablesp. bacon fat, sauté onions till tender.

6. In bowl, beat eggs slightly; then stir in sour cream, ¾ teasp. salt, pepper, chives, onions, and bacon. Pour this mixture into baked (yes, baked) pie shell; sprinkle with caraway seeds. Bake 30 min. Let stand a few minutes before cutting into 8 wedges to serve.

Luscious, nut-rich bars that are wonderful "keepers." Try them for afternoon tea, or for dessert topped with a dollop of whipped cream if you wish.

ELLEN'S VALNÖTS TÅRTA
(Ellen's Walnut Torte)

3½ cups finely ground California walnuts	1¼ cups granulated sugar
	3 teasp. almond extract
6 egg yolks	6 egg whites

Make same day, or several days or weeks ahead, if desired:

1. Start heating oven to 325°F. Grease, line with wax paper, then grease again bottom of 9" x 9" x 2" cake pan. Grind nuts with fine blade of food chopper.

2. In small bowl, with electric mixer at high speed, beat egg yolks until thick and tripled in volume. Gradually add sugar, beating until very thick—about 10 min. Then gradually fold in walnuts and almond extract.

3. In large bowl, with electric mixer at high speed, beat egg whites until stiff but not dry. Fold about one fourth of beaten egg whites into yolk mixture; then gradually fold yolk mixture into remaining egg whites until well blended.

4. Turn batter into pan. Bake 1 hr., or until edges start pulling away from sides of pan. Cool 10 min.; turn out onto wire rack; remove paper; cool.

5. Wrap in foil; then store in tightly covered container, refrigerator, or freezer. Just before serving, cut into 3" x 1" bars; if desired, sprinkle with confectioners' sugar. Makes 27 bars.

These buttery S-, O-, and U-shaped cookies are generations old— from Sweden's kitchens.

ESTER'S SPRITSAR
(*Ester's Spritz Cookies*)

2 cups sifted all-purpose flour	1 cup soft butter or margarine
1 teasp. double-acting baking powder	¾ cup granulated sugar
	1 egg yolk, unbeaten
⅛ teasp. salt	1 teasp. almond extract

Make same day, or up to 2 weeks or so ahead, if desired:
1. Sift together flour, baking powder, and salt.
2. In large bowl, with electric mixer at medium speed, or with wooden spoon, cream butter. Gradually add sugar, beating until *very light and fluffy*. Add egg yolk and almond extract, beating until well blended.
3. With mixer at low speed, gradually add flour mixture, beating just until well mixed. Wrap in wax paper. Refrigerate until easy to handle—about ½ hr.
4. Meanwhile, start heating oven to 350°F. Onto cold, ungreased cookie sheet, force dough through star disk of cookie press,* forming, S, O, and U shapes. Bake 8 to 10 min., or until edges are golden-brown.
5. These may be stored in a tightly covered container or wrapped in foil and refrigerated up to two weeks. Makes about 7 doz.

* A cookie-press set can be purchased in a housewares department.

These thin-as-parchment, crisp, spicy cookies are a favorite with Swedish families all through the year, but especially at Christmas- time.

ELLEN'S PEPPARKAKOR
(*Ellen's Gingersnaps*)

½ cup maple syrup	1 teasp. powdered cloves
½ cup butter or margarine	1 teasp. grated lemon rind
⅓ cup brown sugar, firmly packed	1 tablesp. dark rum
1 teasp. powdered ginger	1 teasp. baking soda
1 teasp. powdered cinnamon	2½ cups sifted all-purpose flour

Make day before, or several weeks ahead, if desired:
1. In saucepan, combine maple syrup, butter, and brown sugar; boil until butter and sugar are melted. Stir in ginger, cinnamon, cloves, lemon rind, rum, and baking soda. Remove from heat; in large bowl, cool until lukewarm.
2. When mixture is lukewarm, gradually stir in flour. Wrap dough in wax paper; refrigerate until easy to handle. Then start heating oven to 350°F.

3. Remove small portion of dough from refrigerator; on a lightly floured surface, roll it out *paper thin*. Cut into desired shapes; place on greased cookie sheets. Bake 5 to 8 min., or until done. Repeat.

4. These may be stored for several weeks in a tightly covered container. Makes about 8½ doz. 2½" cookies.

Swedish Pancakes, hot from the plättpanna, *and topped with lingonberry preserves, are a luscious treat.*

PLÄTTAR
(*Swedish Pancakes*)

1 cup sifted all-purpose flour	Few drops vanilla extract
2 tablesp. sugar	Butter, margarine, or shortening
½ teasp. salt	Lingonberry preserves
3 eggs	Sweetened, flavored whipped
3 cups milk	cream
2 tablesp. melted butter or margarine	

About 2 hr. before serving:

1. Sift flour with sugar and salt. In large bowl, with egg beater, slightly beat eggs; add milk, butter, and vanilla, beating just until well blended.

2. Add flour mixture all at once, beating until well blended; refrigerate.

At serving time:

1. On top of range, start heating seasoned plätt pan; * brush with butter. (You can improvise a plätt pan this way: Fold 3"-wide strips of foil lengthwise in half twice; form into about 7 3" circles, fastening ends together with paper clips or staples. Into rings, on a greased, heated griddle, pour batter as in step 2, below. When batter is set, lift off ring, turn pancake, brown other side. Repeat, using same rings, till all batter is used.)

2. Beat pancake batter slightly. When pan is very hot (drop of water will dance when dropped on it), pour about 1 tablesp. batter into each section of pan, then cook until top is covered with tiny bubbles and underside is *well browned*. Then, using 2 small spatulas, carefully turn each pancake and brown other side; keep warm while making rest of pancakes. (Leftover batter may be refrigerated, covered, for a day or so.)

3. To serve, arrange pancakes on heated platter or individual dessert plates in stacks of 7 or 8 or in overlapping circles. Pass lingonberry or your favorite preserves and, for company, a bowl of whipped cream to spoon over pancakes. Makes 70 3" pancakes.

* Plätt pans may be purchased from Hammacher Schlemmer, 145 East 57th Street, New York, New York.

Switzerland

The perfect answer, when you long to impress! Bubbly shrimp, basking in a subtly spiced curry sauce, with Hollandaise spooned on top.

SCAMPI MODE SEMIRAMIS

2 egg yolks
Salt
Butter
1 tablesp. lemon juice
1 medium onion, peeled, minced
1 small leek, finely sliced
1 clove garlic, peeled, minced
1 medium apple, pared, cored, chopped
1 large tomato, peeled, chopped
¼ teasp. dried thyme
¼ teasp. powdered cinnamon
¼ teasp. black pepper
1 tablesp. curry powder

½ cup flaked coconut
¾ cup canned chicken broth
½ cup heavy cream
¼ cup seedless raisins
1 medium cucumber, pared, chopped
½ green pepper, seeded, chopped
¼ cup toasted slivered almonds
1½ lb. raw jumbo shrimp, shelled, deveined
¼ cup snipped scallions
2 tablesp. cognac
¼ cup dry white wine
Toast triangles

Make about 1 hr. and 15 min. before serving:
1. *Make up Hollandaise sauce as follows:* In small bowl, with electric mixer at medium speed, beat egg yolks till thick; add ¼ teasp. salt, then ¼ cup melted butter, one teaspoon at a time, beating constantly. Combine ¼ cup melted butter and lemon juice; slowly add, about 2 teaspoons at a time, to yolk mixture, beating constantly. Refrigerate.
2. *Make curry sauce as follows:* In large deep skillet melt 2 tablesp. butter; in it sauté onion, leek, garlic, apple, and tomato until tender, stirring frequently. Then stir in thyme, cinnamon, black pepper, curry, coconut, 2 teasp. salt, chicken broth, and cream. Simmer 5 min., then set aside.
3. Soak raisins in hot water to cover. In small skillet heat 1 tablesp. butter; in it sauté cucumber and green pepper until golden, stirring frequently. Then add drained raisins with almonds. Add this to curry sauce.
4. Preheat broiler 10 min., or as manufacturer directs. In large skillet heat 2 tablesp. butter; in it sauté shrimp about 5 min.,

then stir in scallions. Pour cognac over all, then wine, then bring to a boil. Add to curry sauce. Pour into tin-lined copper skillet or shallow Pyroceram utensil. Over top, spoon Hollandaise sauce. Broil 3 to 5 min., or until bubbling and top is golden. Serve with toast triangles. Makes 6 to 8 servings.

This delicate, fragrant Swiss cheese pie is de luxe, indeed, served hot—in generous wedges if for supper, in smaller wedges as an appetizer.

SWITZERLAND CHEESE-AND-ONION PIE

1 unbaked 9″ pie shell, with small fluted edge
2 large onions, peeled, thinly sliced (1 cup)
2 tablesp. butter or margarine
½ lb. natural Swiss cheese, coarsely grated

1 tablesp. flour
3 eggs
1 cup milk or light cream
½ teasp. salt
⅛ teasp. pepper

1. Prepare unbaked pie shell, using favorite pastry. Start heating oven to 400°F.
2. Now, in small skillet, sauté onions tender in butter; turn into pie shell.
3. Toss grated cheese with flour, then sprinkle over onions.
4. Now, with egg beater, beat eggs well. Then stir in milk or cream, salt, and pepper. Pour over cheese.
5. Bake pie at 400°F. 20 min. Now reduce oven heat to 300°F. and bake 25 min. longer, or until knife, inserted in center, comes out clean.
6. Serve pie hot, in wedges, for lunch or supper. Or cut into smaller wedges and serve as an evening snack. Makes 6 servings.

Here the loving Swiss touch adds thin cheese and ham slices to their favorite veal cutlets.

CUTLETS OF VEAL À LA SUISSE

6 thin veal cutlets (about 1½ lb.)
6 thin slices natural Swiss cheese
6 paper-thin slices cooked ham
2 tablesp. flour
Generous dash of paprika
⅓ cup butter or margarine

1 cup sauterne or Rhine wine
1 cup beef gravy (your own or canned)
½ cup light cream
Dash salt
About 6 drops lemon juice

1. Using edge of heavy saucer, pound each cutlet well; then cut each in half.
2. Now, on each of 6 of cutlet halves, place in this order: ½ thin slice cheese, 1 paper-thin slice ham, then ½ thin slice cheese.

3. Top each with second cutlet half and fasten securely with toothpicks.

4. Now mix flour with paprika, then use to coat cutlets.

5. In skillet place butter or margarine. When quite hot, add cutlets and sauté until well browned on each side.

6. Now add ½ cup wine and cook slowly, uncovered, until liquid is almost completely evaporated. Then slowly add, while stirring with wooden spoon, ½ cup wine, beef gravy, and cream.

7. Cover skillet and simmer cutlets 10 min., or until fork-tender. Just before serving, stir in salt and lemon juice, then remove toothpicks. Especially nice with hot fluffy rice. Makes 4 servings.

This handsome Swiss twist is of a delicate, light texture and flavor. It was a New Year's breakfast favorite in the old days.

EIERZOPF
(*Swiss Twist*)

¾ cup milk	4½ cups sifted all-purpose flour
½ cup butter or margarine	2 eggs, beaten (reserve 1 tablesp.
⅓ cup granulated sugar	for later use)
½ teasp. salt	½ lemon, juice and grated rind
1 pkg. active dry, or cake, yeast	(optional)
¼ cup warm water	

Early on the day you're serving it:

1. In small saucepan scald milk; stir in butter or margarine, sugar, and salt. Cool till lukewarm.

2. In large bowl, sprinkle or crumble yeast into warm water; stir until yeast is dissolved.

3. Then stir in lukewarm milk mixture, sifted all-purpose flour, eggs, and lemon juice and rind; mix well. On lightly floured surface, knead dough until smooth. Place in large greased bowl; cover with clean towel. Let rise in warm place (80°F. to 85°F.) until doubled.

4. Punch down dough, turn onto floured surface, divide in half. Roll each piece between hands into strip about 30″ long. Place one strip vertically and the other horizontally, crossing in middle. Now lift top end of vertical strip down to left side of its bottom end. Then lift left end of horizontal strip up and over lower two strips. Repeat this with right end of same strip. Alternate with top left and right strips in this manner until dough is used up; then pinch ends together securely. Place twist on greased large cookie sheet.

5. Brush twist all over with the reserved 1 tablesp. beaten egg. Let rise in warm place until about half double in size. Meanwhile, start heating oven to 325°F.

6. When half double in size, bake twist 10 min. at 325°F.; then

30 to 35 min. at 350°F. When done, remove from cookie sheet with large spatula. Cool on rack. When serving, your twist will taste oven-fresh if you wrap it in aluminum foil and let it heat, low under the broiler, for about 10 to 15 min.

The Swiss are famous for their soups! This is a modern version, combining convenience with the heartiness of old-time cooking.

VEGETABLE SOUP WITH VEAL ROUNDELS

2 slices day-old white bread
1 lb. veal shoulder, ground
1 egg, beaten
1 medium onion, peeled, minced
¼ cup snipped parsley
2 tablesp. all-purpose flour
2 tablesp. pkgd. dried bread crumbs
1 teasp. seasoned salt

½ teasp. salt
⅛ teasp. pepper
1 teasp. Worcestershire
2 envelopes garden-vegetable-soup mix
Few thinly sliced onion rings
Few paper-thin slices raw carrots
2 thin scallions, cut in pieces

About 45 min. before serving:
1. Soak bread slices in hot water to cover, for 1 min., then drain well, squeezing out all excess water.
2. In medium bowl, combine veal, egg, onion, parsley, flour, bread crumbs, seasoned salt, salt, pepper, Worcestershire, and drained bread slices. Mix until thoroughly blended, then form into golf-ball-size balls and place on floured wax paper.
3. In large saucepan place soup mix; add 7 cups water, bring to a boil, then turn heat low.
4. Now drop in meat balls and simmer, uncovered, 15 min. Transfer all to soup tureen, then garnish with onion rings, carrot slices, and scallions. Makes about 6 servings.

This is the friendliest of Swiss dishes—it's a party in itself.

SWISS FONDUE

Crusty French bread
2 tablesp. cornstarch
3 tablesp. Kirsch or brandy
1 clove garlic, peeled, crushed
2 cups dry white wine

Dash pepper
Dash nutmeg
¾ lb. natural Swiss cheese (Emmenthal or Gruyère, or half and half), finely grated (3 cups)

About 30 min. before serving:
1. Cut French bread into small cubes, then heap, in bread basket. Stir together cornstarch and Kirsch until smooth; set aside.
2. Rub inside of earthenware casserole with garlic. Pour in wine,

101

then heat until just below boiling; add pepper and nutmeg. Gradually add cheese, while stirring constantly with a fork. Then add cornstarch mixture and stir until smooth and bubbling. Place over alcohol burner, warm enough to keep it bubbling slightly.

3. Each person heaps some bread cubes on his plate; then, with fork, he dips them, one by one into the fondue, being careful not to lose a piece, because that means he must donate a bottle of wine or provide for the next fondue party. Serve as a main dish for 3 or 4 people.

P.S. If no earthenware casserole is available, prepare fondue in a stainless-steel, oven-glass, or Pyroceram saucepan, or in a chafing dish.

A Swiss teatime treat—flaky cheese twists—that beg to be made from real Swiss cheese as they are at home.

CHÄS-TANGE
(Cheese Sticks)

2 cups sifted all-purpose flour	1 egg, beaten
Salt	1½ cups grated natural Swiss
1 cup butter or margarine	cheese, packed
1 egg	Caraway seeds
2½ tablesp. milk	

1. Into large bowl sift flour with ¼ teasp. salt. With pastry blender cut in butter or margarine until it's like coarse corn meal.
2. Blend in egg, beaten with milk. Wrap this dough in wax paper, refrigerate 1 hr.
3. Start heating oven to 375°F. Grease 2 cookie sheets.
4. On lightly floured surface, roll out half of dough, ⅛" thick; with pastry wheel cut into 5" x ½" strips. Twist 2 strips together; place on sheet; pinch ends together. Repeat with rest of strips.
5. Brush twists with some of beaten egg; sprinkle with ¾ cup grated cheese, then 1 tablesp. caraway seeds and 1 teasp. salt. Bake 15 min., or till golden; then remove.
6. Repeat steps 4 and 5 with rest of dough.
7. Serve warm or cool, with soup or salad or as nibbler. Stored in tight container, these keep nicely several days. Makes about 36.

Like poundcake in texture and flavor, this superb cake, with its sprinkling of raisins, is a traditional favorite at Swiss coffee time.

GUGELHOPF

1 cup plus 2 tablesp. butter	½ cup seedless dark raisins, finely
1¼ cups granulated sugar	snipped
5 eggs, separated	2¼ cups sifted all-purpose flour
Grated rind 1 lemon	2 teasp. double-acting baking
1 tablesp. lemon juice	powder

Make 1 or 2 days ahead as follows:
1. Start heating oven to 325°F. Butter well a 9″ tube pan or 2-qt. turkhead pan. In large bowl, with your mixer at medium speed, beat butter until creamy; beat in sugar, then egg yolks, one at a time, beating until very light and fluffy—about 10 min.
2. Next beat in lemon rind and juice and raisins. Sift together flour and baking powder. Beat egg whites until stiff. Alternately fold flour and egg whites into butter mixture, a third at a time.
3. Turn into prepared cake pan and bake 60 to 65 min., or until cake tester, inserted in center, comes out clean. Cool 10 min., then turn out on rack to cool completely. Serve, cut into wedges, with a steaming cup of coffee.

With its generous layer of cherries on the bottom, and whipped cream on top, you have "fruit and cake," for dessert, all in one!

KIRSCHENKUCHEN
(*Cherry Cake*)

Butter or margarine	2 teasp. double-acting baking
9″ x 3″ spring-form pan	powder
1 1-lb.-14-oz. can and 1 1-lb.-1-oz.	½ teasp. salt
can dark pitted cherries, well	1 cup finely ground, unblanched
drained	almonds
1 cup granulated sugar	1 cup sifted all-purpose flour
4 eggs, separated	Confectioners' sugar
1 teasp. powdered cinnamon	Heavy cream (optional)
¼ teasp. powdered cloves	

Make day before or early on the day:
1. Butter spring-form pan, then line bottom with wax paper. Open cans of cherries; drain. Start heating oven to 350°F.
2. In large bowl, with electric mixer at medium speed, beat 1 cup butter or margarine with sugar until fluffy; beat in egg yolks, one at a time.
3. Now blend in cinnamon, cloves, baking powder, and salt, then almonds with flour. Beat egg whites until stiff; then carefully fold them and cherries into butter-almond mixture.

4. Pour batter into spring-form pan. Bake 1 hr. 15 min., or until cake tester, inserted in center, comes out clean. Let stand 5 min.; loosen sides of cake from pan, remove rim, invert on rack; remove bottom of pan and paper. Cool.

5. Then invert on cake plate so cherry layer rests on bottom. Sprinkle top with confectioners' sugar. Serve, in wedges, with whipped cream. Makes 12 servings.

To kindle a glow in your birthday child's eyes, make the Swiss Torte below. Nutted and rich all the way through, it's much beloved in Switzerland.

JAPONAISTORTE
(Layered Hazelnut Torte)

1¼ lb. shelled hazelnuts (4 cups)	3½ cups sifted confectioners' sugar
10 egg whites	4 egg yolks
2 cups granulated sugar	3 tablesp. instant coffee
⅔ cup sifted cake flour	1½ teasp. hot water
1 cup soft butter or margarine	Decorating bag
1 cup shortening	Pastry tube, number 3

Make torte early on day before serving, as follows:

1. Finely grind 2 cups hazelnuts. Start heating oven to 275°F.

2. On each of 3 squares of wax paper, draw a 9″ circle. Grease papers to a point slightly beyond the circle line, then flour lightly. Place one of the prepared wax-paper squares on each of 2 lightly greased cookie sheets; reserve the third square of paper for later use.

3. Beat egg whites until stiff but not dry; then gradually beat in 1½ cups granulated sugar, while continuing to beat until stiff. Then gently fold in ground hazelnuts and cake flour, blending carefully.

4. Spread one third of hazelnut mixture, just to edge of drawn circle on each of 2 wax-paper squares, keeping sides of circles even. Refrigerate rest of hazelnut mixture.

5. Place 2 cookie sheets in 275°F. oven; bake mixture 1 hr., or until light-brown and dry, switching cookie sheets after 30 min. When done, invert each on a rack, peel off wax paper, turn right side up, then let cool.

6. Place third piece of wax paper on a cool cookie sheet. Spread with rest of hazelnut mixture as in step 4. Bake at 275°F. 1 hr., then remove and proceed as in step 5.

7. Start heating oven to 400°F. Bake 2 cups whole shelled hazelnuts in shallow baking pan 10 min., shaking pan occasionally. Then rub off the skin from 24 of the hazelnuts.

8. Butter large piece of wax paper. In small skillet, over medium heat, melt ½ cup granulated sugar to golden syrup, stirring it

occasionally with a fork. Into syrup drop the 24 hazelnuts, a few at a time, coating all sides. Then drain, lifting one by one with fork to buttered wax paper.

9. Finely grind rest of baked hazelnuts in food chopper. In large bowl, with electric mixer at medium speed, cream butter with shortening until well blended; then gradually beat in confectioners' sugar, blending well. Now add egg yolks, one by one, beating until light and fluffy; then beat in 1¼ cups ground hazelnuts.

10. Refrigerate ½ cup of this frosting. Into another 1¼ cups of same frosting, stir instant coffee dissolved in hot water, then refrigerate.

11. Now stack the 3 baked layers, filling and frosting them with the rest of the frosting. Refrigerate 1 hr., then sprinkle top and pat sides with rest of hazelnuts.

12. With coffee frosting in decorating bag and closed star pastry tube number 3, press out a continuous border of half circles around top edge of cake; repeat, about 1″ in from this border. Make one large rosette in center.

13. Next, with the ½ cup refrigerated frosting in decorating bag and same pastry tube number 3, press out a small rosette wherever half circles join each other, as well as on the center rosette. Then top each of these rosettes with one of the caramelized hazelnuts.

14. With 2 large spatulas transfer torte to cake plate; refrigerate till served. Makes about 16 wedge-shaped servings.

P.S. Use leftover egg yolks in custard sauce, eggnog sauce, gold cake, bread pudding, custard pie, quick lemon pie, or hard-cooked, in salad, etc.

Swiss Walnut Pie! It's a honeyed crush of walnuts, caramelized, within a flaky cookie crust. Present it on a pretty plate, so its deliciousness shows.

ENGADINERTORTE
(*Swiss Walnut Pie*)

Granulated sugar	¼ teasp. salt
2 cups chopped California walnuts	¾ cup butter
2 tablesp. honey	1 egg, beaten
½ cup light cream	1 tablesp. water
2¼ cups sifted all-purpose flour	9″ layer-cake pan

One, two, or three days ahead:
1. In large skillet, over medium heat, melt 1½ cups granulated sugar, while stirring constantly, until it forms a golden syrup. Add chopped walnuts and honey, and mix well; then stir in light cream; let cool.

2. In medium bowl, combine flour and salt. With a pastry blender or 2 knives, scissor-fashion, cut in butter until like corn meal. Add ⅓ cup sugar, beaten egg, and water; mix well. Form into smooth ball; then wrap dough in wax paper and refrigerate until well chilled.

3. Start heating oven to 350°F. Now cut off and reserve a little less than half of dough for later use. On lightly floured surface, roll rest of dough into a circle ¼" thick. Fold it in half, then lift onto ungreased 9" layer-cake pan; unfold and press gently to fit pan. Trim pastry even with top edge of layer-cake pan. Then spread walnut mixture evenly over the bottom of it. Fold sides of pastry down over filling.

4. Roll out reserved dough into a 9" circle. Place on top of pie. With floured fork press edges together slightly. Then prick top with fork. Bake pie 50 min., or until top is golden.

5. Cool pie on wire rack. Then, with spatula, loosen it around edges. Place a plate over top of pie; then invert pie and plate together. Lift off layer-cake pan, place a second plate lightly on bottom of pie, then invert both to turn pie right side up. Refrigerate until time to cut into wedges and serve, topped with vanilla ice cream, if desired.

An irresistible frozen dessert that brings a cool touch of perfection and happy ending to any feast.

SOUFFLÉ GLACÉ AU GRAND MARNIER

5 egg yolks	½ cup plus 2 tablesp. Grand
Granulated sugar	Marnier
2 egg whites	2 cups heavy cream

About 4 to 4½ hr. before serving:

1. In small bowl, with electric mixer at high speed, beat egg yolks with ¼ cup sugar until thick and lemon-colored—about 10 min.

2. Beat egg whites until they form soft peaks; gradually beat in ¼ cup sugar, then beat to a stiff meringue.

3. In large bowl combine egg-yolk mixture and meringue. Into this carefully fold Grand Marnier, then heavy cream, beaten stiff. Pour into 9" x 9" x 2" pan. Freeze about 4 hr., or until well chilled, but still soft. Makes about 8 servings.

P.S. May be done day before and frozen firm for serving.

Yugoslavia

In Yugoslavia they're fond of "solid food," simply and deliciously prepared—the true test of a good cook.

DJUVETSCH
(*Meat-Vegetable Casserole*)

2 to 3 tablesp. shortening
1½ lb. mixed boned pork, beef,
  and veal, in 1" cubes
⅓ cup uncooked regular white rice
2 medium onions, peeled, sliced
1 10½-oz. can condensed beef
  broth, undiluted
2 teasp. paprika

2 teasp. salt
¼ teasp. pepper
2 medium carrots, pared, sliced
1 medium green pepper, seeded,
  sliced
1 large potato, pared, cut into
  eighths
2 medium tomatoes, quartered

About 2½ hr. before serving:
1. In large skillet heat shortening; in it brown meats well on all sides. Place into 2-qt. casserole. Start heating oven to 350°F.
2. To drippings in skillet add rice and onions and sauté until golden. Add beef broth, paprika, salt, and pepper and bring to a boil. Pour over meat in casserole.
3. Top with carrots, green pepper, potato, and tomatoes. Toss lightly to mix ingredients. Bake, covered, 2 hr., or until meat and vegetables are tender. Makes 4 to 6 servings.

Lunch served in the fields, and supper served in the country kitchen, are often similar—hot soup like this one, cheese, eggs, onions, and a sweet cake.

KISELA CORBA
(*Serbian Soup*)

2 tablesp. shortening
1½ lb. boned pork shoulder, in 1"
  cubes
1½ qt. water
4 teasp. salt
¼ teasp. pepper
1 teasp. paprika
1 parsnip, pared, cut into ¼"
  slices

2 medium carrots, pared, cut into
  ¼" slices
2 large onions, peeled, sliced
¼ cup uncooked regular white rice
2 eggs, beaten
½ cup commercial sour cream
1 tablesp. vinegar
Snipped parsley

About 1 hr. and 45 min. before serving:
1. In Dutch oven or large kettle heat shortening; in it brown

pork well on all sides. Then add water; bring to a boil and simmer, covered, 1 hr.

2. Now add salt, pepper, paprika, parsnip, carrots, onions, and rice. Bring to a boil, then simmer, covered, ½ hr., or until meat and vegetables are tender.

3. Add eggs, while stirring with a fork. (The eggs will shred and thicken soup.) Then remove from heat. Beat together sour cream and vinegar. Stir into soup until smooth. Serve, sprinkled with parsley, as a main-dish soup. Makes 6 servings.

In Yugoslavia where cakes vary from the Hungarian torte to the Turkish baklava, perhaps the best known is Potica.

POTICA
(*Raisin-and-Nut Coffeecake*)

1½ pkg. active dry, or cakes, yeast	Sifted all-purpose flour
¼ cup warm water	1 cup butter or margarine
⅔ cup lukewarm milk	Raisin Filling, below
¼ cup granulated sugar	Walnut Filling, below
1 teasp. salt	1 beaten egg
3 egg yolks	

Early on the day, or day before:

1. Sprinkle yeast onto warm water to dissolve. In large bowl combine milk, sugar, salt, and egg yolks; stir in yeast.

2. In another bowl place 4¼ cups sifted flour; with pastry blender, or 2 knives, scissor-fashion, cut in butter until the size of large peas. Add to milk mixture, while beating well with a wooden spoon until smooth.

3. Then knead *well*, while gradually adding 5 to 7 tablesp. flour. Now, on floured pastry board, roll out dough to ½" thickness. Then fold it into thirds; repeat rolling and folding twice.

4. Now form dough into a smooth ball and place in large, floured bowl. Cover with a piece of wax paper, then with a towel. Let rise in warm place (80°F. to 85°F.) until doubled—about 1½ to 2 hr.

5. Punch down dough, then cut it in half. On cloth-covered, well-floured board, roll out one of halves into a rectangle about ⅛" thick. On it spread egg-yolk mixture in step 2 of Raisin Filling, p. 109, to within 1" of edges. Then sprinkle with raisin-rum mixture in step 1 of same filling.

6. Now, starting from long side of rectangle, roll it up, jelly-roll-fashion, using hands, then cloth to help in the rolling. Fold roll in half lengthwise, bringing one half alongside other half; lay to one side in greased baking pan, 14" x 10" x 2".

7. Roll out rest of dough into a rectangle, about ⅛" thick. Spread with walnut mixture in Walnut Filling, p. 109, to within

1″ of edges. Then, sprinkle with its raisin-rum mixture. Roll up and fold as in step 6. Then lay beside first roll in baking pan. Cover with cloth and let rise in a warm place until doubled in bulk. Meanwhile, start heating oven to 350°F.

8. When dough has doubled, brush it with beaten egg. Then bake it 45 min., or until light-brown and done. Let cool 5 min. on rack, then loosen edges with spatula and turn out of pan. Let cool, cut in half lengthwise, then serve, cutting into cross-wise slices. Makes two coffeecakes.

P.S. Leftovers may be wrapped in foil, then reheated in a 400°F. oven for 8 to 10 min.

Raisin Filling:

1. Combine 2⅓ cups seedless dark raisins (12 oz.) and 2 tablesp. rum and let soak.
2. In bowl stir together 3 egg yolks, 1 cup granulated sugar, 1 teasp. vanilla extract, grated rind 1 lemon, 2 tablesp. heavy cream, and 2 tablesp. pkgd. dried bread crumbs until well blended. Set aside until ready to use.

Walnut Filling:

1. Combine ½ cup seedless dark raisins and 1 tablesp. rum or brandy and let soak.
2. Place 3 cups chopped California walnuts (12 oz.) in medium bowl. Place ¾ cup heavy cream and 1 tablesp. butter in sauce-pan, bring to a boil, then pour over walnuts and blend well. Now stir in ⅓ cup granulated sugar, 1 egg, beaten, grated rind of ½ lemon, and ¼ teasp. powdered cinnamon, blending well. Set aside until ready to use.

MIDDLE EAST

ARABIA

ISRAEL

LEBANON

TURKEY

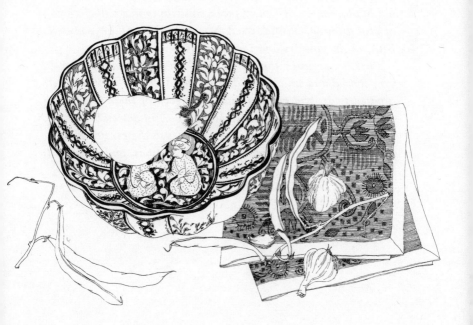

Time was when the countries of the Middle East seemed as remote from the Western world as another planet. Now they are as close as the morning newspaper, the fastest jet plane. Knowing something of the food of these countries holds many rewards.

Traditions, religious regulations, customs, and climate all play an important part in the food picture of these countries. To the people of the Moslem faith, and the Jewish, pork is forbidden, but mutton and lamb are used in abundance. Consequently, recipes for their preparation are varied and many. Methods of serving differ between countries—as well as the number of meals served in a day.

Israel is yet a young country and some foods are still far from plentiful. Consider, too, the many countries from which refugees come to Israel, bringing their own traditions and customs. Paramount, however, is the kosher law of eating—a law centuries old in observance. All these facets contribute to a still-changing or still-forming cuisine. Used in many different ways are the fruits of the country and the seafoods.

Turkey has given the world the shish kebab, pilavs, and a very special and unique kind of coffee; Arabia is known for its candied fruits and pastries—and from each of these fascinating countries of the East comes some unique and delectable recipe. When you share these foods, you share also the centuries of tradition, the strange and interesting customs, and above all, the gracious hospitality that these countries embrace.

Arabia

*Here, that much beloved lamb, as well as vermicelli, add hearti-
ness to a soup that's very subtly fragranced with mint. You'll serve
it again and again!*

ARABIAN LAMB-AND-TOMATO SOUP

2 tablesp. butter or margarine	1 tablesp. snipped mint leaves
3 large onions, peeled, sliced	2 teasp. salt
1½ lb. lamb shoulder	½ teasp. pepper
2 medium tomatoes, cut into	1 qt. water
eighths	2 oz. vermicelli

About 1 hr. and 40 min. before serving:
1. In Dutch oven, heat butter; in it brown onion slices, turning
frequently. Then add lamb, tomatoes, mint, salt, pepper, and
water. Bring to a boil, then simmer, covered, 1 hr. and 15 min.
2. Now add vermicelli and cook 15 min., or until they are tender.
3. Then remove lamb, cut it off the bone into small pieces, then
return to soup. Serve as a main-dish soup. Makes about 4 servings.

*Lamb, when available, is a great favorite on Arabian tables. If not
roasted on skewers, it is often served stuffed, as below.*

KABOURGA
(Stuffed Breast of Lamb)

2 tablesp. butter or margarine	Salt
½ cup uncooked regular white rice	Pepper
2 large cloves garlic, peeled,	½ cup pine nuts
minced	2 lamb breasts (each about 1¼
1 large onion, peeled, chopped	lb.) with pocket for stuffing, and
1 small green pepper, seeded,	bones cracked on one side
coarsely chopped	1 8-oz. can tomato sauce
¼ cup snipped parsley	

About 2½ hr. before serving:
1. Start heating oven to 350°F. In medium skillet heat butter;
in it brown rice, half of garlic, all the onion and green pepper,
turning frequently. Then add parsley, 1 teasp. salt, ¼ teasp.
pepper, pine nuts, and 1 cup water. Bring to a boil, then simmer,
covered, about 8 min., or until all water is absorbed.

2. Use this filling to stuff pockets in both lamb breasts, securing the openings with toothpicks. Place, side by side, in baking dish. Now rub lamb with 1 teasp. salt, ¼ teasp. pepper, and rest of garlic.

3. Pour tomato sauce and 2 cups water over lamb, then bake about 2 hr., or until meat is done, basting it occasionally, and covering with foil for last half hour.

4. In serving, cut lamb with sharp knife into thick slices. Makes 6 to 8 servings.

This refreshing native fruit salad may be served with or without greens—the oranges and ripe olives contributing delightful color and flavor contrasts.

MUNKACZINA
(*Arabian Salad*)

3 oranges, peeled, thinly sliced crosswise	2 tablesp. salad oil
1 3⅞-oz. can pitted ripe olives	1½ teasp. salt
2 medium onions, peeled, thinly sliced	½ teasp. pepper
	2 tablesp. lemon juice
	Lettuce leaves

About 1 hr. before serving:
In bowl combine orange slices, olives, onion slices, salad oil, salt, pepper, and lemon juice. Toss until blended, then refrigerate until well chilled.

Just before serving:
Line salad bowl with lettuce leaves; on them heap salad. Makes about 6 servings.

Israel

An Israeli dinner dish—known the world over—in which short ribs simmer to near-savory tenderness before the bit of barley, potatoes, and limas are added.

CHULENT
(*Lima Bean and Short-Rib Dinner*)

3 lb. short ribs, cut into 2″ pieces
4 medium onions, peeled, chopped
Salt
¾ to 1 teasp. pepper
Paprika

1½ cups water
⅓ cup barley
2 large potatoes, pared, quartered lengthwise
1 16- or 17-oz. can dried lima beans, undrained

About 3 hr. before serving:
1. In Dutch oven, brown short ribs well on all sides.
2. Add onions, then sauté till brown, stirring. Now add 2 teasp. salt, pepper, 1 teasp. paprika, and water; then simmer, covered, 1½ hr. Skim off excess fat.
3. Now add barley, quartered potatoes, 1 teasp. salt, and 1 teasp. paprika. Cook, covered, 30 min.; add limas and cook 10 min. longer, or until short ribs and potatoes are tender. Makes 6 to 8 servings.

Israel's Honey Cake captivates not only with its luscious flavor, but the fact that it's even better a week later—a good keeper!

HONEY CAKE

2 cups sifted cake flour
1 teasp. double-acting baking powder
1 teasp. baking soda
¼ teasp. salt
3 tablesp. butter or margarine

½ cup granulated sugar
¾ cup honey
3 eggs, well beaten
Grated rind 1 orange
½ cup applesauce
1 cup chopped California walnuts

1. Start heating oven to 325°F. Grease a 15″ x 10″ x 1″ jelly-roll pan or shallow roasting pan.
2. Sift together flour, baking powder, baking soda, and salt.
3. With spoon, cream butter, sugar, and honey together well. Then stir in well-beaten eggs until smooth.
4. Next, stir in flour mixture, orange rind, applesauce, and walnuts just until mixed.

5. Turn batter into pan and bake 40 to 45 min., or until a cake tester, inserted in center, comes out clean.

6. Cool 10 min. on wire rack; carefully remove pan, then cool completely on rack. Serve in squares.

Lebanon

The cracked wheat for this flavorsome lamb casserole can be bought in health stores. Get some, so you can try this dish soon.

KIBBEH BI SSANIEH
(Baked Lamb and Wheat Dish)

½ lb. cracked wheat	¼ cup pine nuts
1 tablesp. shortening	Salt
⅔ cup minced onion	Pepper
1½ lb. *lean* lamb, ground	⅛ teasp. powdered cinnamon

About 1 hr. and 30 min. before serving:

1. In medium bowl place cracked wheat; on it pour 1½ cups cold water, then let stand 30 min.

2. Meanwhile, in medium skillet, heat shortening; in it brown ⅓ cup minced onion and ½ lb. lamb, ground, turning frequently. Then add pine nuts, ½ teasp. salt, and ¼ teasp. pepper; set aside. Start heating oven to 350°F.

3. To cracked wheat add 1 lb. lamb, ground, ⅓ cup minced onion, 2 teasp. salt, ¼ teasp. pepper, and cinnamon. Spread half of this mixture on bottom of 8" x 8" x 2" baking dish; on it spread browned-lamb mixture, rest of cracked-wheat mixture.

4. Bake 1 hr., or until nicely browned. Serve, cut into 9 squares.

An apple dessert that couldn't be simpler to fix and bake, and boasts of an enchanting ginger-cinnamon flavor.

BAALBEK APPLES
(Apple Dessert)

2 lb. medium apples	1 teasp. powdered cinnamon
6 tablesp. butter	¼ teasp. powdered ginger
½ cup confectioners' sugar	

About 20 min. before serving:

1. Pare, core, and quarter apples. In large skillet, over medium heat, melt butter; in it sauté apples, turning them frequently, until they are well browned on all sides and tender. Transfer to serving dish.

2. Combine confectioners' sugar, cinnamon, and ginger. Sprinkle over apples. Serve as a dessert. Makes 4 servings.

Whatever the occasion, these small buttery cakes, with their spicy nut filling, will win immediate favor.

CARABEIGE ALEPPO
(Nut Cookies)

1½ cups butter or margarine	⅓ cup granulated sugar
3 cups sifted all-purpose flour	½ teasp. powdered cinnamon
1¼ cups California walnuts, or almonds, finely chopped	1 cup sifted confectioners' sugar

Day before or early on the day:
1. With pastry blender or two knives, scissor-fashion, cut butter into flour until like coarse corn meal; add about ¼ cup water and toss quickly together, forming a smooth ball of dough. Start heating oven to 350°F.
2. From dough break off walnut-size pieces; roll into balls and place on cookie sheet. Make large indentation in center of each, forming little "nests."
3. Combine walnuts, sugar, and cinnamon; use to heap in center of cookies. Bake 25 to 30 min., or until light-brown. Transfer to rack to cool.
4. Stir together confectioners' sugar and 5 teasp. water. Use to dribble over cookies. Store, covered. Makes 40 to 45 cookies.

Turkey

Turks are very fond of rice, which, with fine noodles, chicken broth, and tomato they make into a flavorsome Pilav to serve with their Shish Kebab.

PILAV
(Turkish Rice Dish)

½ cup butter or margarine	¼ teasp. pepper
¾ cup very fine noodles	1 medium tomato, cut up
2 13¾-oz. cans chicken broth	2 cups uncooked processed white rice
½ cup water	
½ teasp. salt	

About 30 min. before serving:
1. In deep skillet heat butter; in it brown noodles, stirring fre-

quently. Then add chicken broth, water, salt, pepper, and tomato and bring to a boil.

2. Now stir in rice, then simmer, covered, over low heat, 20 min., or until rice is tender and water absorbed. (Don't stir rice or remove cover while cooking.) Serve with Shish Kebab. Makes 8 servings.

Lamb, as one of Turkey's national meats, is never more popular than when broiled or grilled on skewers with green pepper and tomato chunks. Shish Kebab, to be sure!

TURKISH ȘIȘ KEBAP
(Shish Kebab)

2½ to 3 lb. boned leg of lamb, trimmed of gristle and most of fat, then cut into 1½″ cubes
3 medium onions, peeled, minced
Salt
½ teasp. pepper
1½ teasp. dried orégano

Olive or salad oil
8 13″ metal skewers
6 to 8 not-too-ripe tomatoes, in large wedges
4 green peppers, seeded, cut into 2″ chunks
Pilav, p. 117

In your kitchen:
About 24 hr. before your shish-kebab party, place lamb in large bowl; then throw in onions, 2 teasp. salt, the pepper and orégano, and 3 tablesp. oil, tossing well. Refrigerate all, covered, turning lamb occasionally.

At the grill:
About 1½ hr. before it's time to eat, start fire. While coals are heating, alternate, on metal skewers, the lamb cubes, tomatoes, and green peppers, allowing ¼″ between pieces; lightly brush vegetables with oil. Then grill shish kebab, 5″ above hot coals, about 30 min., turning frequently and brushing all with enough oil to keep moist. Sprinkle tomato wedges with salt.

At the table:
For each guest, with fork, push a shish kebab from skewer onto dinner plate. Then pass a bowl of Pilav, p. 117. Makes 8 servings.
P.S. If Shish Kebab is done in the broiler, preheat broiler 10 min., or as manufacturer directs. Then broil kebab 12 to 15 min. on each side, brushing frequently with oil.

Turkish cookery deserves to be better known! This Cucumber Salad is one of their many imaginative dishes that you'll be happy you tried.

CACIK
(Cucumber Salad)

1 clove garlic, peeled, crushed	1½ to 2 cups yoghurt
1 tablesp. wine vinegar	3 medium cucumbers
2 teasp. salt	1 tablesp. olive oil
1 tablesp. snipped fresh dill	1 tablesp. snipped mint leaves

About 1 hr. before serving:
1. In salad bowl combine garlic, vinegar, salt, dill, and yoghurt and blend well.
2. Pare cucumbers, quarter them lengthwise, then cut crosswise into thin slices. Blend with yoghurt mixture, then refrigerate until well chilled.
3. Serve, sprinkled with olive oil and mint. Makes about 6 servings.

This so-called Fruit Salad is something like our fruit cup, and when nicely chilled, makes an excellent dessert.

MEYVA SALATA
(Fruit Salad)

1 medium pear, cored, cubed	1 teasp. powdered ginger
1 cup fresh grapes	½ cup brandy
1 pt. strawberries, hulled, quartered	2 tablesp. lemon juice
	½ cup confectioners' sugar
2 oranges, peeled and sliced thin, crosswise	

About 4 hr. before serving:
1. In glass serving bowl or sherbet glasses arrange pear, grapes, strawberries, and oranges.
2. In small bowl combine ginger, brandy, lemon juice, and confectioners' sugar. Pour over fruit and blend well.
3. Refrigerate several hours, tossing occasionally to blend flavors. Serve as a dessert. Makes about 6 servings.

Poland's Sausage Smothered in Red Cabbage
(Kielbaski Duszone W Czerwonej Kapuscie), page 76

FAR EAST

CEYLON

CHINA

HONG KONG

INDIA

INDONESIA

JAPAN

KOREA

MALAYA

PAKISTAN

THAILAND

The man who, a century ago, classed "same old rice" with "same old glimpse of paradise" obviously had never experienced dining in the countries of the Far East. For in these countries rice takes on a hundred different flavors—a hundred different services.

There is the rice of India—with its curries or Kormas, its meat balls; the rice of Ceylon, with accompaniments of coconut, seafood, fruit; and in each of these countries distinctive and delicious sauces.

China gives us the beauty and succulence of crisp vegetables, duck, roast pork, liver, and fish. Japan offers foods that are designed to delight the eye as well as please the appetite. And from all these countries come new ideas for using fruits and melons.

Here too, religious regulations affect food habits and customs, but perhaps the over-all important facet of the subject of food in these countries of the Far East is the abiding belief that food is more than mere bodily sustenance, that what a man eats can exalt or debase his soul. Here too, the art of cookery is recognized for its true worth and its great contribution to the art of living.

Try your hand at some of these recipes. Set your table with grass mats, a lovely flower arrangement, provide chopsticks for the adventurers, and find in your own dining room something of the exotic and charming atmosphere that is characteristic of these countries of the Far East.

Ceylon

This magnificent chicken-and-eggplant casserole is a specialty which the Singhalese reserve for state occasions. Perhaps you'll want to serve it on state occasions, too.

BRINJAL SMOORE
(Eggplant Casserole)

2 3-lb. broiler-fryers, quartered
⅓ cup butter or margarine
Water
1 6-oz. can tomato paste
2 cloves garlic, peeled, finely minced
2 tablesp. sugar
10 whole cloves
1 teasp. salt
2 tablesp. vinegar
½ teasp. turmeric
1 stick cinnamon
2 tablesp. Worcestershire

5 whole cardamoms, peeled
½ teasp. paprika
Fat or salad oil
1 1½-lb. eggplant, unpared
3 tablesp. lemon juice
1 tablesp. salt
2 teasp. turmeric
4 medium onions, peeled, quartered
1 large green pepper, cut into eighths
2 large tomatoes, sliced
Slivered almonds

About 2 hr. before serving:

1. Start heating oven to 425°F. In 13" x 9" x 2" baking dish or large roasting pan, arrange chicken, skin side up, in single layer. Dot with butter. Bake, uncovered, 30 min., or till golden-brown, occasionally brushing with drippings in baking dish.

2. Reduce oven temperature to 350°F. In saucepan, mix 1¼ cups water, tomato paste, garlic, sugar, cloves, 1 teasp. salt, vinegar, ½ teasp. turmeric, cinnamon, Worcestershire, cardamoms, and paprika; bring to a boil and simmer 5 min.

3. Pour 1 cup of this sauce over chicken, coating all pieces; then place remaining sauce in skillet. Bake chicken 20 min., or till tender.

4. Meanwhile, in deep saucepan, put enough fat or salad oil to come halfway up the side. Heat to 375°F. on deep-fat-frying thermometer.

5. Now, cut eggplant into 3" x ½" strips; turn into large bowl; sprinkle with lemon juice; cover with water; let stand 5 min. Remove eggplant; drain well; sprinkle eggplant with 1 tablesp. salt mixed with 2 teasp. turmeric.

6. In hot fat, at 375°F., fry eggplant, a few strips at a time, about 2 min., or till fork-tender; drain well.

7. Meanwhile, in tomato sauce in skillet, simmer onions and green pepper, covered, 10 min., or just until fork-tender.

8. Now arrange eggplant, onions, pepper, and tomato sauce over chicken pieces in skillet.

9. Lay tomato slices on chicken; sprinkle with almonds. Return to 350°F. oven; bake, uncovered, 15 min. longer, or till heated through.

To Serve:

Arrange on heated large serving platter with big bowl of hot fluffy rice tossed with seedless raisins. Makes 8 hearty servings.

Want to curry favor with your family? Try Ginger-Curry Shrimp, served with Egg-and-Onion Sambal, and followed by Banana Puffs. All three hail from balmy Ceylon.

GINGER-CURRY SHRIMP

1¼ lb. cleaned raw shrimp	2 whole ginger roots
2 medium onions, peeled, sliced	1¼ cups milk
2 cloves garlic, peeled, sliced	2 tablesp. salad oil
⅛ teasp. cayenne	2 tablesp. lime juice
⅛ teasp. turmeric	1 teasp. sugar
1½ teasp. salt	1 tablesp. cornstarch
2 cinnamon sticks	Hot fluffy rice

About ½ hr. before serving:

1. In large skillet combine shrimp, 1 sliced onion, sliced garlic, cayenne, turmeric, salt, cinnamon sticks, ginger, and 1 cup milk. Cover and simmer 10 min.

2. In hot salad oil, in small skillet, sauté 1 sliced onion till tender; stir in lime juice and sugar.

3. Into ¼ cup milk stir 1 tablesp. cornstarch; pour into shrimp mixture, while stirring. Add sautéed onion; cook till thickened.

4. Serve over hot fluffy rice, along with Egg-and-Onion Sambal. Makes 6 servings.

EGG-AND-ONION SAMBAL

1 large onion, peeled, thinly sliced	⅓ cup cold water
	1 teasp. sugar
1 medium cucumber, thinly sliced	½ teasp. salt
1 large green pepper, seeded, sliced into rings ⅛" thick	½ teasp. pepper
	3 hard-cooked eggs, shelled, halved
⅓ cup lemon juice	

Early on the day:

1. Arrange onion and cucumber slices and green pepper rings in salad bowl.

2. Mix lemon juice with water, sugar, salt, and pepper; pour over onion-cucumber mixture. Toss well, then refrigerate.

Just before serving:
Toss salad well, then garnish with halved eggs. Makes 6 servings.

BANANA PUFFS

2 cups sifted cake flour	1 large ripe banana
2 teasp. sugar	¼ cup flaked coconut
⅛ teasp. salt	1 teasp. lime juice
½ cup butter or margarine	1 egg white
½ cup buttermilk	Salad oil

1. Into bowl sift flour, sugar, salt; with pastry blender cut in butter until like corn meal. Now blend in ½ cup buttermilk, then knead lightly.
2. Toss banana, cut into ¼" cubes, with coconut and lime juice.
3. Next, on lightly floured surface, roll out dough about ¼" thick. With 2¾" cookie cutter, cut dough into rounds. Then, on each of half of rounds, center 1 tablesp. banana mixture; brush edges with slightly beaten egg white; then top each with second round and press edges together with fork.
4. In large skillet heat 1½" salad oil to 360°F. on deep-fat-frying thermometer. Then fry 5 or 6 puffs at a time till golden, turning once; drain on paper towel; repeat. Serve warm or cold. Makes about 12.

China

It's those delightful surprises in Chinese dishes that tease one's palate. Take Bamboo-Shoot Soup—it blends chicken broth and green peas with tiny slivers of ham and crispy bamboo shoots!

HUO TUI HSUN PIEN TANG
(Bamboo-Shoot Soup)

4 thin slices boiled ham	½ 10-oz. pkg. frozen peas
1½ 13¾-oz. cans chicken broth	¼ teasp. salt
½ 5-oz. can bamboo shoots, sliced, drained	

About 20 min. before serving:
Cut ham into ½" lengthwise strips. Then combine with chicken broth, bamboo shoots, peas, and salt in a saucepan and simmer, uncovered, 15 min. Makes 4 servings.

Far East

One of the delectable dishes the Chinese eat with chopsticks, as a first course, or with clear soup as a main course.

CH'UN CHÜAN
(Chinese Egg Rolls)

1 cup cooked or rinsed canned shrimp, chopped
1 cup drained canned bean sprouts, chopped
1 cup finely chopped celery
½ cup drained canned mushrooms, chopped
1½ teasp. salt

1 teasp. monosodium glutamate
½ teasp. granulated sugar
1 cup sifted all-purpose flour
1 teasp. salt
4 eggs
Cold water
About 2 qt. salad oil
3 tablesp. dry mustard

About 3 hr. before serving: *
1. Make Shrimp Filling as follows: Mix shrimp, bean sprouts, celery, mushrooms, 1½ teasp. salt, monosodium glutamate, and sugar, then refrigerate.
2. Now make batter for Egg-Roll Wrappers, by thoroughly combining flour, 1 teasp. salt, 3 eggs, beaten. Then stir in 1 cup water, a little at a time, until a smooth, thin batter.
3. Now cook the Egg Roll wrappers as follows: Heat 1 teasp. salad oil in a skillet, 7" across bottom, over medium heat. Then pour in 3 tablesp. batter (scant ¼ cup). Rotate skillet until batter covers bottom, then let it cook until surface is set; do not turn. When set, carefully slide it onto paper toweling. (If wrapper sticks, roll one edge of it over and loosen bottom with spatula.)
4. Wipe any particles from bottom of skillet, then repeat step 3 until all batter is used up, letting each wrapper cool on its own piece of paper toweling.
5. Now fill each egg roll as follows: Drain Shrimp Filling well, then place 1 heaping tablespoonful of it, off-center, on one of wrappers. Fold two sides of wrapper over filling, then brush exposed part of wrapper with some of remaining egg, beaten. Next, starting from filling end, roll up filling in wrapper. When all egg rolls are filled, refrigerate them, uncovered, for 1 hr.
6. Then, to fry egg rolls, heat 1" of salad oil in a skillet to 375°F., or until a 1" square of day-old bread browns in 40 seconds. Fry egg rolls, two at a time, until well browned on both sides, draining them on paper toweling.
7. When all the rolls have been fried, reheat them, uncovered, on a cookie sheet in a 400°F. oven about 10 min.
8. Meanwhile, for the Hot Mustard Sauce, stir enough water into dry mustard to make it the consistency of mayonnaise.
9. These Egg Rolls, with the mustard sauce, are delicious before a main dish of frozen or canned chicken chow mein. Fruit and hot tea make nice top-offs.

* If preferred you can make Egg Rolls a week ahead, then wrap and freeze them. Or make a day ahead, then refrigerate them.

Along the coastline, where fish is more plentiful, you'll find it steamed, whole, to delectable tenderness, in tart soy sauce.

CHENG YU
(Steamed Sea Bass)

1 1½-lb. cleaned sea bass
½ teasp. ground ginger
2 tablesp. soy sauce
2 tablesp. dry sherry or rice wine
2 tablesp. salad oil
2 tablesp. lemon juice

1 teasp. salt
½ teasp. pepper
2 scallions, cut in ½" pieces
Lemon slices
Parsley

About ½ hr. before serving:
1. Wipe fish, dry, then lay on double thickness of foil, with edges turned up all around.
2. Combine ginger, soy sauce, sherry, salad oil, lemon juice, salt, pepper, and scallions; pour over fish.
3. Stand 3 6-oz. custard cups in bottom of a large Dutch oven. On them rest a wire rack. Pour 1½" of water into Dutch oven, and heat to boiling.
4. Lay fish, on the foil, on the wire rack, being sure the boiling water does not come up over edge.
5. Steam, covered, about 15 min., or until fish is tender, basting it occasionally with sauce mixture.
6. Serve whole, garnished with lemon slices, parsley, and sauce. Makes 3 or 4 servings.

Vegetables are seldom served separately in China. More often, as in this great favorite, they are cooked briefly, right in the main dish.

PEKING JA
(Peking Duckling)

1 4- to 5-lb. duckling, quartered
½ cup chopped onion
1 6-oz. can sliced mushrooms
2 tablesp. sherry
1 tablesp. soy sauce
1 teasp. ground ginger
1 tablesp. sugar
2 teasp. salt

2 10-oz. pkg. frozen leaf spinach, thawed, or 6 cups Chinese cabbage in ½" crosswise slices
2 tablesp. cornstarch
2 tablesp. water
Preserved kumquats
Mandarin oranges
Flaked coconut

About 1 hr. and 45 min. before serving:
1. In large Dutch oven place duckling, skin side down; sprinkle with onion.
2. Drain canned mushroom liquid into measuring cup; to it add enough water to make 1 cup; pour over duckling.

3. Now to duckling add sherry, soy sauce, ginger, sugar, and salt. Boil, covered, 20 min.; lower heat, simmer 30 min.

4. Remove duckling from Dutch oven; spoon off fat. Return duckling to Dutch oven, skin side up; simmer 30 min., or until very tender.

5. Move duckling to one side of Dutch oven; add spinach and mushrooms; cook, covered, stirring once or twice, 10 min., or until spinach is done.

6. Blend cornstarch with water; add to hot liquid in Dutch oven, a little at a time, stirring constantly; simmer 2 min.

To serve: Over surface of large square or oblong platter arrange spinach with mushrooms; top with duckling pieces, tucking kumquats here and there. Tuck a tiny bowl of mandarin oranges and another of flaked coconut in opposite corners of platter. Makes 4 servings.

The Chinese spare no pains to achieve their subtle, delicate flavors. This Oriental version of roast pork is one example.

CH'A HSIAO
(*Oriental Roast Pork*)

2 teasp. salt
¾ cup soy sauce
½ cup lemon juice
¾ cup granulated sugar
½ teasp. red food color
1 small onion, peeled, sliced

¾ teasp. ground ginger
2 cloves garlic, crushed (optional)
About 3 lb. lean boned pork
   shoulder, in one piece
Hot fluffy rice

Day before or early on the day:
In medium bowl combine salt, soy sauce, lemon juice, sugar, food color, onion, ginger, and garlic. Place pork, fat side up, in this marinade; refrigerate.

About 3½ hr. before serving:
1. Start heating oven to 325°F. Remove pork shoulder from marinade, reserving marinade; roll up pork, then tie it securely with string. Place it on wire rack in shallow roasting pan which has been lined with foil. Insert roast-meat thermometer into center of its meaty section.

2. Roast pork about 3 hr., or until roast-meat thermometer registers 185°F., basting meat with reserved marinade several times during this roasting period.

3. When pork is done, remove and discard onion. Slice pork into ¼" slices, then arrange them on a heated platter. Serve with hot fluffy rice. Makes about 6 servings.

*This savory main dish is in the real Chinese sweet-and-sour tra-
dition, the meat balls being welcome made of beef or pork.*

TIEN SUAN ZOU WAN
(Sweet-and-Sour Meat Balls)

3 large green peppers, seeded	2 tablesp. butter or margarine
4 canned pineapple slices	1 cup canned chicken broth
1 lb. lean pork or beef, ground	½ cup juice from canned pine-
4 teasp. soy sauce	apple slices
Salt	¼ cup vinegar
1 teasp. seasoned salt	2 tablesp. cornstarch
¼ teasp. pepper	1 tablesp. sugar
1 tablesp. flour	Hot fluffy rice

About 1 hr. before serving:

1. Wash, then cut each seeded pepper into 6 pieces; cook, in
boiling water to cover, 3 min.; drain. Cut each pineapple slice
into 6 pieces; drain.
2. Combine pork, 2 teasp. soy sauce, ¾ teasp. salt, seasoned salt,
pepper; blend well. Shape into 16 small balls; roll balls in flour.
3. In hot butter, in skillet, over medium heat, brown balls well
on all sides; cover; simmer 5 min., or until no longer pink
in center; remove to hot platter; keep warm.
4. To butter in skillet, add ⅓ cup chicken broth, green peppers,
pineapple pieces. Cover; simmer 8 min. Meanwhile, combine ⅔
cup broth, pineapple juice, vinegar, cornstarch, sugar, 2 teasp.
soy sauce, ½ teasp. salt; add to green-pepper mixture; stir constantly till thickened and clear.
5. Pour pepper mixture over meat balls. Serve hot, with fluffy
rice. Makes 4 servings.

*Dessert is not too important in the Chinese meal, fruit—fresh
or preserved—and almond cookies or litchies being the usual.*

SHUI KUO PIN PANG
(Fruit Bouquet)

Finely crushed ice *	12 melon chunks
4 canned or fresh pineapple	12 plump dried figs
slices, cut into 24 chunks	16 fresh grapes
24 pitted dates	16 canned mandarin oranges or
24 preserved kumquats	orange slices

About 3 hr. before serving:

Prepare or buy enough finely crushed ice to make a pyramid 7″
high and 12″ across; refrigerate. Get all the fruits ready; refrigerate.

* You may omit ice and group fruits on an oval platter.

129

About 1 hr. before serving:

1. In large serving dish, with deep rim to keep ice from dripping over, shape a pyramid of ice, 7″ high and 12″ across.
2. Press fruits around pyramid in rows, securing with toothpicks if needed. Refrigerate bouquet.
3. Just before dessert time, take bouquet from refrigerator and set on buffet table. With bamboo picks, guests help themselves to pieces of fruit. Makes 6 servings.

Yes, these are those same crisp, almondy cookies that the Chinese like to serve at snacktime—anytime—along with a fragrant cup of green or black tea.

HSING JEN PING
(*Almond Cookies*)

2½ cups sifted all-purpose flour
¾ cup granulated sugar
¼ teasp. salt
1 teasp. double-acting baking powder
¾ cup soft shortening

1 whole egg
2 tablesp. water
1 teasp. almond extract
⅓ cup blanched almonds
1 egg yolk
1 tablesp. water

1. Sift together flour, sugar, salt, and baking powder. Using electric mixer at medium speed, or spoon, mix shortening with egg until creamy. Add 2 tablesp. water and extract; mix.
2. Gradually add flour mixture, stirring with fork till mixture draws away from sides of bowl. Knead to blend; refrigerate 1 hr.
3. Now start heating oven to 350°F. Form dough into 1″ balls; using palm of hand, flatten each to ¼″ thickness.
4. Place balls on greased cookie sheet, ½″ apart. Press almond in each; brush with yolk, beaten with 1 tablesp. water. Bake 25 min., or until golden. These keep well. Makes 3 doz.

Hong Kong

Hong Kong's cookery is great, and a delight to travelers. All styles of Chinese cookery may be found, as these three samples attest.

HOP PO GAI DING
(*Chicken with Walnuts*)

1 teasp. sugar
1 teasp. salt
1 tablesp. soy sauce
3 tablesp. sherry
1 2½- to 3-lb. broiler-fryer,
  skinned and boned
Cornstarch
1 egg, beaten

¼ cup salad oil
1 cup California walnut halves
½ teasp. powdered ginger
2 cloves garlic, peeled, minced
1 teasp. monosodium glutamate
1 5-oz. can sliced bamboo shoots,
  drained
Hot fluffy rice

About 45 min. before serving:
1. In medium bowl combine sugar, salt, soy sauce, and sherry. Cut chicken into bite-size pieces (about 1½″), then let stand in sherry mixture 15 to 18 min.
2. Remove chicken, reserving sherry mixture. Lightly sprinkle chicken with cornstarch, then toss with beaten egg.
3. In skillet heat salad oil; in it lightly brown walnuts, turning often; remove walnuts. To remaining oil in skillet add ginger, garlic, and chicken pieces; sauté until chicken pieces are well browned on all sides.
4. Add ¾ cup water, monosodium, sherry mixture. Simmer, covered, 20 min.; then stir in bamboo shoots and walnuts and simmer 5 min. Serve over hot fluffy rice. Makes 6 servings.

SKILLET BEEF AND CELERY

Salad oil
2 medium onions, peeled,
  chopped
2 cups finely sliced celery stalks
1½ lb. chuck, fat removed, then
  cut into thin 1″ to 1½″ slices

½ teasp. salt
¼ teasp. pepper
2 tablesp. soy sauce
1 teasp. monosodium glutamate
2 teasp. cornstarch
Hot fluffy rice

About 1 hr. before serving:
1. In large skillet heat 2 tablesp. salad oil; in it sauté onions and celery until golden, then remove.
2. In same skillet heat 2 tablesp. salad oil; add chuck and brown

well. Then stir in salt, pepper, soy sauce, monosodium glutamate, and 1 cup water. Simmer, covered, 35 min.

3. Add onion-celery mixture and cook 10 min. Combine cornstarch with ¼ cup water. Add to meat in skillet and bring to a boil. Serve over hot fluffy rice. Makes 6 servings.

FRIED RICE

1½ cups uncooked regular white rice
Salt
Salad oil
1 lb. boned lean pork shoulder, cut into very thin, narrow strips

1 clove garlic, peeled, minced
2 medium onions, peeled, chopped
4 scallions, snipped
3 eggs, beaten
3 to 4 tablesp. soy sauce

About 45 min. before serving:

1. Boil rice in plenty of boiling salted water for about 10 min., or until *just* tender. Drain in colander, then rinse thoroughly with cold water.

2. In large skillet heat 2 tablesp. salad oil; in it sauté pork until tender—about 8 to 10 min., turning frequently; then remove.

3. To same skillet add 2 tablesp. salad oil; in it sauté garlic, onions, and scallions until golden. Now add beaten eggs and cook, stirring, until just set, *but not dry;* then remove.

4. To same skillet add 2 tablesp. salad oil; add rice and toss until hot. Next add soy sauce and pork and egg mixture, blending well. Serve, passing more soy sauce, if desired. Delicious luncheon or light dinner dish. Makes 6 generous servings.

India

Especially popular in North India, the balls for this Kofta are made from minced beef or chicken, as well as from lamb.

NARGISI KOFTA
(*Indian Egg-Meat Balls*)

4 medium eggs, hard-cooked
2 lb. lean, square-cut lamb shoulder, trimmed, boned, ground
2 teasp. dried mint flakes, crumbled
2 teasp. salt
¼ teasp. pepper
¼ cup butter or margarine

1 large onion, peeled, sliced thin
½ fresh red pepper, cut into ½" strips (optional)
¼ to ½ teasp. chili powder
1 teasp. turmeric
1 teasp. powdered ginger
¼ teasp. garlic salt
½ cup canned chicken broth

About 30 min. before serving:
1. Cut shelled hard-cooked eggs in half crosswise. Mix ground lamb with mint, 1½ teasp. salt, and pepper. Divide meat into 8 parts; mold each into a thin patty, then wrap it around each egg-half to cover it completely.
2. In 2 tablesp. butter or margarine, in large skillet, sauté meat balls (kofta) until brown on all sides.
3. Meanwhile, in medium skillet, melt 2 tablesp. butter or margarine; in it fry onion and red pepper until onion is transparent; add chili powder, turmeric, ginger, garlic salt, ½ teasp. salt, chicken broth; heat.
4. Place meat balls in serving dish with sauce over them. Or, if preferred, pass sauce separately. Makes 4 servings. For 8 servings, double recipe.

*Many Indian dishes are quite possible for you to copy—with even
a touch of Eastern splendor. Here is a traditional curry, as well
as one of the picturesque Indian breads.*

MURGI CURRY*
(Chicken Curry)

2 tablesp. salad oil
2 large onions, peeled, chopped
2 cloves garlic, peeled, minced
1 teasp. chopped green ginger, or
  ½ teasp. powdered ginger
1 tablesp. powdered coriander
  seed
1 teasp. turmeric

1 teasp. powdered cumin seed
½ teasp. powdered cinnamon
½ teasp. powdered cardamom
2 teasp. chili powder
1 2½- to 3-lb. broiler-fryer, cut up
1 cup yoghurt
½ cup commercial sour cream
2 tomatoes, chopped

About 1 hr. before serving:
1. In large skillet heat salad oil; in it sauté onions and garlic
until golden. Then stir in 1 teasp. salt, ginger, coriander, turmeric,
cumin seed, cinnamon, cardamom, and chili powder.
2. Rub chicken pieces with 2 teasp. salt; arrange in skillet and
brown lightly. Beat together yoghurt and sour cream; add, with
tomatoes, to chicken.
3. Bring to a boil, then simmer, covered, 40 to 45 min., or until
chicken is tender. Serve with fluffy dry rice, our Indian bread,
below, chutney, and cucumber salad (diced cucumbers, mixed
with yoghurt, salt, and a little pepper). Makes 4 to 6 servings.

* If desired substitute 5 teasp. curry powder for ginger, coriander, turmeric,
cumin, cinnamon, cardamom, and chili powder.

POORI
(An Indian Bread)

2 cups whole-wheat flour
2 teasp. double-acting baking
  powder

1 teasp. salt
Salad oil
1 cup cold water

About 1½ hr. before serving:
1. In bowl thoroughly combine the wheat flour, baking powder,
salt, 2 tablesp. salad oil, and water. Roll into 1½" to 2" balls.
2. On board roll out each ball into ⅛"-thick circle, using some
wheat flour to prevent its sticking.
3. Into skillet pour salad oil to a depth of 1½". Heat to 380°F.
Drop in bread circle; with tip of wooden spoon hold it beneath
oil until bubbly and puffy. Cook until light brown, turning once;
drain on paper towel. Repeat with rest of circles.
4. Serve hot, piled on plate, along with any Indian main dish,
such as curried chicken. Makes about 15.
P.S. If desired, bread may be made up early on the day or day
before, then wrapped in foil and reheated in a hot oven of about
400°F. before serving.

Indonesia

AN INDONESIAN RIJSTTAFEL

The rijsttafel is an old East Indian custom. Literally, it means "rice table."

Fluffy white rice is its basis, with help-yourself toppings of spicy fish, meat, and vegetable dishes that build up into a symphony of subtly different tastes. No bread is necessary. Iced tea makes a fine complement, though in Java cold beer is considered a classic accompaniment. And for dessert nothing is more fitting than cool slices of pineapple.

All the dishes for this famous feast, including a suggested list of condiments, follow. Set your table for buffet or sit-down service with serving dishes for the featured rice in the center, and the toppings and condiments around it, so each can help himself. (In Indonesia they have a boy carry each dish in a sort of procession.)

It will be easier for you as cook and hostess if you start making the dishes in the order we give them, and at the time indicated.

CONDIMENTS

Day before: Arrange your choice of the condiments that follow in serving dishes, then refrigerate: Toasted coconut, salted peanuts, chutney, India relish, pickled hot peppers, fingers of pared cucumbers, green beans in bottled oil-and-vinegar dressing, preserved orange peel, shredded, and bottled shrimp wafers.

SHRIMP SAMBAL

1 tablesp. peanut oil	1¼ teasp. salt
⅛ teasp. crushed (not ground) red pepper	24 raw shrimp, shelled and deveined
2 tablesp. peanut butter	1 teasp. sugar
1 small onion, peeled, minced	3 tablesp. water

Day before:
In skillet, heat oil; add crushed pepper, peanut butter, onion, and salt; cook until mixture bubbles. Then add shrimp, sugar, and water; simmer, stirring often, for about 5 min., or until shrimp are cooked. Refrigerate. Serve cold, sprinkled with paprika, if desired. Makes 12 rijsttafel servings.

CORN FRITTERS

1 12-oz. can shoe-peg white corn, drained
1 egg, beaten
1 tablesp. minced scallions
1 clove garlic, peeled, minced
1 tablesp. minced celery
2 tablesp. flour

1 tablesp. snipped parsley
¼ teasp. pepper
¾ teasp. salt
4 blanched almonds, crushed with rolling pin
⅓ cup peanut oil

Day before:
Combine all ingredients except oil. Drop, by heaping tablespoonfuls, into hot oil in skillet. Sauté till brown on one side; turn and sauté till brown and crisp on other side. Drain on paper towels; cool; refrigerate.

Fifteen minutes before serving:
Place fritters on sheet of foil on cake rack. Bake at 400°F. 15 min. Makes 16 rijsttafel servings.

SAUTÉED BEEF IN COCONUT MILK

¾ cup flaked coconut
½ cup milk
2 medium onions, peeled, chopped
1 clove garlic, peeled, minced

1¼ lb. boned sirloin
2 tablesp. peanut oil
¾ teasp. salt
¾ teasp. chili powder

Day before:
Add coconut to milk; wrap onions with garlic in foil. Refrigerate both.

About 1¼ hr. before serving:
Cut steak into ¾" cubes; sauté in hot peanut oil, in skillet, till browned. Move meat to one side of skillet; add onions and garlic; sauté till tender. Sprinkle salt and chili powder over meat; turn down heat; add coconut-milk mixture; allow to simmer, uncovered, 5 min., stirring frequently. Place meat mixture on piece of heavy-duty foil; cover with second piece of foil; turn up edges; pinch together; bake on cookie sheet at 400°F. 45 min., or till tender. Makes 12 rijsttafel servings.

BAKED BANANAS

4 ripe bananas
2 tablesp. melted butter or margarine

Salt

Twenty-five minutes before serving:
Start heating oven to 400°F. Peel bananas; cut in halves lengthwise, then crosswise. Arrange on heavy-duty foil; turn up edges.

Brush with melted butter; sprinkle with salt. Bake about 15 to 20 min., or till bananas are easily pierced with fork.

Just before serving:
Broil baked bananas about 1 min. Makes 16 rijsttafel servings.

SPICED BAKED BASS

¼ teasp. salt	½ cup butter or margarine,
⅛ teasp. pepper	melted
1 clove garlic, peeled, minced	3 tablesp. soy sauce
1 lemon, sliced	3 tablesp. lime juice
2 lb. boned striped bass	¼ teasp. crushed (not ground) red
	pepper

Day before:
Wrap salt, pepper, garlic in one piece of foil; lemon in another. Refrigerate.

About 45 min. before serving:
Start heating oven to 400°F. Meanwhile, place striped bass, cut side up, in 13" x 9" x 2" baking dish; rub salt mixture into bass. Combine butter, soy sauce, lime juice, red pepper; pour over bass.

About 30 min. before serving:
Bake bass, basting occasionally with soy mixture, till fish flakes easily with a fork and is still moist. Cut fish into 4" squares; arrange on heated platter; pour sauce over it. Garnish with lemon. Makes 12 rijsttafel servings.

CHICKEN IN LIME

1 tablesp. minced onion	½ teasp. salt
1 clove garlic, peeled, minced	⅛ teasp. pepper
¼ teasp. crushed red pepper	¼ cup peanut oil
½ teasp. powdered cumin	2 tablesp. soy sauce
½ teasp. coriander seeds, crushed	2 tablesp. lime juice
¼ teasp. turmeric	1 lime, quartered or cut into
1 2½-lb. broiler-fryer, cut into	sixths
very small pieces	

Day before:
Wrap onion and garlic in foil; refrigerate. Wrap crushed red pepper with cumin, coriander, and turmeric.

About 40 min. before serving:
Sprinkle chicken with salt and pepper; sauté in oil in skillet till browned. Push chicken to one side; put onion and garlic in skillet; sauté till golden. Add red-pepper mixture and soy sauce.

Cook, covered, *stirring frequently,* about 20 min., or till chicken is tender.

Just before serving:
Sprinkle chicken with lime juice; add lime quarters; heat. Makes 12 rijsttafel servings.

BAKED EGGPLANT

1 small eggplant	6 tablesp. melted butter or mar-
1 teasp. salt	garine
Dash pepper	Snipped parsley

Thirty minutes before serving:
Start heating oven to 400°F. Pare eggplant; cut into 1″ cubes. Arrange cubes on sheet of heavy-duty foil; turn up sides; sprinkle with salt, pepper. Then brush the eggplant cubes with 3 tablesp. melted butter. Bake 20 min.

Just before serving:
Turn range heat to "broil." Brush eggplant cubes with 3 tablesp. melted butter; then broil them until they are browned. Now top with snipped parsley. Makes 16 rijsttafel servings.

JAVANESE OMELET

1 onion, peeled, sliced	⅛ teasp. crushed (not ground) red
1 tomato, sliced	pepper
¼ cup snipped parsley	⅛ teasp. salt
½ cup slivered boiled ham	4 eggs, beaten
2 tablesp. peanut oil	2 tablesp. soy sauce

Day before:
Halve slices of onion and tomato; wrap in foil, with parsley and ham; refrigerate.

Twenty minutes before serving:
In skillet place peanut oil, then onion and tomato slices, parsley, ham, red pepper, and salt. Sauté in skillet till tender-crisp; turn heat *very* low; pour beaten eggs on top; cover. When eggs are just set, pour soy sauce on top. Cut omelet into strips; heap on platter. Makes 12 rijsttafel servings.

HOT FLUFFY RICE

Time for cooking depends upon kind of rice. Follow label directions closely. Plan to have 2 cups hot rice ready for each serving. Add no salt or butter in cooking or serving.

P.S. You may want to ask a friend to be co-hostess and prepare the bass, eggplant, and bananas on the day of the party. By using foil, you can fit baked dishes in same oven: top rack, bass; below, beef, bananas, eggplant. Fritters are set on foil-covered rack on bass dish.

JAVA'S NASI GORENG

From Indonesia, too, comes Nasi Goreng—a dish of curried fried rice tossed with shrimp and meat balls.

Each guest helps himself to the Nasi Goreng, then tops it with his choice of these condiments: crumbled crisp bacon, canned fried onion rings, slivered crystallized ginger; Sambal Oelik (crushed red peppers soaked in peanut oil), raisins, plumped up in water, as well as peanuts and that old Far Eastern stand-by—chutney. A Sate or two go at the side of each guest's plate.

Cut-up, fresh pineapple, tossed with fresh and frozen fruit, and served in a hollowed-out pineapple shell makes a fitting finale.

NASI GORENG
(Curried Fried Rice)

½ lb. chuck beef, ground once
2 tablesp. pkgd. dried bread crumbs
1 egg, unbeaten
1¼ cups chopped onion
Salt
Pepper
Butter or margarine

1 cup diced celery
3 tablesp. salad oil
½ lb. shelled, deveined fresh shrimp
2 tablesp. curry powder
2 cups canned chicken broth
2 cups pkgd. precooked rice

1. Combine chuck, bread crumbs, egg, ¼ cup chopped onion, ½ teasp. salt, and ⅛ teasp. pepper. Form into tiny meat balls, using 1 tablesp. of mixture for each; set aside.
2. In large skillet, melt 2 tablesp. butter. Add 1 cup chopped onion and celery; sauté till golden; then remove from skillet.
3. In same skillet, heat salad oil; add shrimp; sauté 3 to 5 min., or until cooked; remove from skillet.
4. In same skillet, brown meat balls well, keeping them round by rotating skillet over heat as they cook.
5. In medium saucepan, melt 2 tablesp. butter; add curry, 1 teasp. salt, ⅛ teasp. pepper, and chicken broth; bring to boil. Add rice; cover; remove from heat; let stand 5 min., or as label directs.
6. Now add celery-onion mixture, shrimp, and rice to meat balls in skillet. Cover and heat until piping hot. Serve, heaped in a bowl or on a platter with or without condiments. Makes 4 to 6 servings.
NOTE: For a Nasi Goreng party toss in strips of Javanese Omelet, p. 138.

SATES
(*Skewered Broiled Pork*)

4 medium onions, peeled, chopped
2 cloves garlic, peeled, minced
4 teasp. crushed coriander seeds (optional)
1 teasp. black pepper
Dash cayenne pepper

3 tablesp. lemon juice
2 tablesp. brown sugar
¼ cup soy sauce
1½ lb. boned pork shoulder
6 to 8 9″ metal skewers
Hot fluffy rice

About 2 hr. before serving:
1. In large bowl toss onions, garlic, coriander seeds, 1 tablesp. salt, pepper, cayenne.
2. Add lemon juice, brown sugar, and soy sauce, and toss. Trim fat from pork; cut pork into ½″ cubes, then add to onion-and-soy-sauce mixture. Let stand at room temperature about 1 hr., so flavors penetrate pork.

About ½ hr. before serving:
Preheat broiler 10 min., or as manufacturer directs. Meanwhile, onto each skewer string about 9 pork cubes. Broil 8 min. per side, or until no pink shows when largest pork cube is slit. Serve on bed of hot rice. Makes 6 to 8 servings.

Japan

Do as the Japanese do, and cook this fascinating dish in an electric skillet, chafing dish, or hibachi, right before your guests. Its natural crispness and fragrance are never lost—the cooking times are so brief!

SUKIYAKI

½ cup soy sauce
3 tablesp. sugar
¾ cup canned chicken broth
About ½ head Chinese cabbage
About ½ lb. fresh spinach
12 scallions
1 large onion, peeled
2 large mushrooms

1 or 2 canned bamboo shoots
About ⅓ can bean curd (optional)
1 cup canned shirataki (optional)
1 lb. very thinly sliced beef tenderloin or sirloin
2″ square suet or 2 tablesp. salad oil
Hot fluffy rice

One hour before company comes:
1. In pitcher combine soy sauce, sugar, and broth; then set it aside.
2. Next, prepare 3 cups of cabbage in diagonal slices, ½″ wide. Then snip 3 cups spinach and slice scallions into 2″ lengths.
3. Now cut onion in half lengthwise, then into ¼″ slices. Also slice mushrooms and bamboo shoots and cut bean curd into 8 small cubes.
4. Next arrange all the vegetables, shirataki, and the thinly sliced meat on a platter or tray. Carry it, suet, and the pitcher of soy sauce to the table, which has been set with an hibachi and skillet or an electric skillet.
5. Then, when everyone's seated, the ceremony begins at the table! Heat the suet in the skillet; into it, with long fork, push from tray all but meat and spinach. Then pour on sauce, and let cook over high heat 8 min.
6. Now push spinach and meat onto vegetables, then let it all simmer 2 min. Then push them down into sauce, cook all 3 min., and serve with hot fluffy rice and hot green tea. Makes 6 servings.
P.S. Japanese food items may be ordered from: Katagiri & Co., 224 East 59th Street, New York City.

In Japanese tempura restaurants you can watch the cooks dip fish and vegetable morsels in batter, fry them light and crisp, then serve them up as unforgettable delicacies.

TEMPURA
(Batter-Fried Food)

2 large onions, peeled, in ¼″ rings
2 carrots, pared, in 3″ by ¼″ sticks
3 celery stalks, in 3″ by ¼″ sticks
¼ lb. green beans, in 3″ to 4″ lengths
2 large green peppers, seeded, in ¼″ rings
1 large sweet potato, pared, sliced ⅛″ thick
1 lb. large shrimp, shelled, deveined, with tails left on
1 lb. sea scallops

½ cup soy sauce
½ cup water
2 teasp. sugar
½ teasp. salt
2 tablesp. sherry or white wine
2 tablesp. drained horse-radish or 2 teasp. ginger
2 cups sifted all-purpose flour
8 eggs
½ cup cold water
Salad oil
Hot fluffy rice

Day before or early on the day:
1. Clean, prepare for frying, and then refrigerate onions, carrots, celery stalks, green beans, green peppers, and sweet potato.
2. Split shrimp in half lengthwise, up to tails. Refrigerate.
3. Cut scallops in half, making discs; refrigerate.
4. Make Tempura Sauce: In saucepan combine soy sauce, water,

sugar, salt, sherry or wine, and horse-radish. Bring to boil, while stirring; cool; refrigerate until needed.

5. Line 2 large cookie sheets with paper towels. Get ready 6 to 8 small bowls for Tempura Sauce, also one large serving platter.

Two hours before serving:

1. Start heating oven to 350°F. In large bowl, combine flour, eggs, cold water. With fork or pastry blender, stir till it has consistency of batter.

2. In large skillet, heat 1½″ salad oil to 350°F. on deep-fat-frying thermometer.

3. Dip 5 or 6 onion rings in batter; then fry in hot oil till golden. Remove with tongs or slotted spoon onto paper towels on cookie sheets. Repeat; keep rings warm in oven.

4. Now dip and then fry carrot and celery sticks, green beans, green peppers, sweet potato, shrimp, and scallops in same way.

5. In several heated small serving dishes, or on one heated large platter, group vegetables and sea food. Pour Tempura Sauce into bowls.

6. Each guest helps himself to some Tempura. Then, with chopsticks, if desired, he dips each piece into his Tempura Sauce before eating. Hot fluffy rice is a nice go-along. Makes 6 to 8 servings.

Korea

Koreans, too, prefer their foods cut into thin strips and pieces, so that cooking can be brief, and natural crispness and fragrance preserved.

KOKI-KUK
(Beef-Spinach Soup)

2 tablesp. salad oil	½ teasp. salt
1 clove garlic, peeled, minced	¼ teasp. pepper
1 tablesp. sesame seeds	1 tablesp. cornstarch
4 scallions, snipped	½ lb. fresh spinach, or 1 10-oz.
½ lb. chuck, cut into thin strips	pkg. frozen leaf spinach
¼ cup soy sauce	

About 40 min. before serving:

1. In large saucepan heat salad oil; in it sauté garlic, sesame seeds, and scallions until golden; then add chuck and cook until it loses its red color. Next stir in soy sauce, salt, pepper, and 1 qt. water.

2. Bring to a boil, then simmer 25 min., or until meat is almost tender. Combine cornstarch with 2 tablesp. water, add to soup with spinach. Cook about 5 min., or until spinach is tender. Makes 4 to 6 servings.

In this irresistible version of sautéed beef liver, you can see that Korean housewives use spice and seasoning generously. But it's so exquisite!

KAN-CHUPSI
(*Liver Piquant*)

2 tablesp. salad oil	1½ tablesp. flour
1 large clove garlic, peeled, minced	¼ teasp. pepper
1 large onion, peeled, chopped	1 tablesp. sugar
2 tablesp. sesame seeds	¾ to 1 teasp. salt
1 lb. beef liver, cut into thin strips	2 tablesp. soy sauce
	1 cup water
	Hot fluffy rice

About 15 min. before serving:
1. In large skillet heat salad oil; in it sauté garlic, onion, and sesame seeds until golden. Then add liver and cook, while stirring, until it loses its red color.
2. Sprinkle on flour, then stir in pepper, sugar, salt, soy sauce, and water. Bring to a boil, then cook 1 to 2 min. Serve at once with hot fluffy rice. Makes about 4 servings.

Another quick and easy Korean hearty, in which the "bits" of pork, chicken, and vegetables are cooked with jealous care for their delicate color, flavor touches, and food values.

TOYAJI-KOGI WA TARK-KOGI
(*Chicken-and-Pork Skillet Dish*)

2 cups water	1 cup thinly sliced white radishes
Salt	3 medium tomatoes, in wedges
1 lb. lean boned pork shoulder, in 1½″ cubes	¼ teasp. pepper
1 2-lb. broiler-fryer, cut up	⅛ teasp. cayenne pepper
2 tablesp. salad oil	3 tablesp. soy sauce
2 cloves garlic, peeled, minced	1 tablesp. cornstarch
1 large onion, peeled, sliced	1 lb. fresh peas, shelled, or 1 10-oz. pkg. frozen peas
2 tablesp. sesame seeds	

About 1 hr. before serving:
1. In large saucepan bring water and 1 teasp. salt to a boil. In it place pork and chicken; bring to a boil, then simmer 15 min. Drain, reserving broth, pork, and chicken.
2. In large skillet heat salad oil; in it sauté garlic, onion, and sesame seeds until golden. Then add pork and chicken pieces and brown lightly.
3. Next add radishes, tomatoes, 1½ teasp. salt, pepper, cayenne, soy sauce, and ¾ cup reserved broth. Simmer, covered, 30 min.

143

4. Combine cornstarch with ¼ cup reserved broth, then add, with peas, to chicken-pork mixture. Cook 5 to 8 min., or until peas, chicken, and pork are tender. Makes 6 servings.

This four-fruit cocktail, with its delicate mingling of fruit, cinnamon, and nut flavors, is a holiday favorite.

WHASHAI
(Korean Fruit Salad)

¾ cup water
¼ to ⅓ cup granulated sugar
½ teasp. cinnamon
2 large oranges, peeled, sectioned
2 large unpared pears, halved, thinly sliced

2 large peaches, peeled, halved, thinly sliced
½ lb. fresh cherries, or 1-lb.-1-oz. can pitted dark cherries, drained
¼ cup lime juice
¼ cup pine nuts

Several hr. before serving:
1. In small saucepan combine water, sugar, and cinnamon; simmer about 5 min., or until a light syrup is formed; cool slightly.
2. In large bowl combine oranges, pears, peaches, cherries, lime juice, and sugar syrup. Cover and refrigerate until well chilled.
3. Serve in pretty glass dish, sprinkled with pine nuts. Makes about 6 servings.

Malaya

Let the fragrance of this Malayan curry bridge international boundaries. Anyone can make it!

LAMB CURRY

2 tablesp. salad oil
2 medium onions, peeled, chopped
2 lb. lean, boned lamb shoulder, in 1″ cubes
1 tablesp. curry powder
1 3½-oz. can flaked coconut

1⅓ cups milk
1 tablesp. flour
2½ teasp. salt
Butter or margarine
1 tablesp. lemon juice
Hot fluffy rice

About 1 hr. before serving:
1. In Dutch oven heat salad oil; in it sauté onions until golden; then add lamb and curry and sauté about 10 min., turning frequently.

2. In saucepan combine coconut and milk; bring to a boil, then simmer over low heat about 2 min., stirring occasionally. Drain, pressing out excess moisture and reserving both coconut milk and coconut flakes.

3. Beat together flour and ¼ cup water; add, with coconut milk and salt to lamb. Simmer, covered, 40 to 45 min., or until lamb is tender.

4. Meanwhile, if desired, melt 2 tablesp. butter in skillet; in it sauté coconut flakes until golden. When lamb is tender, stir in lemon juice. Then serve with hot fluffy rice and sautéed coconut. Makes about 6 servings.

Sea fish, including crabs and shrimp, are plentiful in Malaya—this cucumber-and-shrimp version making a justly famed appetizer on crackers, or luncheon salad.

TIMUN SALAD
(*Cucumber-and-Shrimp Salad*)

2 large cucumbers	½ teasp. powdered ginger
1 lb. cooked, shelled, deveined shrimp	¼ cup salad oil
	¼ cup vinegar
3 hard-cooked eggs, shelled, sliced	2 to 3 teasp. curry powder
4 teasp. salt	⅛ teasp. cayenne pepper

A few hr. before serving:

1. Split unpared cucumbers lengthwise; remove seeds. Cut each cucumber half lengthwise into thirds, then thinly slice each third crosswise. (You should have about 4 cups, sliced.) Place in bowl.

2. Cut shrimp into small pieces. Add to cucumber, with sliced eggs, salt, ginger, salad oil, vinegar, curry powder, and cayenne pepper; toss until well blended. Refrigerate until chilled.

3. Serve as first course at a buffet. Or, if desired, serve on lettuce leaves as a light luncheon dish. Makes 4 to 6 servings.

This piquant fish bake makes use of three of Malaya's fresh staples—fish, coconut, and pineapple. But you can make it too!

MALAYAN FISH BAKE

1½ lb. haddock or cod fillets	¼ cup all-purpose flour
1 8½-oz. can pineapple slices	1 teasp. curry powder
1 3½-oz. can flaked coconut	1 tablesp. chopped chutney
1⅓ cups milk	¼ teasp. crushed red pepper
Butter or margarine	Hot fluffy rice

About 45 min. before serving:

1. Cook fish in salted water until just done—about 10 min.; drain,

reserving 1 cup liquid. Arrange fish on bottom of 10″ x 6″ x 2″ baking dish; over it arrange pineapple slices, reserving juice. Start heating oven to 400°F.

2. In saucepan combine coconut and milk, bring to a boil, then simmer over low heat about 2 min., stirring occasionally; drain, reserving liquid and coconut.

3. In saucepan melt 3 tablesp. butter; stir in flour, then add coconut milk, reserved fish stock, and pineapple juice. Cook, while stirring, until thickened. Next stir in curry, chutney, 1 teasp. salt, and pepper.

4. Pour over fish in baking dish. Down center sprinkle some of reserved coconut flakes. Bake 15 to 20 min., or until bubbling. Meanwhile, in skillet, melt 2 tablesp. butter; in it sauté rest of coconut flakes until golden. Serve along with fish. Delicious with hot fluffy rice. Makes about 4 servings.

Pakistan

Widen your world and enjoy the difference of Pakistan's chicken, steeped in a yoghurt-ginger-onion marinade, then filled with a fabulous potato stuffing.

MURGH-I-MUSALLAM
(*Stuffed Chicken*)

1 medium onion, peeled, grated
1 teasp. powdered ginger
1 tablesp. pepper
2 teasp. salt
1 cup yoghurt
1 4½-lb. roasting chicken
4 cups diced cold cooked potatoes

3 hard-cooked eggs, shelled, coarsely chopped
½ cup seedless raisins
⅓ cup chopped blanched almonds
¼ cup lemon juice
3 tablesp. butter or margarine

About 3½ hr. before serving:

1. In large bowl stir together onion, ginger, pepper, 1 teasp. salt, and yoghurt.
2. Now cut all fat from chicken.
3. Next, with two-tined fork, pierce surface of chicken well on all sides.
4. Then set chicken in yoghurt mixture, and, with spoon, coat it well on all sides with this mixture.
5. Cover bowl of chicken and refrigerate for 1 hr.
6. Meanwhile, toss diced cold cooked potatoes with coarsely chopped hard-cooked eggs, seedless raisins, chopped almonds, 2 tablesp. lemon juice, and 1 teasp. salt or onion salt. Cover, then refrigerate till needed.

7. At end of 1 hr., lift chicken from yoghurt mixture and wipe dry with paper towels.

8. Stuff its body cavity and neck opening with potato mixture.

9. Fasten neck skin to back of bird with skewer. Push drumsticks under band of skin at tail, or tie to tail.

10. Next, in melted butter or margarine, in Dutch oven, over medium heat, brown chicken well on all sides.

11. Then cover Dutch oven and simmer chicken, turning frequently, for 1½ hr., or till delightfully tender.

12. Now lift chicken to a heated large platter; remove skewers.

13. Then into butter mixture left in Dutch oven, stir 2 tablesp. lemon juice.

14. Serve this gravy over chicken. Makes 4 to 6 servings.

Your buffet guests will welcome the novel flavor of this Pakistan eggplant relish as a partner for most any meat.

EGGPLANT-SOUR-CREAM SALAD

5 to 6 tablesp. butter or margarine

1 large or 2 small eggplants (about 1¾ lb.), pared, cut into ½" cubes

1 teasp. chili powder

1 small clove garlic, peeled, minced

1½ teasp. salt

½ cup commercial sour cream

Several hours before serving:

1. In large skillet melt butter; in it sauté eggplant cubes until golden, turning often.

2. Transfer eggplant to bowl. Add chili powder, garlic, salt, and sour cream, blending well. Refrigerate until chilled.

3. Serve as salad, on lettuce leaves if desired, and sprinkled with parsley. Makes 4 to 6 servings.

This delectable creamy rice pudding boasts of the fragrance of rose water added just before it's chilled.

FIRNI
(Rice Pudding)

4 cups milk

1½ teasp. salt

½ cup uncooked regular white rice

½ cup seedless raisins

1 cup light cream

½ cup granulated sugar

¼ cup rose water

¼ cup pistachio nuts, chopped

Early on the day:

1. Bring milk to a boil, then add salt and rice. Cook over low heat,

uncovered, 30 min., stirring occasionally. Meanwhile, soak raisins in hot water to cover.

2. To rice add light cream, sugar, and drained raisins; cook 10 to 15 min., or until thickened. Then remove from heat and add rose water. Pour into serving dish; sprinkle with pistachio nuts.

3. Refrigerate until well chilled. Makes about 6 servings.

Thailand

The cuisine of Thailand (or Siam as it once was called) is beautifully suited to our tropical days, too. As summer approaches, do try their Chicken Sour and Sweet, served with hot fluffy rice and chow-mein noodles. And the flavors in their Shrimp Salad may be new to your family, too.

KAI PRIAO WAN
(Chicken Sour and Sweet)

2 tablesp. shortening
3 cloves garlic, peeled, crushed
1½ medium chicken breasts, thinly sliced
5 chicken livers, quartered
2 large carrots, pared, sliced ⅛″ thick
1 large cucumber, pared
3 small tomatoes, peeled
1 large onion, peeled
½ cup canned condensed chicken broth, undiluted
1 tablesp. flour
2 tablesp. granulated sugar
¼ cup soy sauce
¼ cup vinegar
Hot fluffy rice
Chow-mein noodles

About ¾ hr. before serving:
1. In shortening, in large skillet, sauté garlic till golden.
2. Add chicken-breast slices, quartered chicken livers, sliced carrots. Cook over medium heat, while stirring, for 5 min.
3. Next, add cucumber, split lengthwise, then sliced crosswise ⅛″ thick, tomatoes cut into eighths, onion cut into ¼″ wedges, and chicken broth. Cover and simmer 5 min.
4. Meanwhile, in small bowl, combine flour, sugar, soy sauce, and vinegar. Pour over chicken and vegetables in skillet while stirring; cook till thickened.
5. Serve in heated large bowl with rice and chow-mein noodles. Makes 6 servings.

KUNG YAM
(Shrimp Salad)

1 cup grated fresh or canned
  flaked coconut, firmly packed
1 cup light cream
2 lb. shelled, deveined shrimp
2 cups boiling water
2 teasp. salt
1 large bay leaf
1 tablesp. olive oil

2 cloves garlic, peeled, minced
3 shallots, chopped
2 large green peppers, seeded,
  chopped
2 apples, pared, coarsely grated
½ cup broken pecans
¼ cup soy sauce
Lettuce leaves

Two hours before serving:
1. Combine coconut and cream; bring to boil. Cool 30 min.; drain off cream; refrigerate it.
2. Meanwhile, cook shrimp in boiling water with salt and bay leaf, covered, about 5 min. Drain; split in halves lengthwise; refrigerate.
3. In olive oil in skillet, sauté garlic and shallots till golden. Combine peppers, apples, pecans, garlic mixture, soy sauce, reserved cream; toss; refrigerate 45 min.
4. On large platter, arrange lettuce; on it, place shrimp, then apple mixture. Makes 6 servings.

AFRICA

EGYPT

GUINEA

MOROCCO

SOUTH AFRICA

SUDAN

The cook who finds herself baffled by the preparation of a simple meal of two or three courses would stand in awe of African dining customs. Imagine being a Moroccan cook with sixty courses to prepare for a special-occasion dinner! Or an Egyptian supper which is served on a very low table with the guests probably reclining on rugs and cushions and helping themselves to the bountiful array of food.

Because of the tremendous area of this continent and the varied peoples who inhabit it, it is virtually impossible to talk about food in relation to the entire area. Egyptians, for example, breakfast well and abundantly in contrast to other countries of the Mediterranean and then eat very lightly until the evening meal.

In the North Coast region, various national backgrounds— French, Spanish, Italian—as well as the influence of Mohammedanism and the regional foodstuffs influence the food customs. In the Union of South Africa, the modern cities of Capetown and Johannesburg offer still another way of eating—largely reminiscent of Dutch, Indian, and British foods.

There is, of course, wild game prepared in many ways, particularly in the central area of Africa. Mutton is the most usual meat, and in South Africa, the langouste, *known to many countries now as the South African lobster tail, is eaten broiled or sautéed in butter and served with noodles.*

Throughout the African countries there is a vast respect for true hospitality and whether it is in the home of a South African family with its foods that reflect both British and Dutch influence or in an Egyptian home with fabulous tropical fruits and vegetables served with the native fish dishes, the visitor finds courtesy and warmth.

The hostess who wants to be truly outstanding will find a way of telling her guests something of the background of the countries of their origin when she serves the recipes that are typical of this area of the world.

Egypt

Basically Egyptian, with American accents, are the pot roast and salad which follow. Lamb, as well as mutton, is widely used in Africa—yoghurt too.

SAKHDAT-KHAROUF-MEHAMMARA
(*Egyptian-Style Lamb Pot Roast*)

1 to 1½ lb. green beans	Salt
2 lb. small potatoes	Pepper
1 1- to 1¼-lb. eggplant	Garlic salt
About 1 lb. long, thin zucchini	Paprika
1 garlic clove, peeled, cut	2 onions, peeled
1 boned rolled leg of lamb (6 lb. before boning, rolling)	3 medium tomatoes

1. In 1″ boiling, salted water, cook whole green beans 5 min. Drain; measure liquid; add water if necessary to make 2½ cups.

2. Now start heating oven to 375°F. Pare potatoes. Cut eggplant into ½″ crosswise slices; pare, then quarter slices. Wash zucchini; cut into ½″ crosswise slices.

3. Next, with cut clove of garlic, rub lamb on all sides; sprinkle with 2 teasp. salt and ¼ teasp. pepper.

4. Place lamb in center of large shallow open pan (about 15″ x 10½″). Arrange potatoes, beans, eggplant, and zucchini around meat, making two piles of potatoes and one each of other vegetables.

5. Sprinkle vegetables with about 2 teasp. salt, then with about ¼ teasp. each pepper and garlic salt. Sprinkle potatoes well with paprika.

6. Pour reserved bean liquid into pan with lamb. Slice onions; place on top of meat and vegetables. Lastly, cut tomatoes into quarters; with hands, squeeze juice over meat and vegetables; discard pulp.

7. Bake lamb, uncovered, 2½ hr., frequently basting both meat and vegetables with pan juices.

8. At end of baking time, place meat on large platter; partly slice it. Arrange vegetables around it. If desired, thicken pan juices and pass. Makes 6 servings, with meat left over.

Africa

SALATA-ZABADY
(Creamy Cucumber Salad)

1 large cucumber (¾ to 1 lb.)
1 teasp. salt
½ pt. yoghurt
1 tablesp. salad oil

¼ teasp. salt
⅛ teasp. pepper
1 clove garlic, peeled, minced

1. Pare, then slice cucumber very thin. Sprinkle with salt.
2. Let stand 30 min.; then, with hands, squeeze out as much water as possible.
3. Now, with spoon, beat yoghurt until creamy. Stir in salad oil, salt, pepper, and garlic.
4. Add drained cucumbers, and refrigerate about 1 hr. Makes 6 servings.

Guinea

Native to Guineans, too, are peanuts or groundnuts which they use generously in their cookery. Here we approximate four of their tasty dishes, using our own peanuts and peanut butter.

GUINEAN CHICKEN STEW

1 2¾-lb. broiler-fryer, cut up
Salt
½ teasp. pepper
3 tablesp. peanut or olive oil
2 cloves garlic, peeled, minced
2 medium onions, peeled, chopped

1 6-oz. can tomato paste
2 medium tomatoes, cut up
½ teasp. crushed red pepper
½ cup chunk-style peanut butter
1 10-oz. pkg. frozen okra

About 1 hr. before serving:
1. Rub chicken pieces with 1 teasp. salt and pepper. In large skillet heat oil; in it brown chicken well on all sides, then remove.
2. To drippings in skillet add garlic and onions and sauté until golden. Stir in tomato paste, tomatoes, red pepper, 1 teasp. salt, and 1½ cups water; in this lay chicken pieces.
3. Bring to a boil, then simmer, covered, 40 min. Blend peanut butter with ½ cup water. Add with okra to chicken, blending well. Cook 8 to 10 min., or until chicken and okra are tender. Makes 6 servings.

PORK-AND-GROUNDNUT SOUP

3 tablesp. peanut or olive oil
½ lb. boned lean pork, cut into small cubes
1 tablesp. flour
2 teasp. salt
½ teasp. crushed red pepper

1 cup canned salted peanuts
1 small eggplant, pared, finely chopped
1 large tomato, finely chopped
2 medium onions, peeled, chopped

About 1 hr. and 15 min. before serving:
1. In Dutch oven heat oil; in it place pork, then sprinkle with flour. Brown well on all sides, turning frequently.
2. Now add salt, red pepper, and 1 qt. water. Bring to a boil, then simmer, covered, ½ hr.
3. Meanwhile, in skillet, lightly toast peanuts, then finely grind them. Add with eggplant, tomato, and onions to soup. Simmer, covered, ½ hr. Then serve as a luncheon dish with crackers and a mixed green salad. Makes 4 to 6 servings.

GUINEAN BEEF STEW

2 tablesp. peanut or olive oil
1½ lb. boned chuck, cut into 1" cubes
1 10½-oz. can condensed consommé, undiluted
2 large tomatoes, chopped
3 medium onions, peeled, chopped

1 10-oz. pkg. frozen chopped spinach
1 teasp. salt
Dash cayenne
½ cup chunk-style peanut butter
Hot fluffy rice

About 1 hr. and 45 min. before serving:
1. In Dutch oven heat oil; in it brown chuck well on all sides. Then add consommé and simmer, covered, 1 hr.
2. Now stir in tomatoes, onions, spinach, salt, cayenne, and peanut butter. Simmer, covered, ½ hr., or until chuck and vegetables are tender. Serve with hot fluffy rice. Makes about 6 servings.

GROUNDNUT MUFFINS

½ cup butter or margarine
¼ cup granulated sugar
2 eggs
1 cup sifted all-purpose flour

½ teasp. double-acting baking powder
¼ teasp. salt
½ cup plus 2 tablesp. chopped salted peanuts

Make early on the day, or 1 hr. before serving:
1. Start heating oven to 425°F. Grease 8 muffin-pan cups (2½" across top). In small bowl, with electric mixer at medium speed,

beat butter with sugar until creamy. Add eggs, one at a time, beating until light and fluffy.

2. Sift flour with baking powder and salt. Add, with ½ cup chopped peanuts, to butter mixture.

3. Divide the mixture evenly between muffin cups. Sprinkle tops with 2 tablesp. chopped peanuts. Bake 12 to 15 min., or until golden and done. Makes 8 muffins.

Bananas—a staple food in Africa—are one of the four luscious fruits combined in this unusual jam.

FOUR-FRUIT JAM

8 bananas, peeled, thinly sliced
4 large oranges, peeled, quartered, thinly sliced
1 large grapefruit, peeled, quartered, thinly sliced

3 lemons, peeled, quartered, thinly sliced
5 cups granulated sugar

In large kettle combine bananas, oranges, grapefruit, lemons, and sugar. Stir until well blended, then cook over medium heat, uncovered, 40 to 45 min. Pour at once into sterilized jelly glasses; seal each with a thin layer of hot paraffin. Cover and store in a cool, dry place. Fills 6 to 8 medium glasses.

Morocco

Here is Morocco's national dish—a hearty, in several versions, that's worthy of any party. Rice may replace the farina.

COUSCOUS
(Lamb-and-Chicken Stew)

¼ cup butter or margarine
2 lb. lamb riblets, cut up
1 2- to 2½-lb. broiler-fryer, cut up
3 medium onions, peeled, chopped
Salt
Pepper
¼ teasp. cayenne pepper

½ medium head cabbage, cut into 6 wedges
3 carrots, pared, cut into 1″ pieces
1 green pepper, seeded, then cut into sixths
1 1-lb.-4-oz. can chick peas
⅔ cup farina

About 2 hr. before serving:
1. In large Dutch oven melt butter; add riblets; brown well. Remove, then in same butter brown chicken well; remove. Add

onions; sauté until browned. Return lamb and chicken to Dutch oven; sprinkle with 2 teasp. salt, 1 teasp. pepper, cayenne. Add 2 cups water; simmer, covered, 1 hr.

2. Remove chicken, pour off 1 cup broth and reserve. On top of lamb arrange cabbage, carrots, green pepper, and undrained chick peas. Top with chicken. Cook, covered, about 25 min., or until all vegetables are tender.

3. Meanwhile, in saucepan, bring reserved 1 cup broth with 1 cup water to boil; stir in farina and 1 teasp. salt. Cook, while stirring, for 3 min., or until thickened. Turn off heat; cover and keep warm.

4. To serve, place bowl of farina in center of serving dish; surround it with vegetables, chicken, lamb. Skim fat from gravy; pass gravy. Makes 6 servings.

The stuffing for this top-stove roast chicken is fluffy white rice, rich with a blend of ginger, pepper, cinnamon, and saffron, as well as walnuts and raisins.

STUFFED CHICKEN À LA MOROCAINE

½ cup dark seedless raisins	Powdered ginger
1½ cups uncooked regular white rice	Ground pepper
Salt	Powdered cinnamon
	Saffron
½ cup chopped California walnuts	2 3-lb. broiler-fryers
	¼ cup butter or margarine

About 1 hr. and 45 min. before serving:
1. Make this stuffing: Cover raisins with boiling water; set aside. To 3 cups boiling water, add rice, 2 teasp. salt; simmer 12 min., or until rice is *just* tender and liquid absorbed. Drain raisins; with fork toss rice with walnuts, raisins, and ¼ teasp. each of ginger, pepper, cinnamon, and saffron.

2. Use to stuff chickens; tuck leg ends under band of skin or tie together at ends. In large Dutch oven melt butter or margarine; in it brown chickens well on all sides.

3. Combine 2¼ teasp. salt, ¼ teasp. saffron, and ½ teasp. each ginger, pepper, and cinnamon with 1¼ cups water. Pour over chickens, then simmer, covered, for 1 hr., or until fork-tender.

4. Arrange chickens on large platter, with some of gravy poured over them; pass rest. Makes 8 servings.

Another tasty from Morocco! Tajine, a kind of stew, that can be made with many different ingredients. Here it's a tajine with beef.

BEEF TAJINE WITH PEAS
(Beef Stew with Peas)

3 tablesp. butter or margarine
1 large onion, peeled, chopped
½ cup snipped parsley
2 lb. boned chuck, cut into 2" pieces
1 bay leaf, crushed

2 tablesp. flour
2 teasp. salt
1 teasp. ground cumin seed
½ teasp. pepper
2 lb. fresh, or 2 10-oz. pkg. frozen green peas, thawed and drained

About 2 hr. and 20 min. before serving:
1. In Dutch oven heat butter; in it sauté onion and parsley until golden. Then add chuck, bay leaf, and flour and brown while turning frequently.
2. Now add salt, cumin seed, pepper, and 1¾ cups water. Bring to a boil, then simmer, covered, 1 hr. 45 min. Add fresh peas and cook 15 min., or until meat and peas are tender. (Or, if frozen peas, cook meat 10 min. longer, and peas only 5 min.) Makes about 6 servings.

South Africa

You'll never find a more delicious deep-dish vegetable, ham, and chicken pie! It's flaky, juicy, has a golden crust. And with salad and fruit, it's a lovely way to end the day.

HOENDER PASTEI
(Boer Chicken Pie)

2 3-lb. stewing chickens, quartered
1 teasp. whole allspice
1 teasp. whole peppercorns
3 bay leaves
3 medium carrots, pared, halved
3 celery stalks, halved
3 medium onions, peeled, quartered
About 10 parsley sprigs
¼ lb. cooked ham, sliced, then quartered

4 hard-cooked eggs, shelled, sliced
¼ cup butter or margarine
¼ cup flour
⅓ cup sherry
2 tablesp. lemon juice
¼ teasp. powdered mace
¼ teasp. pepper
2 egg yolks
1 pkg. piecrust mix
1 egg, beaten

Early on the day or day before:
1. In a large kettle bring chickens to a boil in 1 qt. water with 1

tablesp. salt, allspice, peppercorns, and bay leaves. Add carrots, celery, onions, and parsley; simmer, covered, ½ hr., or until vegetables are tender-crisp.

2. Remove vegetables and chicken from kettle; strain broth. Slice carrots and celery diagonally ½″ thick. Carefully cut chicken from bones in chunks, removing skin. In 12″ x 8″ x 2″ baking dish, arrange chicken, vegetables, ham, and eggs.

3. In saucepan melt butter or margarine; stir in flour, then gradually add 2 cups chicken broth, sherry, lemon juice, mace, 1 teasp. salt, and pepper. Cook, while stirring, until thickened.

4. Beat egg yolks, then slowly stir into sauce; heat, while stirring, until thickened, *but do not boil.* Pour over chicken. Prepare piecrust mix as label directs, then roll into 14″ x 10″ rectangle. Fold in half, crosswise; unfold, as top crust, over chicken. Turn overhang under; press firmly to edge of dish, then make scalloped edge.

5. In center of top crust, with knife, cut out a rectangle 7″ x 3″. At each corner of rectangle make a ½″ diagonal slit, then turn its piecrust edges up to form a scalloped edge. With remaining dough and small cookie cutter, cut out small designs; arrange over top of piecrust; then refrigerate.

About 45 min. before serving:
Start heating oven to 425°F. Brush pie with beaten egg. Bake 30 min., or until golden and hot. Makes 8 servings.
FOR A FOURSOME: Make half the recipe, using a 10″ x 6″ x 2″ baking dish.

Not too long ago, the great shellfish specialty of South Africa was quite unknown to the rest of the world. Today, South African lobster tails are frozen and shipped far and wide. Since we, in America, eat many of them, this dish should please!

STUFFED ROCK-LOBSTER TAILS

6 8-oz. rock-lobster tails, thawed	⅛ teasp. cayenne pepper
Salt	3 egg yolks
Butter	2 cups light cream
2 tablesp. minced onion	1 3½- to 4-oz. can button mush-
⅓ cup sherry	rooms
3 tablesp. flour	

About 1 hr. before serving:
1. Drop lobster tails into boiling salted water, then cook 9 min., or until just tender; drain. Remove meat and cut into small pieces, reserving shells. Start heating oven to 425°F.

2. In saucepan melt 3 tablesp. butter; in it lightly sauté onions, then add sherry and lobster meat, and heat but do not boil. Sprinkle with flour, 1½ teasp. salt, and cayenne.

3. Beat together egg yolks and cream; stir into lobster mixture. Heat, while stirring, until thickened. Place lobster shells in shallow baking dish; fill with lobster mixture. Sauté mushrooms in 1 tablesp. butter until golden. Place here and there on lobsters.
4. Bake 10 to 12 min., or until lightly browned. Serve with saffron rice and a tossed green salad. Makes 6 servings.
p.s. Steps 1, 2, and 3 may be done early on the day or day before; then refrigerate filled lobster shells until ready to bake.

Yes, it's your favorite hamburger, spiced up with curry, bay leaves, lemon, etc., baked in a deep 10″ pie plate, then garnished with a ring of lemon slices.

BOBOTIE
(Hamburger Baked as Pie)

3 tablesp. butter or margarine	2 tablesp. plum jam
1½ cups chopped onion	2 tablesp. lemon juice
2 cups fresh bread crumbs	¼ cup canned ground blanched
½ cup milk	almonds
3 lb. chuck beef, ground 3 times	3 bay leaves
1 egg	2 lemons, sliced
1 to 2 tablesp. curry powder	Lemon leaves
2 teasp. salt	2 pimento strips

1. Start heating oven to 350°F.
2. In small skillet, melt butter; add onion and sauté until golden.
3. Soak bread crumbs in milk.
4. Thoroughly combine chuck, egg, onion, curry powder, salt, plum jam, lemon juice, almonds, and bread-crumb mixture.
5. On bottom of an ungreased 10″ pie plate or round baking dish, lay bay leaves. On top, arrange meat mixture, patting it with fork to fit plate.
6. Bake 1 hr.; then drain off any excess moisture.
7. Garnish with lemon slices and leaves, arranged in a border around edge of meat pie. On center top, lay a lemon slice that has been cut halfway through and twisted, with a thin pimento strip on either side.
8. Serve in wedges. Makes 8 to 10 servings.

The kind of cookie that always fits in—whether it be for coffee time, teatime, or dessert.

SOETKOEKIES
(Spice-Nut Cookies)

1 cup butter or margarine	½ teasp. powdered ginger
2 cups light-brown sugar	1 cup chopped, shelled almonds
4 cups sifted all-purpose flour	1 egg
¾ teasp. baking soda	¼ cup red wine
1½ teasp. powdered cinnamon	1 beaten egg

Make two or three days ahead:
1. In large bowl, with electric mixer at medium speed, beat butter with sugar until creamy. Meanwhile, sift flour with baking soda, cinnamon, and ginger; add almonds.
2. To butter mixture add flour mixture, alternately with 1 egg and wine, blending well. Form into a ball, wrap in wax paper, then refrigerate until well chilled.
3. Start heating oven to 400°F. On floured board roll out part of dough to ¼″ thickness. With cookie cutter cut out shapes. Place on cookie sheet; brush with beaten egg. Bake 7 to 8 min., or until golden. Remove to rack to cool. Repeat with rest of dough. Store in cookie jar. Makes 6 to 7 doz.

Sudan

This recipe combines two African favorites—lamb and okra. (Incidentally, okra is an African name. They introduced it to us.)

BANI-BAMIA
(Lamb-Okra Stew)

2 tablesp. butter	⅓ cup canned tomato paste
2 medium onions, peeled, sliced	1½ cups water
2 cloves garlic, peeled, minced	2 teasp. salt
1½ lb. boned lean lamb shoulder, in 1½″ pieces	½ teasp. black pepper
	1 10-oz. pkg. frozen okra

About 1 hr. and 15 min. before serving:
1. In Dutch oven melt butter; in it sauté onions and garlic until golden; then add lamb and brown it on all sides.
2. Stir together tomato paste and water; add to lamb with salt and pepper. Bring to a boil, then simmer, covered, 1 hr.
3. Now add okra and cook, covered, 8 to 10 min., or until lamb and okra are tender. Makes 4 servings.

Africa

In Sudan chicken is reserved for special occasions and parties.

CHICKEN-POTATO SKILLET DISH

1 2½-lb. broiler-fryer, cut up
2 teasp. salt
½ teasp. black pepper
2 to 3 tablesp. butter or margarine
2 medium onions, peeled, sliced

2 cloves garlic, peeled, minced
⅓ cup canned tomato paste
1½ cups water
About 8 small potatoes, pared

About 1 hr. before serving:
1. Sprinkle chicken with salt and pepper. In large skillet heat butter; in it sauté chicken pieces, onions, and garlic until golden.
2. Stir together tomato paste and water. Add to chicken, bring to a boil, then simmer, covered, 20 min.
3. Add potatoes and simmer, covered, 30 min., or until chicken and potatoes are tender. Makes 4 to 6 servings.

Yoghurt is a dressing par excellence in the Middle East, Far East, and Africa. You'll be an enthusiast, too, when you try this recipe.

SALADA
(Cool-and-Crisp Salad)

1 cup yoghurt
1 tablesp. vinegar
¼ cup salad oil
½ teasp. crushed red pepper
2 teasp. salt
1 clove garlic, peeled, minced
  (optional)

3 to 4 cups lettuce, in bite-size
  pieces
2 medium tomatoes, cut into
  eighths
6 large scallions, sliced

About 15 min. before serving:
1. In large salad bowl, stir together yoghurt, vinegar, salad oil, red pepper, salt, and garlic.
2. Add lettuce, tomatoes, and scallions and toss until well blended. Makes 4 to 6 servings.

CARIBBEAN ISLANDS

HAITI

JAMAICA

PUERTO RICO

VIRGIN ISLANDS

When one sees the islands of the Caribbean from the air at night it is difficult to believe that the sparkling strings of lights can be anything but a fairyland. They look like nothing else but jeweled necklaces against the black velvet of the sea. Then, next morning, seeing them in the brilliant sunshine—the luxuriant foliage and flowers—the pastel buildings—the old-world atmosphere—surrounded by the incredibly beautiful waters of the Caribbean, one is even surer that here is a land of enchantment.

Exotic fruits and certain vegetables are typical of all these islands, yet each island has its own distinctive foods and food customs. Each is influenced by the traditions of the people who first settled there and by the country with which it is affiliated. Thus throughout the islands one finds traces of English, French, Spanish, African, and Indian culture—the old and the new.

Among the foods one finds certain specialties such as the plantain, the large green banana that is always cooked before eating—one delightful way being the thinly sliced, crisply fried chips served with drinks—the delicious coconut ice cream, the tropical fruits—mango, guava, papaya. Less exciting, but an indispensable part of the diet, is the native dish of rice and beans.

Learning about their foods, trying their recipes, are rewarding experiences. To the person who has visited these lovely islands, our dishes will bring back many happy memories. To the one who has not been there, they will be, hopefully, an interesting preview of a future visit.

Haiti

Since black mushrooms are not readily available, we substituted our fresh ones in this dish, with ever-so-tasty results.

RICE AND MUSHROOMS

½ lb. fresh mushrooms
Salad oil
½ lb. diced lean pork
2 oz. diced lean salt pork
1 tablesp. snipped scallions
Salt

Dried thyme
1 clove garlic, peeled
1 green pepper, seeded
1 cup uncooked regular white rice
3 frankfurters

1. Cut up mushrooms into bowl, then pour on 2½ cups hot water. With one hand, squeeze mushrooms in water to make water dark-colored.
2. Now, in skillet, heat 1 tablesp. salad oil. Add diced pork and salt pork. Sprinkle with scallions, 1½ teasp. salt, and ¼ teasp. dried thyme.
3. Mince garlic (or use a garlic press) and add to skillet. Cook, stirring often, until pork and salt pork are nicely browned.
4. Add mushrooms in their liquid; bring to boil. Then add halved green pepper and rice. Cover and cook over low heat, stirring occasionally with fork, 15 min., or until all liquid is absorbed.
5. Slice frankfurters; add to rice mixture; cook, uncovered, 1 min., or so as to heat franks. Serve at once. Makes 4 to 6 servings.

You can share the sparkle and vividness of Haiti via its peppery Ragout of Veal, or Sweet-Potato Loaf.

RAGOUT OF VEAL WITH CASHEWS

3 tablesp. salad oil
2 lb. veal shoulder, cut into 1"
   cubes
1 teasp. flour
¼ teasp. black pepper *
1 teasp. salt

1 large clove garlic, peeled,
   minced
1 tablesp. Worcestershire
1 8-oz. can tomato sauce
½ cup salted cashew nuts
Snipped parsley

About 1½ hr. before serving:
1. In medium Dutch oven heat salad oil; in it brown veal well

* In Haiti they would use ½ to ¾ teasp. black pepper.

on all sides; then stir in flour, pepper, salt, garlic, Worcestershire, tomato sauce, cashew nuts, and 2 cups water.

2. Bring to a boil, then simmer, covered, 1¼ hr., or until veal is tender, stirring occasionally.

3. When done, transfer veal mixture to a serving bowl; sprinkle with snipped parsley. Delicious with hot cooked rice. Makes 4 servings.

SWEET-POTATO LOAF

1½ cups mashed sweet potatoes	¼ teasp. powdered nutmeg
3 ripe bananas	¼ teasp. powdered cinnamon
1 cup milk	3 eggs, beaten
3 tablesp. granulated sugar	Dark corn syrup or maple syrup
¾ teasp. salt	Whipped cream (optional)
⅓ cup dark seedless raisins	

About 2 hr. before serving:
1. Start heating oven to 350°F. Grease well a 9″ x 5″ x 3″ loaf pan.
2. In medium bowl combine sweet potatoes, mashed bananas, and milk; then add sugar, salt, raisins, nutmeg, cinnamon, and eggs, stirring until well blended.
3. Pour into prepared loaf pan. Bake 1 hr. 20 min., or until firm and golden on top.
4. Carefully loosen edges of loaf with spatula, then invert on serving dish. Let potato loaf cool a bit, then spoon corn or maple syrup over it as a glaze. Cut into serving pieces. Pass more syrup and some whipped cream for an American touch. Makes about 12 slices.

Haiti's market stalls are colorful with island fruits, including avocados, which grow freely there. Don't miss this salad!

AVOCADO SALAD

½ lb. cooked shrimp, in shells	⅓ cup olive oil
1 teasp. prepared mustard	1 tablesp. lemon juice
1½ teasp. salt	1 14-oz. can hearts of palm, cut
½ teasp. black pepper	into about ¾″ slices
½ teasp. garlic salt	3 avocados
3 tablesp. wine vinegar	Few sprigs parsley
1 small onion, minced	Few lettuce leaves

About 1 hr. before serving:
1. Shell and devein shrimp, then split lengthwise.
2. In bowl combine mustard, salt, pepper, garlic salt, vinegar, onion, olive oil, and lemon juice. Add hearts of palm, shrimp.
3. Cut avocados in half lengthwise; remove pits. With a teaspoon

scoop out meat, then add to shrimp mixture. Now toss everything carefully together, then use to fill avocado halves.

4. Garnish each avocado half with a parsley sprig, then arrange on lettuce leaves on pretty serving platter or individual plates. Refrigerate until chilled.

5. Serve as a salad or appetizer. Makes 6 servings.

Jamaica

Here we present an "interesting local soup specialty."

PEPPERPOT

1½ lb. boned chuck, in 1" cubes
1 tablesp. salt
½ teasp. black pepper
Few dashes Tabasco
1 lb. cabbage, coarsely chopped
1 leek, sliced
1 large onion, peeled, sliced
1 tablesp. flour
1 10-oz. pkg. frozen okra

About 2 hr. before serving:

1. In large kettle place chuck, 3 cups water, salt, pepper, and Tabasco. Bring to a boil, then simmer, covered, 1½ hr.

2. Next add cabbage, leek, and onion, and cook, covered, 20 min. Blend flour with 3 tablesp. water until smooth. Stir into meat, then add okra and cook, covered, 10 min., or until meat and vegetables are tender. Makes 4 to 6 servings.

In the West Indies the cookery is primarily Creole, of which this tasty chicken dish is an example.

CHICKEN IN THE SKILLET

1 2½-lb. broiler-fryer, cut up
2 tablesp. lemon juice
2 teasp. salt
½ teasp. pepper
¼ cup all-purpose flour
3 tablesp. butter or margarine
2 medium onions, peeled, sliced
1 cup fresh or canned chicken broth
1 large tomato, cut into wedges

About 1 hr. before serving:

1. Place chicken pieces in large bowl; toss with lemon juice, salt, pepper, and flour until well coated.

2. In large skillet heat butter; in it brown chicken and onions well on all sides. Next add chicken broth and tomato, then simmer, covered, 45 min., or until chicken is tender. Makes 4 to 6 servings.

The Island of Jamaica is lush and tropical—and the best desserts are fruits eaten au naturel, *or in ice cream, puddings, or pies.*

GRAPEFRUIT PIE

2 grapefruits, sectioned
½ cup light-brown sugar
Sifted all-purpose flour
2 tablesp. melted butter

1 teasp. double-acting baking powder
¼ teasp. salt
¼ cup butter or margarine
3 tablesp. milk

About 50 min. before serving:
1. Carefully toss grapefruit sections with brown sugar, 2 tablesp. flour, and melted butter, then arrange on bottom of 9″ fluted pie plate, 2″ deep. Start heating oven to 400°F.
2. Sift together 1 cup flour, baking powder, and salt. With pastry blender or 2 knives, scissor-fashion, cut in butter until like coarse corn meal.
3. Add milk, then toss quickly together, forming a smooth ball. On floured board, roll pastry into a circle, slightly larger than pie plate.
4. Place circle of pastry on top of grapefruit mixture, then turn its edges under, making a scalloped edge. Prick top with fork. Bake about 30 min., or until top is golden. Serve warm, cut into wedges. Makes 8 servings.

Puerto Rico

An intriguing skillet dish of rice, pork (the favorite meat in Puerto Rico), sausage, and ham.

RICE GUISADO
(Rice-and-Meat Skillet Dish)

2 tablesp. shortening
1 lb. boned pork shoulder, in 1″ cubes
2 medium onions, peeled, chopped
2 cloves garlic, peeled, minced
1 bay leaf, finely crushed
2 tablesp. snipped parsley
2 teasp. salt

¼ teasp. pepper
3 cups water
2 Italian-style sweet sausages, cut up
¼ lb. cooked ham, in ½″ cubes
1 cup uncooked processed white rice

About 1 hr. and 15 min. before serving:
1. In large skillet or Dutch oven heat shortening; in it brown

pork well on all sides. Now add onions and garlic and sauté until golden.

2. Next stir in bay leaf, parsley, salt, pepper, and water. Bring to a boil, then simmer, covered, 35 min.

3. Meanwhile, in skillet, brown sausages and ham, turning frequently. Add, with rice, to pork in skillet; then simmer, covered, about 25 min., or until meat and rice are tender. Makes 4 to 6 servings.

Asopao (a soupy rice) is perhaps the favorite Puerto Rican dish. Incidentally, it can be made with shrimp as well as chicken.

ASOPAO
(Chicken-and-Rice Dish)

1 2½-lb. broiler-fryer, cut up
1 teasp. dried orégano
¼ teasp. pepper
Salt
1 tablesp. lime juice
4 to 5 bacon slices, cut up
2 tablesp. salad or olive oil
1 green pepper, seeded, cut up
1 sweet red pepper, seeded, cut up
2 cloves garlic, peeled, minced
¼ lb. cooked ham, in thin strips

1 medium onion, peeled, chopped
1 tomato, chopped
12 pitted green olives
1 tablesp. bottled capers
1 tablesp. juice from capers
1 cup uncooked processed white rice
2½ cups water
1 10-oz. pkg. frozen green peas, thawed

About 1 hr. before serving:

1. Rub chicken pieces with orégano, pepper, 2 teasp. salt, and lime juice.

2. In large skillet or Dutch oven, fry bacon until crisp. Then add oil, green and red peppers, garlic, ham, and onion and sauté 5 to 10 min.

3. Next add chicken and sauté until golden. Then stir in tomato, olives, capers, caper juice, 1 teasp. salt, and rice. Sauté a few minutes, while turning frequently.

4. Now add water and cook, covered, 35 min. Stir in peas and cook 5 min., or until chicken and peas are tender. Makes 4 to 6 servings.

There are many varieties of yams found in Puerto Rico—white, yellow, and red—which the Puerto Ricans prepare in numerous succulent ways.

YAM CURRY

2 lb. fresh yams or sweet potatoes
¼ cup butter or margarine
1 medium onion, peeled, chopped
1 teasp. curry powder
1 teasp. salt

¼ teasp. pepper
¾ cup fresh or canned chicken broth
1 tablesp. lime juice

About 45 min. before serving:
1. Cook yams in plenty of boiling water until just tender. Drain, then peel and cut into small cubes or thick slices.
2. In saucepan heat butter; in it sauté onion until golden; then stir in curry, salt, pepper, chicken broth, and lime juice. Bring to a boil, while stirring, then add yams and simmer, covered, about 5 min., or until yams have absorbed part of liquid. Makes 6 servings as a vegetable.

This fragrant spicecake from Puerto Rico keeps well and becomes more flavorful the longer it is held.

BIZCOCHO DE ESPECIES
(*Spicecake*)

3½ cups sifted cake flour
3 teasp. double-acting baking powder
1 tablesp. powdered cinnamon
1 tablesp. powdered cloves
1 tablesp. powdered nutmeg

1 cup butter or margarine
2¼ cups dark-brown sugar
6 eggs, unbeaten
1 cup milk
⅓ cup sweet Madeira wine
Confectioners' sugar

1. Start heating oven to 350°F. Lightly grease 9″ angel-food tube pan. Sift together flour, baking powder, cinnamon, cloves, and nutmeg.
2. In large bowl, with electric mixer at medium speed, cream butter, while gradually adding brown sugar; beat until well blended.
3. Add eggs, one at a time, with 1 tablesp. flour mixture, to butter mixture; beat well. Alternately add remaining flour mixture and milk; then add wine.
4. Beat well; pour into tube pan. Bake 1 hr., or until cake tester, inserted in center, comes out clean.
5. Cool cake in pan 10 min.; then remove it from pan, inverting on wire rack. When cake is cool, sprinkle top with confectioners' sugar. Store in covered cake box.

Virgin Islands

One version of this hearty chicken dinner in a nutshell comes from—where else—the Virgin Islands.

CHICKEN PORTELLO

6 fresh coconuts
6 bacon slices, diced
1½ cups cut fresh corn (3 ears)
3 onions, peeled, sliced
1½ cups chopped, seeded green peppers
Salt

Pepper
1 clove garlic, peeled, minced
6 small tomatoes, peeled, cut into sixths
4 cups cooked- or canned-chicken chunks

1. With long nail or ice pick, puncture three indentations at one end of each coconut; drain milk from these holes.
2. From punctured end of each coconut, saw off approximately 1½" to make lid. With sharp knife, remove coconut meat from each lid in large chunks; then peel and grate coconut meat.
3. In large skillet, sauté bacon until crisp; mix in corn, ¼ cup grated coconut, onions, green pepper, 1 teasp. salt, ¼ teasp. pepper, and garlic. Cook until tender. Sprinkle tomatoes with some salt and pepper, then add, with chicken, to corn mixture; cook 5 min.
4. Start heating oven to 350°F. Now spoon chicken mixture into coconut shells. Top with lids; then wrap each coconut completely in foil.
5. Place coconuts in roasting pan with 1" water. Bake 1 hr. 15 min. Serve in shells, topped with grated fresh coconut. Makes 6 hearty servings.

OCEANIA

Who among us has not succumbed, mentally and emotionally, to tales of the islands of the Pacific ocean! When it comes to food, most of us are likely to think in terms of the Hawaiian luau and stop there. And a luau is good thinking—and good eating! But consider some of the other countries in this group and the foods they offer.

Australia, far away as it is, clings to a form of cookery that is basically English. Too busy at first, settling in this vast country, to think much about creature comforts, Australians were content with plain, nourishing foods. Gradually, individual touches were added to the meats and vegetables and today Australians are rapidly becoming gourmets. Indeed, their excellent lamb, unusual fish, luscious fruits and vegetables make this inevitable.

New Zealand, too, appreciates plain food but its cooks show their creativeness in the truly delectable seafood dishes they serve and in their excellent use of the abundant wild game available to them.

In this group of recipes is ample opportunity for sampling new foods and bringing into your own home the romance and adventure of these exotic islands of the Pacific.

Australia

Australians love meat. Lamb is first choice, but beef is almost as popular.

BEEF-AND-VEGETABLE CASSEROLE

1½ lb. lean chuck, in 1½″ cubes	2 tablesp. salad oil
1 cup red wine	2 large onions, peeled, sliced
1 bay leaf, finely crushed	3 medium carrots, pared, in 1″
¼ teasp. dried thyme	slices
¼ teasp. dried marjoram	2 celery stalks, sliced
3 teasp. salt	2 tablesp. flour
¼ teasp. pepper	¾ cup water

Day before:
Place chuck in medium bowl. Combine wine, bay leaf, thyme, marjoram, salt, and pepper. Pour over chuck, then refrigerate, covered.

About 2½ hr. before serving:
1. Start heating oven to 350°F. Drain meat, reserving liquid. In large skillet heat salad oil; in it brown meat well on all sides. Place in 2-qt. casserole along with onions, carrots, and celery stalks.
2. Into drippings in skillet stir flour; brown lightly. Then add reserved liquid and water. Bring to a boil while stirring.
3. Pour over meat and vegetables, then bake, covered, 2 hr., or until meat is tender. Makes about 4 servings.

And they sometimes surround their dish of Curry Hot Pot with potato chips.

CURRY HOT POT

1½ lb. boned chuck	1 tablesp. flour
2 tablesp. salad oil	1 10½-oz. can condensed beef
2 medium onions, peeled, sliced	broth, undiluted
1 medium apple, pared, cored,	2 teasp. salt
cut into small cubes	¼ teasp. pepper
1 tablesp. curry powder	1 tablesp. brown sugar
2 medium tomatoes, chopped	2 hard-cooked eggs, shelled, sliced
¼ cup seedless dark raisins	Snipped parsley

About 1 hr. before serving:
1. Cut chuck lengthwise into 1½″ strips, then crosswise into

very thin slices. In large skillet heat salad oil; in it brown chuck, turning frequently.

2. Next add onions, apple, and curry, and sauté a few minutes. Then stir in tomatoes, raisins, flour, beef broth, salt, pepper, and brown sugar.

3. Bring to a boil, then simmer, covered, 40 min., or until meat is tender. Transfer to serving dish, then garnish with sliced eggs and sprinkle with parsley. Makes 6 servings.

Australians and New Zealanders like pies! You'll see why when you try Ribbon Pie: two layers—the bottom lemony and lovely, reminiscent of England; the top of coconut and the newness of Australia.

RIBBON PIE
(*Lemon-Coconut Pie*)

Granulated sugar	1 tablesp. cornstarch
6 tablesp. butter or margarine	1 cup milk
3 eggs, beaten	¼ teasp. salt
Juice and grated rind of 2 lemons	1 teasp. vanilla extract
1 baked 9″ pie shell	¼ cup flaked coconut

Early on the day:

1. In top of double boiler cream 1 cup sugar with butter. Then stir in beaten eggs, lemon juice, and half of lemon rind. Cook over boiling water, while stirring constantly, until thickened.

2. Pour into baked pie shell and let cool. In small saucepan combine cornstarch, 3 tablesp. sugar, milk, salt, and vanilla. Bring to a boil, while stirring, then cook until thickened; stir in coconut.

3. Pour over lemon mixture in pie shell. Garnish with rest of lemon rind. Refrigerate until well chilled. Serve, cut into wedges. Makes 8 servings.

Tea is the national drink in Australia, so after you sample this banana triumph have a "cuppa."

BANANAS WITH CARAMEL SAUCE

1 cup light-brown sugar	¼ cup light rum
Heavy cream	6 ripe bananas
2 tablesp. butter or margarine	Slivered blanched almonds

Early on the day:

In skillet place sugar, 3 tablesp. heavy cream, and butter. Heat, while stirring, until smooth. Then cook a few minutes, or until caramelized. Remove from heat and stir in rum. Pour into bowl and refrigerate until well chilled.

Just before serving:
Cut peeled bananas in half lengthwise, then crosswise into 2″ pieces; divide evenly between 6 nappy dishes. Pour on caramel sauce. Garnish with ½ cup heavy cream, whipped, and some slivered almonds. Makes 6 servings.

Hawaii

The ancient manner of cooking in Hawaii was in an underground oven and this is still used at their luaus, when roast pig is the mainstay.

For a mainland luau, let your guests enjoy Chicken Luau, along with Pork-and-Pineapple Packages, Teriyaki, and small baked sweet potatoes. Have this entire main course on a leaf-covered table, when dinner's announced. Plan Ice-Cream Aloha (balls of ice cream in coconut or pineapple shells) for dessert; or top off with the fresh fruits that grace the table. And do as they do in Hawaii—let the guests sip fruit punch and nibble on Macadamia nuts throughout!

CHICKEN LUAU

1 2½-lb. broiler-fryer, cut up
Flour
½ cup butter or margarine
1 teasp. salt
1 cup water
1 cup hot milk

1 3½-oz. can flaked coconut
2 lb. fresh spinach, washed
2 tablesp. minced onion
½ teasp. salt
¼ cup water

Lightly dust chicken with flour. In hot butter, in large skillet, cook it until evenly browned. Add 1 teasp. salt and 1 cup water. Cover and simmer about 30 min., or until chicken is tender. Meanwhile, pour milk over coconut; let stand 15 min.; then simmer 10 min. Cut spinach into big pieces; cook with onion and ½ teasp. salt in ¼ cup water about 5 min.; drain. Add, with coconut and milk, to chicken; simmer 3 min. Makes 8 luau servings, or 4, if served alone. (Provide forks.)

PORK·AND·PINEAPPLE PACKAGES

2 lb. fresh pork shoulder (some fat left on), cut into 2" pieces
1¾ teasp. onion or garlic salt
⅛ teasp. pepper
½ teasp. powdered ginger

1 1-lb.-4-oz. can pineapple chunks, drained
2 green peppers, seeded, quartered
8 small tomatoes

Start heating oven to 350°F. On wax paper, place pork; sprinkle with onion salt, pepper, and ginger. On each of 8 12" squares of foil, place some of pork, pineapple, green peppers, and tomatoes. Gather each piece of foil together at top; arrange on shallow baking pan. Bake 2 hr. Makes 8 packages.

TERIYAKI

1 1-lb.-4-oz. can pineapple chunks
⅛ cup soy sauce
1 clove garlic, peeled, minced
¾ teasp. powdered ginger

1 lb. tender top-round or sirloin beef slices, ¾" thick
22 wooden skewers

Drain juice from pineapple. In medium bowl, combine pineapple juice, soy sauce, garlic, and ginger. Add beef; let stand 1 hr. Preheat broiler 10 min., or as manufacturer directs. Cut beef into ¾" cubes. On skewers, alternate beef and pineapple. Broil, 3" from heat, turning once, 10 to 12 min. Makes 22. (Serve 2 or 3 apiece.)

In modern Hawaii, our fiftieth state, they like to serve this dessert, featuring pineapple.

PINEAPPLE·SNOW PUDDING

3½ cups canned pineapple juice
3 env. unflavored gelatine
6 tablesp. granulated sugar
⅛ teasp. salt
2 teasp. grated lemon rind
¼ cup lemon juice
1½ cups heavy cream

1½ cups flaked coconut
4 cups halved fresh strawberries, or 2 10-oz. pkg. frozen strawberries, thawed
4 canned pineapple slices, quartered

Make day before, or early on the day:
1. Into 1 cup pineapple juice, in small bowl, stir gelatine, sugar; let stand 5 min. Set bowl in boiling water; stir till gelatine is dissolved.
2. In large bowl combine 2½ cups pineapple juice, salt, lemon rind, lemon juice; then stir in gelatine mixture. Refrigerate till like unbeaten egg white.

3. With electric mixer at high speed, beat gelatine mixture till fluffy. Whip cream; quickly fold it and ¾ cup coconut into gelatine. Pour into 2-qt. mold; refrigerate till set.

Just before serving:
Unmold pudding onto large serving dish; sprinkle top with some coconut and strawberries; arrange some quartered pineapple slices, strawberries, and rest of coconut around base. Pass rest of pineapple and strawberries. Makes 8 servings.

New Zealand

A new steak taste for your menfolks—steaks stuffed with onions and bacon—right from New Zealand, too.

STUFFED STEAK, NEW ZEALAND STYLE

8 slices bacon, snipped	2 teasp. salt
¾ cup minced onion	⅛ teasp. pepper
¼ cup pkgd. dried bread crumbs	1 cup canned beef consommé,
3 tablesp. catchup	undiluted
6 4-oz. cube steaks	1½ tablesp. flour

About 1 hr. and 30 min. before serving:
1. In skillet, sauté bacon with onion until bacon is crisp and onion golden; pour off all fat. With onion mixture blend bread crumbs and catchup. Start heating oven to 400°F.
2. Rub cube steaks with salt and pepper. On each steak place some of bacon-onion mixture; roll up, fasten each with toothpick. Place in medium baking pan.
3. In small saucepan, heat ¾ cup undiluted consommé; pour over steak rolls. Cover pan with foil, then bake steak rolls 60 to 70 min., or until meat is tender. Blend flour with ¼ cup undiluted consommé; stir into gravy in baking pan, return to oven and let come to a boil.
4. Transfer meat to serving dish, remove toothpicks. Spoon gravy over it. Makes 6 servings.

New Zealanders have a great fondness for pies. Fresh fruits are so plentiful, too. Hence this luscious Melon-Cream Pie.

MELON-CREAM PIE

1 baked 9″ pie shell
2 tablesp. cornstarch
Grated rind ½ lemon
2 tablesp. lemon juice
½ cup granulated sugar

2 eggs, separated
1½ teasp. unflavored gelatine
3 cups diced cantaloupe
Vanilla ice cream

Early on the day:
1. Make and bake pie shell with high fluted edge; then let cool on rack at room temperature.
2. In double-boiler top, mix cornstarch with 2 tablesp. cold water; stir in lemon rind and juice, sugar, egg yolks, and gelatine.
3. While beating with spoon, add 1 cup boiling water. Cook over boiling water, beating constantly, until thickened. Refrigerate until cool. Now fold in cantaloupe and stiffly beaten egg whites. Turn this mixture into pie shell.
4. Refrigerate pie several hours, or until set. Serve, cut into wedges, and topped with ice cream. Makes 8 servings.

And speaking of pies—whether for family or guests—for supper, luncheon, barbecue, or cocktail party—this wonderful open bacon-and-egg pie of theirs always fits in.

TOMATO-CHEESE PIE

Butter or margarine
1 cup sifted all-purpose flour
1 medium tomato
4 oz. natural Cheddar cheese
6 bacon slices, crisp-fried

3 eggs, beaten
1¼ cups milk
½ teasp. salt
¼ teasp. pepper
¼ cup snipped parsley

About 1 hr. and 15 min. before serving:
1. With pastry blender or two knives, scissor-fashion, cut 6 tablesp. butter into flour until like coarse corn meal; add 2 tablesp. water and toss quickly together, forming a smooth ball. Use this pastry to line 9″ pie plate, making a fluted edge.
2. Start heating oven to 350°F. Cut tomato into 8 wedges; arrange in a circle, equidistantly, on bottom of pie shell. Grate cheese, crumble bacon, sprinkle over tomato. Blend eggs, milk, salt, pepper, and parsley. Pour over cheese; bake 50 min., or until firm.
3. Let pie stand for 10 min. Then serve, in wedges.

*New Zealand women are proud of their bakings—and quite justly!
These two-spice muffins with their delicate molasses flavor are one
of their specialties.*

DOUBLE-SPICE MUFFINS

½ cup butter or margarine	1 teasp. baking soda
½ cup granulated sugar	1 teasp. double-acting baking
2 eggs	powder
½ cup milk	1 teasp. powdered cinnamon
½ cup dark molasses	½ teasp. powdered nutmeg
2 cups sifted all-purpose flour	½ teasp. salt

About 45 min. before serving:
1. Grease well 12 3″ cups of muffin pan (measured across the top).
In large bowl, with electric mixer at medium speed, beat butter
or margarine with sugar until light and fluffy. Gradually beat in
eggs, milk, and molasses. Start heating oven to 400°F.
2. Sift together flour, baking soda, baking powder, cinnamon,
nutmeg, salt. Stir into sugar-egg mixture, until well blended.
3. Fill each cup about half full with batter. Bake about 15 min.,
or until cake tester, inserted in center, comes out clean. Now carefully loosen edges with spatula, then remove muffins from pan,
transfer to rack; let cool.
4. Serve hot, with butter, as bread; or cool a bit and serve as
dessert, topped with ice cream or whipped cream. Makes 12.

Philippines

*While pork, and pork with chicken, are great favorites in the
Philippines, people of the islands are also fond of chicken and
fish, served these ways.*

CHICKEN ADOBO

1 2½- to 3-lb. broiler-fryer, cut up	1 bay leaf
Salt	½ cup vinegar
¼ teasp. black pepper	2 cups water
1 clove garlic, peeled, minced	

About 1 hr. before serving:
1. In large, deep skillet place chicken pieces, 2 teasp. salt, pepper,
garlic, bay leaf, vinegar, and water. Bring to a boil, then simmer,
uncovered, about 40 min., or until all liquid has evaporated.

2. Now brown chicken well on all sides (there will be enough chicken fat in skillet to brown it in). Then sprinkle with salt and serve. Makes 4 to 6 servings.

P.S. For an especially delightful potato accompaniment, cut 2 or 3 pared large potatoes into very thin strips; dry with paper towel. Then fry in about 1″ of hot salad oil until crisp and golden; drain on paper towels, then sprinkle with salt and serve.

ESCABECHE
(*Fish, Philippine-Style*)

1 2-lb. dressed red snapper, blue fish, or bass (head removed)
Salt
All-purpose flour
¼ cup butter or salad oil
1 large onion, peeled, sliced
1 large green or red pepper, seeded, sliced

2 cloves garlic, peeled, minced
1½ cups water
1 tablesp. vinegar
1 tablesp. sugar
2 tablesp. soy sauce
¼ to ½ teasp. powdered ginger

About 25 min. before serving:

1. Sprinkle fish with 1 teasp. salt, then flour it lightly. In large skillet heat butter or oil; in it brown fish well on all sides; then remove. (If fish does not fit into skillet, cut in half crosswise.)

2. To drippings in skillet add onion, green or red pepper, and garlic; sauté until golden. Next stir in 1 tablesp. flour, water, vinegar, sugar, soy sauce, ginger, and ½ teasp. salt.

3. Bring to a boil, return fish to skillet, then cook, covered, 8 to 10 min., or until fish flakes easily with fork, but is still moist. Makes 4 servings.

Polynesian Islands

POLYNESIAN LUAU

A Polynesian feast can lend an exotic, informal flavor of the South Seas to your entertaining. The Island dishes which follow are adapted for serving together, luau style—the entire main course being on the table when guests are called. Or, if you have help, the baked shrimp and Rumaki may be served as a first course.

SHRIMP BAKED IN COCONUT

1½ lb. raw shrimp	¾ cup light cream
2 teasp. salt	1 3½-oz. can flaked coconut

Day before:
1. Remove shells but not tails from shrimp; then devein them. Sprinkle them with salt, then refrigerate.
2. Pour cream over coconut; refrigerate.

About 45 min. before serving:
Start heating oven to 350°F. Arrange shrimp in 13" x 9" x 2" baking dish; sprinkle moist coconut, lifted from cream, on top; pour on cream. Bake 40 min., then serve as first course. Makes 8 servings.

RUMAKI
(Oriental Nibblers)

Melted butter or margarine	Canned water chestnuts, drained
Chicken livers (one for each nib-bler)	(one for each nibbler)
	Bacon (½ slice for each nibbler)

Early in the day:
In melted butter or margarine, in skillet, sauté chicken livers until golden; then cool. For each nibbler, wrap 1 chicken liver and 1 drained water chestnut with ½ bacon slice; fasten with toothpick. Refrigerate.

At serving time:
Broil nibblers until bacon is crisp. Then serve, very hot, on toothpicks.

STEAK WITH MUSHROOMS AND BEAN SPROUTS

1½- to 2-lb. flank steak
2 tablesp. soy sauce
1 large clove garlic, peeled, minced
½ teasp. pepper

1 onion, peeled, minced
2 tablesp. butter or margarine
½ lb. mushrooms, sliced
2 tablesp. salad oil
1 16-oz. can bean sprouts, drained

Day before:
Slice flank steak, paper-thin, diagonally across grain. Toss meat strips with soy sauce, garlic, pepper, and onion; refrigerate.

About 1 hr. before serving:
1. In butter, in skillet, lightly sauté sliced mushrooms about 5 min.; remove from skillet, reserve.
2. In salad oil, in same skillet, sauté flank-steak strips until lightly browned. Then cover and simmer 45 min., or until tender.
3. Add mushrooms and bean sprouts and heat. Makes 8 servings.

GINGER PANCAKES WITH CRAB MEAT

2 tablesp. butter or margarine
½ cup minced onion
1 10½-oz. can condensed cream-of-mushroom soup, undiluted
⅓ cup milk

½ teasp. curry powder
1 6-oz. pkg. frozen King-crab meat, thawed, drained *
1 cup pkgd. pancake mix
1 teasp. powdered ginger

About 30 min. before serving:
1. In melted butter, in skillet, sauté onion until tender. Stir in undiluted mushroom soup, milk, and curry, then crab meat; heat.
2. Combine pancake mix with ginger, then prepare as label directs, making 8 pancakes; keep warm till served.
3. Fold each pancake in half, with a spoonful of crab mixture as filling. Arrange, overlapping, on platter. Makes 8 servings.

* If desired, garnish finished dish with an extra package of crab meat.

CHICKEN IN PINEAPPLE SHELLS

2 fresh pineapples
2 tablesp. salad oil
1 cup minced onion
2 cloves garlic, peeled, minced
4 cups seasoned cooked white rice

½ cup bottled barbecue sauce †
Boned, skinned breasts from 2 chickens
4 teasp. honey
4 teasp. sesame seeds

Day before:
1. Halve pineapples lengthwise. Discard hard core; remove meat;

† Or substitute ½ teasp. curry powder and ½ teasp. powdered ginger for barbecue sauce, tossing them with rice.

refrigerate pineapple shells and pineapple meat. (Serve pineapple meat at later meal.)

2. In salad oil, in skillet, sauté onion and garlic until golden; add cooked rice and ¾ teasp. salt, then toss. Refrigerate.

About 1 hr. and 15 min. before serving:

1. Start heating oven to 350°F. Fill pineapple halves with rice mixture; spoon barbecue sauce over them. Cut each breast of chicken in half lengthwise. Set a half breast on each pineapple half; sprinkle each with ¼ teasp. salt; place in roasting pan; add ½″ water.

2. Bake pineapples 45 min.; then spread with honey and sprinkle with sesame seeds; bake 15 min., or until chicken is tender. Makes 4 servings.

P.S. For 8 servings, cut filled pineapple in half lengthwise before serving.

BARBECUED SPARERIBS WITH KUMQUATS

About 2 lb. spareribs (14 to 16 ribs)	½ teasp. prepared mustard
½ cup light molasses	¼ teasp. salt
½ cup catchup	¼ teasp. pepper
½ cup minced onions	1 tablesp. bottled thick meat sauce
1 clove garlic, peeled, minced	½ teasp. Worcestershire
3 whole cloves	¼ teasp. Tabasco
4 narrow strips of orange rind, diced	1 tablesp. butter or margarine
Juice ½ orange	1½ cups preserved kumquats, or 1 13- or 14-oz. can pineapple chunks, drained
1 tablesp. vinegar	
1 tablesp. salad oil	

Day before:

1. Start heating oven to 325°F. Place spareribs in shallow open pan; cover with foil; roast ½ hr.

2. Pour off fat; roast 45 min. longer.

3. Meanwhile, make this sauce: Combine molasses with rest of ingredients except kumquats; boil 5 min. Pour all fat from ribs; cover ribs with sauce.

4. Now continue to roast the spareribs, uncovered, basting often, for 45 min., or until fork-tender, very brown and glazed. Toss with kumquats. Cover with foil. Refrigerate.

About 1 hr. and 15 min. before serving:

Place spareribs in 350°F. oven, along with Chicken in Pineapple Shells, p. 184, for 1 hr., or until heated through. Cut into 1-rib portions. Makes 7 or 8 servings.

NORTH AMERICA

CANADA

MEXICO

PANAMA

UNITED STATES OF AMERICA

Nothing more conclusively points out the vastness of North America than to realize that it encompasses countries so far away from each other geographically and in customs and traditions as Panama, the United States, Canada, and Mexico.

Even within the boundaries of the United States, cookery and food customs vary enormously. The sugarless corn bread, the rich Pecan Pie, the well-done meats of the deep South are strange indeed to the New Englander who dotes on boiled dinners and Boston baked beans, and neither is comprehensible to the followers of Pennsylvania Dutch cookery with its "cup" cheese, "rich" and "poor" soups, dried apples, and dumplings. And a dozen other regional differences could be listed. Imagine, then, the hopelessness of trying to give a fair sample of this, plus the Indian heritage of Mexico's tortillas, "mole de guajolate," and excellent chocolate, Canada's meat pies, cheeses, and homemade breads, and the cosmopolitan flavor of Panama.

All we can hope to do is to create in the reader an interest in this wonderfully wide and exciting range of foods—an interest that will send her on to further discoveries and delights for her table.

Canada

Canadians like the hearty Beefsteak-and-Kidney Pie, p. 21, as well as this tasty variation.

BEEFSTEAK PIE

All-purpose flour
Salt
¼ teasp. pepper
½ teasp. dry mustard
½ teasp. celery salt
1½ lb. boneless chuck, in 1½"
  cubes
Shortening
2 beef-bouillon cubes

3 medium carrots, pared, in 1"
  cubes
2 medium onions, peeled, sliced
1 medium potato, pared, in 1"
  cubes
2 teasp. double-acting baking
  powder
¼ cup milk
½ cup grated natural Cheddar
  cheese

About 2½ hr. before serving:

1. In medium bowl combine ¼ cup flour, 1 teasp. salt, pepper, mustard, and celery salt. Add chuck and toss until well coated.
2. In Dutch oven heat 3 tablesp. shortening; in it brown chuck well on all sides. Add 2 cups water and bouillon cubes; bring to a boil, then simmer, covered, over low heat, 1 hr. Next add carrots, onions, and potato; then simmer 30 min., or until meat and vegetables are tender.
3. Meanwhile, combine 1 cup sifted all-purpose flour, ¼ teasp. salt, and baking powder. With pastry cutter or 2 knives, scissor-fashion, cut in ¼ cup shortening until like coarse corn meal. Add milk and toss together, forming a smooth ball of dough. Start heating oven to 425°F.
4. Roll dough into a rectangle, about ¼" thick; sprinkle with cheese. Roll up, jelly-roll-fashion, then cut crosswise into ¾" rolls.
5. Now pour meat mixture into 1½-qt. casserole. Top with cheese rolls, then bake about 20 min., or until they are golden and done. Makes about 5 servings.

From generation to generation, French Canadians have handed down recipes unchanged. Like this Tourtière de Noël, served at many a French-Canadian Christmas feast.

TOURTIÈRE DE NOËL
(Christmas Pie with Pork, Veal, and Chicken)

Sifted all-purpose flour
½ teasp. salt
Butter or margarine
1 cup chopped, peeled, onions
2 cloves garlic, peeled, minced
½ lb. ground veal
½ lb. ground lean pork
1 teasp. salt

¼ teasp. pepper
½ teasp. allspice
1 teasp. seasoned salt
2 teasp. Worcestershire
½ cup milk
2 cups diced, cooked chicken
1 egg, beaten

Early on the day, or about 2 hr. before serving:

1. In medium bowl mix 2 cups flour, ½ teasp. salt; with pastry blender or two knives, used scissor-fashion, cut in ¾ cup butter or margarine, until like corn meal. Now add 2½ to 3 tablesp. water, toss quickly together, then form into a smooth ball.
2. Use part of this dough to completely line 9″ pie plate; then trim pastry even with edge. Refrigerate rest of dough.
3. In medium skillet heat 2 tablesp. butter or margarine; in it sauté onions and garlic until light-brown. Now add veal and pork; brown lightly; blend in 1 teasp. salt, pepper, allspice, seasoned salt, Worcestershire, and 1 tablesp. flour; add ½ cup water, milk, and bring to a boil while stirring.
4. Pour meat mixture into lined pie plate, spreading it evenly; over it arrange chicken. Start heating oven to 375°F.
5. Roll out almost all of remaining dough into a circle, slightly larger than pie plate. Place on top of pie filling; trim its edges ½″ larger than bottom crust, then turn it under bottom crust; lightly press edges of top and bottom crusts together, in scalloped effect. Brush top with egg, then cut a few slits in it to allow steam to escape.
6. With small star-shaped cookie cutter, cut out a few stars from remaining dough, arrange on piecrust, brush with egg.
7. Bake 1 hr., or until top pastry is golden. Let stand 10 min. Serve hot or cold, in wedges, at a buffet supper or luncheon, with a mixed salad. Makes 8 servings.

The Canadian Indians enjoy dried blueberries; Nova Scotians, Blueberry Grunt (a dumpling dish); and now you can enjoy this crumbly-topped Canadian Blueberry Pudding.

BLUEBERRY PUDDING

4 cups fresh blueberries	⅓ cup light-brown sugar
⅓ cup granulated sugar	⅓ cup sifted all-purpose flour
1 tablesp. lemon juice	¾ cup quick-cooking oatmeal
¼ cup butter or margarine	Pour cream or vanilla ice cream

Make about 2 hr. before serving, as follows:
1. Start heating oven to 375°F. Place blueberries in 1½-qt. casserole; toss with granulated sugar and lemon juice.
2. In small bowl beat butter with brown sugar until blended and fluffy; with fork stir in flour and oatmeal. Sprinkle this mixture over blueberries. Bake 30 min., or until top is golden and blueberries are cooked.
3. Remove from oven and cool 1 hr. Then serve, slightly warm, with pour cream or vanilla ice cream. Makes about 6 servings.

Some fourth- and fifth-generation Canadian Scots still have porridge and tea for breakfast. Thanks to them we have this delightful, filled oatmeal cookie square.

OATMEAL SQUARES

2 cups finely snipped, pitted dates	1 teasp. vanilla extract
1½ cups light-brown sugar	1 teasp. baking soda
Sifted all-purpose flour	2 cups quick-cooking oatmeal
1 cup hot water	¾ cup butter or margarine

Make day before, as follows:
1. In small saucepan combine dates, ½ cup brown sugar, and 1 tablesp. flour. Add water, then simmer 10 min., or until thickened. Stir in vanilla extract. Start heating oven to 375°F.
2. Combine 1 cup brown sugar with 1 cup flour, baking soda, and oatmeal; then stir in butter until well blended.
3. Spread half of oatmeal mixture on bottom of 12" x 8" x 2" baking dish. Cover with date mixture, then sprinkle with remaining oatmeal mixture. Pat with a spoon.
4. Bake 20 min., or until light-golden. Cool in pan, then cut into 24 squares.

Mexico

In Tamales, the moist ground corn meal is spread on a corn husk, covered with chili-seasoned filling, then rolled, tied, and steamed. An easier, but tasty, version of the famous tamale is the Tamale Pie.

TAMALE PIE

2 cups white corn meal	2 15-oz. cans chili con carne with-
1 teasp. salt	out beans
5 cups hot water	Grated natural sharp Cheddar
	cheese

1. In double boiler combine corn meal, salt, and hot water. Cook, covered, stirring occasionally, 30 min., or till it's fairly stiff.
2. Start heating oven to 350°F. Heat chili con carne.
3. Now line bottom and sides of 2-qt. earthenware casserole with two-thirds of mush. Pour in chili.
4. Dot top of chili with rest of mush; then bake 30 min. In serving, sprinkle top of pie with grated cheese. Makes 8 servings.

Mole sauce (pronounced moh-leh) sounds complicated, but it's not really difficult to make. The blend of spices and other flavors (like chocolate!) gives individuality and goodness to one of Mexico's most famous dishes.

CHICKEN MOLE

Butter or margarine	Dash pepper
2 2½-lb. broiler-fryers, cut up	¼ teasp. whole coriander
Salt	1 sq. unsweetened chocolate,
1½ cups canned chicken broth	grated
1 green pepper, seeded	⅓ cup ground almonds
¾ teasp. anise seeds	1 to 1½ tablesp. chili powder
1 tablesp. sesame seeds	3 large tomatoes, peeled
3 cloves garlic, peeled	4 cups hot cooked rice
Dash powdered cloves	2 whole pimentos, quartered
⅛ teasp. powdered cinnamon	

1. In ¼ cup hot butter, in large skillet, brown chicken well on all sides, a few pieces at a time; add more butter as needed. Remove browned chicken to 3-qt. earthenware or oven-glass casserole; sprinkle pieces with salt. Start heating oven to 375°F.
2. In electric blender, combine 1 teasp. salt, ½ cup chicken broth, green pepper, anise seeds, sesame seeds, garlic, cloves, cinnamon, pepper, coriander, chocolate, almonds, chili powder, tomatoes; blend till they make well-combined sauce.
3. In skillet in which chicken was browned, combine sauce with 1 cup chicken broth; simmer, stirring, 10 min.; pour over chicken. Bake, covered, about 1½ hr. Serve along with rice tossed with pimentos. Makes 6 to 8 servings.

Or do as they do in Mexico and use fresh green chili peppers. Three of these might taste as mild as a green bell pepper, the fourth from the same batch may bring tears to your eyes.

CHILIS RELLENOS
(Stuffed Green Peppers)

10 medium green peppers or 12 fresh green chili peppers *	2¾ teasp. salt
½ cup olive oil	½ cup finely chopped canned blanched almonds or peanuts
2 lb. chuck beef, ground once	Fat or salad oil
½ cup canned tomato paste	¼ cup all-purpose flour
5 cloves garlic, peeled, minced	3 eggs
6 teasp. chili powder	1½ cups pkgd. dried bread crumbs

1. Cut around stem of each pepper; with fingers, pull out seeds and pulp; discard. Cook whole peppers in boiling salted water to cover for 5 min.; drain; let cool 5 min.
2. Meanwhile, in skillet, heat oil; add chuck, tomato paste, garlic, chili powder, salt, and almonds. Sauté over low heat, stirring constantly, for 5 min. Let cool slightly.
3. In automatic skillet or saucepan, heat 1¼" fat or salad oil to 375°F. on deep-fat-frying thermometer. Meanwhile, stuff peppers with meat mixture; lightly sprinkle meat with flour. In pie plate, beat eggs with fork; dip each pepper into egg, then into bread crumbs.
4. Fry peppers in hot fat, turning once, until browned on all sides. Makes 10 servings.
Serve hot, in a ring; heap canned red beans, to which sautéed onions have been added, in the center; use fresh tomato wedges as a garnish, if desired.

* Broil chilis on all sides. When well blistered, place in a paper bag; close tightly; let stand 15 min. Peel off skin; cut off tops and remove seeds.

North America

In Mexico, where a meal is not a meal unless beans are served in some form, cooking them is an art, and usually they are served as a separate course just before dessert.

CHILI BEANS

¼ lb. suet, cut into small pieces
1 medium onion, peeled, chopped
1 lb. chuck, ground
2½ teasp. chili powder
1 teasp. salt
⅛ teasp. pepper

¼ to ½ teasp. crushed red pepper
1 8-oz. can tomato sauce
2 1-lb.-1-oz. cans kidney beans
½ cup shredded, natural Cheddar cheese

About 1½ to 3½ hr. before serving:
1. In large skillet sauté suet until light-brown, then add onion and sauté until golden. Next add chuck, then brown it, while turning frequently.
2. Stir in chili powder, salt, pepper, red pepper, and tomato sauce. Cook, covered, 20 min. Then add kidney beans and cook, covered, about 1½ hr. (Or up to 3 hr. if you like them mushy, as the Mexicans do.)
3. While beans are cooking, stir them every half hour, adding a little water if necessary. Just before serving, sprinkle with cheese. Makes 4 to 6 servings.

When Mexicans serve salad they put it on the table on a platter or in a garlic-rubbed bowl, along with the main course. The most popular Mexican salads are made of avocado, like this Guacamole, or a combination of vegetables.

GUACAMOLE
(Avocado Salad)

1 small tomato, finely chopped
1 very small onion, peeled, minced
6 avocados
2½ teasp. salt
2 teasp. lemon juice

2 tablesp. mayonnaise
1 teasp. salad oil
4 drops Tabasco
Shredded lettuce

About ½ hr. before serving:
1. Place tomato and onion in medium bowl. Cut avocados in half, remove pits. With spoon scoop out all their meat, then cut meat into small pieces; add to tomato.
2. Next add salt, lemon juice, mayonnaise, salad oil, and Tabasco. Toss until blended. Arrange on a large bed of shredded lettuce. Serve as salad. Makes 8 generous servings.

Assortments of cookies are often served for dessert, but cakes as we know them are not as popular. (And if all Mexican cookies are as crisp and buttery as these, it is easy to see why.)

MEXICAN WEDDING CAKES

1 cup butter or margarine	2 cups sifted all-purpose flour
Confectioners' sugar	1½ cups ground Brazil nuts,
½ teasp. salt	pecans, or filberts
1 teasp. almond extract or	
2 teasp. vanilla extract	

One or several days ahead:
1. In small bowl, with electric mixer at medium speed, beat butter with ½ cup confectioners' sugar until creamy. Next beat in salt, extract, flour, and nuts until well blended. Refrigerate dough until easy to handle.
2. Start heating oven to 350°F. With fingers shape dough into 1″ balls. Place on cookie sheet. Flatten balls with bottom of tumbler, dipped in flour.
3. Bake balls 10 to 15 min., or until golden. Sprinkle with confectioners' sugar, then remove to rack to cool. Store in container; they keep well. Makes 5 to 6 dozen.

Panama

Sancocho, the soup stew with meat and vegetables, is a truly delicious native dish.

SANCOCHO
(Meat-and-Vegetable Stew)

2 lb. boned chuck, in 2″ cubes	2 medium onions, peeled, cut in half
½ lb. lean pork, in 2″ cubes	1 medium summer squash, in 1″ chunks
5 teasp. salt	
¼ to ½ teasp. black pepper	2 large celery stalks, sliced
2½ qt. water	2 medium potatoes, pared, quartered
1 large carrot, pared, in 1″ cubes	
1 large beet, pared, in 1″ cubes	2 to 3 medium tomatoes, quartered
3 wedges cabbage (about ¾ lb.)	
½ lb. green beans, ends snipped	

About 2½ hr. before serving:
1. In large kettle place chuck, pork, salt, and pepper; add water, then bring to a boil. Skim surface, then simmer, covered, 1½ hr.; skim fat from surface.

2. Add carrot, beet, cabbage, beans, and onions; bring to a boil, then cook 20 min. Add squash, celery, potatoes and cook 15 min.
3. Add tomatoes and cook 5 min. Serve in open soup plates as a main-dish stew. Makes about 8 servings.

A fish dish like Pescado con Alcaparros is very frequently served as a separate course in Panama and is so delicious that it deserves to be.

PESCADO CON ALCAPARROS
(Baked Fish with Caper Sauce)

1 2½- to 3-lb. striped bass, sea bass, or sea trout	2 cloves garlic, minced
Salt	3 medium tomatoes, chopped
Pepper	1 large green pepper, chopped
Butter or margarine	3 tablesp. bottled capers
1 large onion, peeled, chopped	2 teasp. flour

About 45 min. before serving:
1. If desired, remove head from fish; rub cavity and outside with 1 teasp. salt and ¼ teasp. pepper. Place in 13″ x 9″ x 2″ baking dish. Start heating oven to 400°F.
2. In medium skillet heat 2 tablesp. butter; in it sauté onion and garlic until golden; then stir in tomatoes, green pepper, 1 teasp. salt, ¼ teasp. pepper, capers, flour, and ½ cup water. Bring to a boil and boil 5 min. Pour around fish; brush fish with 2 tablesp. butter; then bake fish 25 min., or until it is easily flaked with a fork, but still moist.
3. At table split fish down side of backbone to loosen fillets. Makes 6 servings.

In Panama they are very fond of a salad of radishes, which goes well with the zucca and the beans-with-rice, eaten at every meal.

ENSALADA DE RABANOS
(Radish Salad)

¼ cup olive oil	3 cups sliced red radishes
2 tablesp. lemon juice	1 small onion, peeled, chopped
1½ teasp. salt	1 tablesp. chopped fresh mint
¼ teasp. black pepper	leaves
2 medium tomatoes, peeled, chopped	Lettuce pieces

About 1 hr. before serving:
1. In small bowl beat together olive oil, lemon juice, salt, and pepper.

196

2. Drain tomatoes slightly, then combine with radishes, onion, and mint leaves. Add olive-oil mixture; toss until just blended. Refrigerate until ready to toss with lettuce. Makes 6 servings.

United States of America

Originally this lusty stew-like dish was made in 20-gallon black pots and served to hundreds at picnics.

TENNESSEE BRUNSWICK STEW

4 cups water
1¼ lb. chuck, in 1″ cubes
½ broiler-fryer (1½ lb.)
2 teasp. salt
2 medium potatoes, pared
2 medium onions, peeled
½ cup uncooked regular rice
½ pkg. frozen okra
1 16- to 17-oz. can cream-style corn

1 1-lb.-4-oz. can tomatoes (2½ cups)
1 tablesp. sugar
3 teasp. salt
½ teasp. pepper
Pinch cayenne pepper
½ teasp. celery seeds

Early in day:
In Dutch oven, combine water, chuck, chicken, and 2 teasp. salt; simmer, covered, 1 hr., or till chuck and chicken are tender. Remove chuck and chicken from broth. Skin and bone chicken; cut chicken meat into small pieces. Set aside 1 cup chicken broth (use rest when desired). Refrigerate all.

About 1¼ hr. before serving:
Boil potatoes and onions, covered, about 20 min., or until partially cooked; drain. In Dutch oven, combine 1 cup chicken broth, chicken, chuck, rice, okra, corn, tomatoes, sugar, 3 teasp. salt, peppers, and celery seeds. Add diced potatoes and chopped onions. Simmer, covered, ¾ hr. Serve at once (or refrigerate; then reheat next day). Makes 6 to 8 servings.

There are two schools of thought when it comes to clam chowder —the milk chowder of New England and the tomato chowder of Manhattan—and each likes his the very best.

BOSTON CLAM CHOWDER

3 doz. shucked raw soft-shell clams, with strained liquid
2 cups cold water
¼ lb. diced salt pork, or 2 tablesp. butter or margarine
2 medium onions, peeled, sliced
2 tablesp. flour

¼ teasp. celery salt
¼ teasp. pepper
2 teasp. salt
3 cups diced, pared potatoes
3 cups scalded milk
1½ teasp. salt
1 tablesp. butter or margarine

1. Snip off necks of clams; cut fine with scissors; leave soft parts whole.
2. In saucepan, place clams (necks and soft parts) with liquid. Add water; bring to boil. Drain, reserving liquid and clams.
3. In large kettle, sauté salt pork until golden. Add onions; cook until tender.
4. Into onions, stir flour, celery salt, pepper, 2 teasp. salt, clam liquid, potatoes.
5. Cook, covered, 8 min., or until potatoes are tender. Add milk, clams, 1½ teasp. salt, butter.
6. Ladle into big soup bowls, or into mugs if you're serving out of doors. Makes 8 servings.

The South and Southwest started it. Now the entire nation can't get enough of that barbecue flavor, whether cooked indoors or outdoors over hot coals.

BARBECUED CHICKEN

2 teasp. salt
¼ teasp. pepper
1½ cups canned tomato juice
¼ teasp. cayenne pepper
¼ teasp. dry mustard
1 bay leaf
4½ teasp. Worcestershire
¾ cup vinegar

1 teasp. sugar
3 cloves garlic, peeled, minced
3 tablesp. butter, margarine, or salad oil
2 2½- to 3-lb. broiler-fryers, halved or quartered
3 medium onions, peeled, thinly sliced

Early in day or day before: Make barbecue sauce by combining, in saucepan, salt, pepper, tomato juice, cayenne, mustard, bay leaf, Worcestershire, vinegar, sugar, garlic, butter. Simmer, uncovered, 10 min. Refrigerate.

About 1½ hr. before serving: Start heating oven to 425°F. Arrange chickens, with skin sides down, in single layer in shallow open pan. Sprinkle lightly with some salt and pepper. Arrange onions on chicken, tucking a few slices under wings, legs. Pour on barbecue sauce. Bake, uncovered, basting often, ½ hr.; turn; bake, basting often, 45 min., or until fork can be inserted easily into leg. Makes 4 to 6 servings.

FOR 2: Use one 1½-lb. broiler-fryer and same amount of sauce.

Chili con carne is a favorite national dish. It originated in the Southwest where it's consumed by the bowl as often as hamburgers and hot dogs are eaten in the North.

CHILI CON CARNE

2 tablesp. fat or salad oil
½ cup thinly sliced onions
2 tablesp. diced green pepper
½ lb. round, rump, or chuck, ground
½ cup boiling water
1 cup canned tomatoes
1½ tablesp. chili powder

2 tablesp. cold water
¼ teasp. salt
1 teasp. sugar
1½ small cloves garlic, peeled, minced
2 cups cooked or canned kidney beans, undrained

In hot fat in skillet, cook onions and green pepper until tender. Add meat; cook, uncovered, until meat starts to sizzle and brown. Add boiling water, tomatoes, chili powder mixed with cold water till smooth, salt, sugar, garlic. Simmer, covered, 1 hr. Uncover; simmer ½ hr. Add a little hot water if mixture thickens too much. Add beans; heat. Serve in soup bowls, with rolls or crackers and a salad. Or serve over hot or toasted split corn bread, buttered spaghetti, or fried mush.

To vary: If you prefer a slightly thinner chili con carne, stir in about ¼ cup hot water just before serving. Or replace canned tomatoes with 1⅓ cups diced fresh tomatoes.

A one-plate meal from New England, simple and satisfying.

NEW ENGLAND BOILED DINNER

1 7- to 8-lb. corned-beef brisket
1 large onion, peeled, sliced
6 whole cloves
4 whole peppercorns
1 bay leaf
½ teasp. dried rosemary
1 clove garlic, peeled
1 stalk celery, cut up

1 carrot, pared, sliced
2 parsley sprigs
12 new potatoes
12 whole carrots, pared
1 large head cabbage, cut into 6 wedges
2 16-oz. cans whole beets

About 5½ hr. before serving:
1. Place corned beef in large kettle; cover with cold water; add

sliced onion, whole cloves, peppercorns, bay leaf, rosemary, garlic, celery, sliced carrot, and parsley sprigs. Bring to boil, then simmer, covered, 4 to 5 hr., or until meat is fork-tender. Remove to large heated platter and keep warm.

2. Strain liquid from kettle; return 6 cups liquid to kettle. Then add potatoes and whole carrots; place cabbage on top of them. Bring to boil, then simmer, covered, 30 min., or until vegetables are just tender-crisp.

3. Meanwhile, in saucepan, heat beets.

4. Slice meat, then arrange drained vegetables around it. Pass mustard pickles, chili sauce, or horse-radish. Makes 12 servings.

FOR 6: Use a 3½- to 4-lb. corned-beef brisket and half of remaining ingredients. Cook as in step 1 for 3 to 4 hr., or until tender. Then proceed as directed.

The waters of Alaska abound with salmon; it's the Alaskans' favorite catch and naturally they are masters at preparing it.

CREAMY ALASKAN SALMON

6 slices fresh salmon (about 2½ lb.)	2 tablesp. butter or margarine
Salt	2 tablesp. flour
¼ teasp. pepper	1 cup light cream
1 bay leaf, finely crushed	1 cup milk
¼ teasp. dried thyme	6 lemon wedges
¼ teasp. dried savory	Parsley sprigs

About 45 min. before serving:

1. Start heating oven to 400°F. In large skillet cook salmon in 1 cup water until fish is easily flaked with fork, but still moist—8 to 10 min. Drain, then place slices, side by side, in 13" x 9" x 2" baking dish. Sprinkle with 1 teasp. salt, pepper, bay leaf, thyme, and savory.

2. In saucepan melt butter. Stir in flour, then cream, milk, and ½ teasp. salt. Bring to a boil, then cook until thickened.

3. Pour over salmon in baking dish. Bake 20 min., or until bubbling. Garnish with lemon wedges and parsley sprigs, then serve. Makes 6 servings.

From the Southlands—a soufflé-like bread, so delicate it's spooned from the casserole to the dinner plate to top with butter and eat with a fork.

SPOON BREAD

1 qt. milk	2 tablesp. butter or margarine
1 cup corn meal (yellow or white)	4 eggs
1½ teasp. salt	

In double boiler, heat milk; gradually stir in corn meal mixed with salt; cook, stirring, until smooth and thick. Cover; cook till mushy. Meanwhile, start heating oven to 425°F. Remove the mush from heat; add butter. In bowl, beat eggs till well blended; slowly stir into mush. Pour into well-greased 1½-qt. casserole. Bake, uncovered, 50 to 55 min. Serve at once from casserole, spooning some onto each plate. Eat instead of bread, with lots of butter or margarine. Makes 4 or 5 servings.

A New Orleans specialty—a stew-like mixture of tomatoes, shrimp, onions, peppers, and seasonings, served on fluffy rice.

SHRIMP CREOLE

1½ green peppers, seeded, chopped	½ teasp. dried rosemary
3 or 4 cloves garlic, peeled, minced	½ teasp. paprika
	6 dashes Tabasco
3 large onions, peeled, chopped	2 1-lb.-13-oz. cans tomatoes (about 6 cups)
6 tablesp. salad oil	
4 cups hot seasoned cooked rice	3 lb. raw shrimp, shelled, deveined
1 tablesp. salt	
⅛ teasp. pepper	1 cup snipped parsley

1. Into automatic skillet (or large regular skillet), put green peppers, garlic, and onion; add salad oil. Sauté vegetables at 375°F. (medium heat) until tender.
2. Meanwhile, start cooking rice as label directs.
3. To tender vegetables, add salt, pepper, rosemary, paprika, Tabasco, and tomatoes. Cook all at 225°F. (medium-low heat) 15 min., stirring occasionally. Now add shrimp and cook just until shrimp turn pink. Then turn automatic skillet to 150°F.
4. Add parsley to rice. Arrange rice in ring around Shrimp Creole either in skillet or serving dish. Makes 8 to 10 servings.
FOR 4: Halve all ingredients.

A delightful New England hot bread, dotted with blueberries, which tastes wonderful any time of day.

BLUEBERRY MUFFINS

1 cup fresh blueberries	1 teasp. salt
Granulated sugar	1 egg
2 cups sifted all-purpose flour	1 cup milk
3 teasp. double-acting baking powder	6 tablesp. melted shortening

1. Wash and drain berries; pat dry on paper towels; sweeten to

taste with 2 or 3 tablesp. sugar; set aside. (Or use 1 cup frozen blueberries; don't sweeten.)

2. Start heating oven to 425°F. Grease 14 2½″ muffin-pan cups well. Into mixing bowl, sift flour, baking powder, salt, 2 tablesp. sugar.

3. Beat egg till frothy; add milk and shortening; mix well. Make small well in center of flour mixture; pour in milk mixture all at once. Stir quickly and lightly—*don't beat*—*until just mixed, but still lumpy.* Quickly stir in berries.

4. Quickly fill muffin cups two-thirds full with batter; wipe off any spilled drops. (If batter does not fill all cups, fill empty ones with water to keep grease from burning.) Sprinkle tops of muffins with 4 teasp. granulated sugar. Bake 25 min., or until cake tester, inserted in center of a muffin, comes out clean. Then run spatula around each muffin to loosen it; lift out into napkin-lined basket and serve piping hot. Makes about 14.

P.S. If muffins are done before rest of meal, loosen, then tip slightly in pans and keep warm, right in pans, so they won't steam and soften.

FOR 2: Use 1 egg; halve rest of ingredients.

This unique salad became the rage on the West Coast, served as a first course, California-style.

CAESAR SALAD

1 clove garlic, peeled
¼ cup salad oil
2 cups ¼″ fresh bread squares
1 large head each romaine and iceberg lettuce (3 qt. bite-size pieces)
¼ cup grated Parmesan cheese
¼ cup crumbled Danish blue cheese

½ cup salad oil
1 tablesp. Worcestershire
¾ teasp. salt
¼ teasp. freshly ground black pepper
1 egg
¼ cup lemon juice

Early in day: Quarter garlic; drop into ¼ cup oil; set aside. Toast bread squares in shallow pan at 300°F. 20 min., or until golden, tossing often with fork. Tear greens into bite-size pieces into salad bowl. Refrigerate all.

Just before serving: Sprinkle greens with cheeses; drizzle on ½ cup salad oil, mixed with Worcestershire, salt, pepper. Toss gently until every leaf glistens. Break whole raw egg onto greens; pour lemon juice over all; toss until egg specks disappear. Now pour the ¼ cup oil you set aside (remove garlic) over bread squares; toss; sprinkle over greens. If desired, add 8 cut-up anchovies. Toss salad; serve at once. Makes 4 or 5 servings.

Cabbage salads are almost without end. Here's a colorful, decidedly American, Midwestern version.

COLESLAW

½ cup mayonnaise or salad dressing
¾ teasp. salt
Speck pepper
Dash paprika
½ teasp. sugar
1 tablesp. vinegar
1 tablesp. milk

4 cups finely shredded green cabbage
1 tablesp. minced onion
⅓ cup diced celery
⅓ cup slivered green pepper
⅓ cup grated raw carrot
¼ cup sliced radishes

1. In small bowl blend mayonnaise, salt, pepper, paprika, sugar, vinegar, and milk.
2. In large bowl combine cabbage, onion, celery, green pepper, carrot, and radishes.
3. Pour on mayonnaise mixture, then, using a two-tined fork, toss all together.
4. Pile lightly in salad bowl and serve. Makes 4 servings.

There are many cheesecakes in this land. This is the one, high and smooth, that is famous on Broadway as an after-theater snack.

DE-LUXE CHEESECAKE

1 cup sifted all-purpose flour
¼ cup granulated sugar
1 teasp. grated lemon rind
¼ teasp. vanilla extract
½ cup soft butter or margarine
3 egg yolks
5 8-oz. pkg. soft cream cheese
1¾ cups granulated sugar

¼ teasp. vanilla extract
½ teasp. grated orange rind
3 tablesp. flour
¼ teasp. salt
½ teasp. grated lemon rind
5 medium eggs
¼ cup heavy cream

COOKIE MIXTURE: Mix 1 cup flour, ¼ cup sugar, 1 teasp. grated lemon rind, ¼ teasp. vanilla. With pastry blender or 2 knives, scissor-fashion, cut in butter and 1 egg yolk. Shape into ball; wrap in wax paper; refrigerate 1 hr. Start heating oven to 400°F. Roll about one third of dough between floured pieces of wax paper into 9½" circle. Place on bottom of 9" spring-form pan; trim to fit. Bake about 10 min., or till golden; cool. Grease side of spring-form pan; fit over filled base. Roll rest of dough into 15" x 4" rectangle; cut in half lengthwise; use to line side of pan, patching if necessary.

CHEESE FILLING: Increase oven temperature to 500°F. With electric mixer or spoon, beat cheese until fluffy. Combine 1¾ cups sugar with ¼ teasp. vanilla, orange rind, 3 tablesp. flour, salt,

½ teasp. lemon rind; slowly add to cheese, beating till smooth. Add eggs and 2 egg yolks, one at a time, beating after each addition. Stir in cream. Turn into lined pan. Bake at 500°F. 12 min., or till dough is golden. Reduce oven temperature to 200°F.; bake 1 hr. Cool on rack away from drafts. Remove side of pan; refrigerate until cold.*

To serve: Sprinkle cake with chopped, toasted nuts. Or cover with ¼" layer of commercial sour cream; refrigerate. Or spread strawberry, peach, apricot, or cherry jam or preserves on top. Or top wedges with canned crushed pineapple, sliced peaches, or fresh or thawed frozen strawberries. Makes 12 servings.

* Even better if refrigerated 24 hr.

Rich, syrupy pecan pie, once a Southern favorite, is now equally popular in the Midwest, beloved in New England, and, in fact, in all the U.S.A.

PECAN PIE

Unbaked 9" pie shell
2 eggs, beaten
1 cup dark corn syrup
⅛ teasp. salt
1 teasp. vanilla extract

1 cup granulated sugar
2 tablesp. melted butter or margarine
1 cup coarsely broken pecans †

Start heating oven to 400°F. Mix eggs with syrup, salt, vanilla, sugar, butter; add pecans; pour into shell. Bake at 400°F. 15 min.; then reduce oven heat to 350°F. and bake 30 to 35 min. Cool. Serve, cut into small wedges, with whipped cream or small bunches of grapes.

† If salted nuts are used, omit salt.

This luscious meringue-topped lemon pie gets votes nationwide, but probably the West Coast makes it most.

LEMON MERINGUE PIE

Baked 8" or 9" pie shell
Granulated sugar
¼ cup cornstarch
Salt
1¼ cups warm water
Grated rind 1 lemon

¼ cup lemon juice
3 egg yolks, slightly beaten
1 tablesp. butter or margarine
3 egg whites
Vanilla extract

1. Make and bake pie shell.
2. In double boiler, combine 1 cup sugar, cornstarch, ⅛ teasp. salt. Slowly stir in water, then lemon rind and juice, egg yolks, butter. Cook, stirring, until smooth and thick enough to mound

when dropped from spoon. Remove from heat. Cool thoroughly.

3. Start heating oven to 350°F. Place egg whites in medium bowl; add ¼ teasp. salt and ½ teasp. vanilla extract; beat until frothy throughout. Then add 6 tablesp. sugar, a little at a time, beating well after each addition, until stiff peaks are formed.

4. Spoon lemon filling into cooled pie shell. With spoon, place mounds of meringue around top edge of filling, spreading it so it touches inner edge of crust *all around,* to prevent shrinking. Heap rest of meringue in center, then push out to meet meringue border. Bake 12 to 15 min. Cool, then serve.

Rich and chewy like candy, these cookie squares are a favorite often sent to camps and colleges to remind the young folks of home.

BROWNIES

¾ cup sifted cake flour
½ teasp. double-acting baking powder
¾ teasp. salt
1 cup granulated sugar
½ cup soft shortening
2 eggs, unbeaten

1 teasp. vanilla extract
2 to 2½ sq. unsweetened chocolate, melted
1 cup chopped California walnuts, almonds, pecans, Brazil nuts, pistachio nuts, or peanuts

1. Start heating oven to 350°F. Grease 8" x 8" x 2" pan. Sift flour with baking powder and salt.

2. Gradually add sugar to shortening, mixing until *very light and fluffy.* Add eggs, vanilla; mix till smooth. Mix in chocolate, then flour mixture and nuts. (If desired, save half of nuts to sprinkle on top of batter before baking.)

3. Turn into pan. Bake 30 to 35 min., or until done. Cool slightly; cut into 16 squares or bars; sprinkle with confectioners' sugar if desired. Store right in pan.

And, we salute our newest state, Hawaii. Some of their traditional and new Hawaiian dishes appear on p. 177.

SOUTH AMERICA

ARGENTINA

BOLIVIA

BRAZIL

CHILE

COLOMBIA

PERU

URUGUAY

VENEZUELA

Here lies a land of legend and romance, of contrast in climate ranging from the rarefied altitudes of Bolivia to the tropical jungles of Venezuela, of contrast in economics from vast wealth to direst poverty, of contrast in civilization from the sophistication of Rio de Janeiro to the utter primitiveness of the Inca Indians.

Yet certain customs prevail throughout the different countries —a love of fine food, the five- or six-o'clock tea hour, the very late dinner, the excellent coffee. Argentina, traditionally the land of beef, has many interesting ways of cooking steak and of making meat soups and stews. In Bolivia, where cooler weather accompanies the higher altitude, the taste is for hot spicy foods, similar to those found in Peru and Chile.

Brazil offers, along with its superb coffee, rare fruits and fine seafood. Here too, bean dishes are favorites and here one finds that great delicacy, hearts of palm. Visitors to Chile are amazed at the range of fine foods available and surely every taste can be pleased among the seafood dishes, the plentiful game and native fruits.

Fortunately for us, many of these strange and delightful dishes can be made in our own kitchens. And while the food cannot take us bodily to see the heart-stopping beauty of the harbor of Rio de Janeiro or the colorful and ancient land of the Incas, it can feed our imaginations as it feeds our bodies and takes us in spirit to these faraway and exciting countries.

Argentina

Argentina, and indeed most of South America, eats a great deal of the excellent beef produced there. Here, their short ribs star, with a chicken variation.

PUCHERO DE CARNE
(*Boiled Beef Dinner*)

2½ lb. short ribs
2 qt. water
4 teasp. salt
1 teasp. pepper
2 large onions, peeled, halved
3 carrots, pared, halved crosswise
3 cabbage wedges (about ½ lb.)
3 sweet or hot Italian or Spanish sausages
2 to 3 cloves garlic, peeled, minced

2 large potatoes, pared, cut in half
1 yellow summer squash, cut into large chunks
1 green pepper, seeded, cut into large strips
2 ears corn
2 tomatoes, quartered
1 1-lb.-4-oz. can chick peas, drained (optional)

About 2 hr. and 15 min. before serving:

1. In large kettle place short ribs, water, salt, and pepper. Bring to a boil, then skim surface with a large spoon. Now simmer ribs, covered, 1 hr. 30 min.

2. Add onions, carrots, cabbage wedges, sausages, garlic, and potatoes; bring to boil, then simmer, covered, 20 min. Add squash and green pepper and cook 10 min.

3. With sharp knife scrape kernels from ears of corn; add, with tomatoes and chick peas, to soup. Simmer 5 min.

4. Carefully pour off broth, leaving vegetables and meat in covered kettle. Skim fat from broth if desired, then serve broth as a first course, with buttered toast.

5. Cut meat into serving pieces; arrange with vegetables on large serving platter and serve as main dish. Makes about 6 servings.

PUCHERO DE POLLO (BOILED CHICKEN DINNER): Substitute 1 3-lb. broiler-fryer, cut up, for short ribs. Simmer in 2 qt. water with 4 teasp. salt and 1 teasp. pepper for 30 min., then proceed as in steps 2 to 5 above. Makes about 6 servings.

Two meal-in-a-dish favorites that you'll wish to introduce at your table. Spanish or Italian sausages add a subtle taste touch.

ESTOFADO
(Beef Stew)

2 tablesp. olive oil
2 lb. chuck, in 1½" pieces
½ lb. Spanish or sweet Italian sausages, quartered
1 large onion, peeled, chopped
3 large cloves garlic, peeled, minced
1 6-oz. can tomato paste

2 large tomatoes, chopped
1 cup dry white wine
½ lb. fresh mushrooms, quartered
¼ cup snipped parsley
½ teasp. dried thyme
2 bay leaves, crushed
2 teasp. salt
½ teasp. pepper

About 2 hr. before serving:
1. In Dutch oven heat olive oil; in it brown chuck and sausages on all sides; then add onion and garlic and sauté a few minutes.
2. Stir in tomato paste, tomatoes, wine, mushrooms, parsley, thyme, bay leaves, salt, and pepper. Cook, covered, 1 hr. 30 to 40 min., or until meat is tender; skim off fat, if desired. Makes about 6 servings.

Favorite appetizers of the Argentine are Empanadas—hot or cold pastry turnovers filled with meat or sweet fillings; try some, next time you're having guests.

EMPANADAS
(Fruit-and-Meat Turnovers)

2 cups sifted all-purpose flour
¼ teasp. salt
1¾ teasp. cinnamon
Granulated sugar
¾ cup butter or margarine

1 egg yolk
2 tablesp. sherry
2½ tablesp. milk
Fruit-and-Meat Filling, p. 211
1 egg, slightly beaten

Early on day, or 2 hr. ahead:
1. Into large bowl sift flour with salt, ¼ teasp. cinnamon, and ¼ teasp. sugar. With pastry blender or 2 knives, scissor-fashion, cut in butter till like corn meal.
2. Blend well egg yolk, sherry, milk. Add to flour mixture; then, with pastry blender or fork, mix till a dough. Wrap in wax paper, foil, or saran; refrigerate.
3. Grease two or three cookie sheets. Make Fruit-and-Meat Filling.

Just before baking:
1. Start heating oven to 400°F. On lightly floured surface, roll out half of dough ⅛" thick; with 4" cookie cutter, cut into rounds.

On half of each round place two rounded teaspoonfuls of Fruit-and-Meat Filling.

2. Brush edge of each round with beaten egg; then fold over, making semicircle; press edges together with tines of fork; arrange on cookie sheet. Repeat with rest of dough.

3. Brush tops of Empanadas with beaten egg; sprinkle with ⅓ cup sugar mixed with 1½ teasp. cinnamon. Bake 20 min., or till golden; remove to rack.

4. Serve hot, as a finger-style appetizer or as first course at a sit-down dinner. Makes about 28.

FRUIT-AND-MEAT FILLING: In 1 tablesp. melted butter in skillet, sauté 3 tablesp. chopped onion till golden; add ½ lb. chuck, ground; cook, while stirring, 2 min.; turn into bowl. Mix with ½ cup chopped green pepper, ½ cup chopped tomatoes, ½ cup chopped ripe fresh peaches, ¾ cup chopped pared fresh pears, 2 teasp. snipped chives, ½ teasp. salt, 1 tablesp. sugar, 2 tablesp. sherry. Refrigerate.

Bolivia

Bolivians, in their rather chilly land, high above sea level, grow such luscious fruits as bananas, avocados, cherimoyos, pineapples, etc. Quite understandably, they favor spicy, warming cooking like this.

AJÍ DE CARNE
(Pepper Pork)

¼ cup olive oil

3 cloves garlic, peeled, minced

4 medium onions, peeled, coarsely chopped

2 lb. pork shoulder, cut into ¾" cubes

3 tablesp. uncooked regular white rice

3 medium tomatoes, coarsely chopped

¼ teasp. crushed red pepper

¼ teasp. powdered cinnamon

⅛ teasp. powdered cloves

1½ teasp. salt

¼ teasp. saffron

1 10½-oz. can condensed consommé, undiluted

1 to 2 green bananas, peeled, quartered

3 medium potatoes, pared, quartered

¼ cup heavy cream

1 tablesp. molasses

¼ cup finely chopped peanuts

About 1 hr. and 15 min. before serving:

1. In large Dutch oven heat olive oil; in it sauté garlic and onions 5 min., turning often. Add pork and rice, then brown well on all sides.

2. Now stir in tomatoes, red pepper, cinnamon, cloves, salt, saffron, and consommé. Simmer, covered, for 30 min. Stir in bananas and potatoes and simmer 15 min. Add heavy cream, molasses, and peanuts, and simmer until meat and potatoes are tender—about 15 min. Makes 6 servings.

Bolivian avocados are small and round. But just buy some of ours and serve this salad—say on a midsummer Friday night. You've a treat in store!

PALTAS RELLENAS
(*Stuffed Avocados*)

½ cup mayonnaise	2 cups coarsely snipped lettuce
½ teasp. salt	1½ cups flaked cooked fish (1 lb.) *
¼ teasp. pepper	3 avocados
1 tablesp. lemon juice	Few lettuce leaves
¼ to ½ teasp. crushed red pepper	1 hard-cooked egg, shelled
1 tablesp. bottled capers	

About 1 hr. before serving:
1. In medium bowl combine mayonnaise, salt, pepper, lemon juice, red pepper, and capers. Stir in snipped lettuce and fish.
2. Cut avocados in half lengthwise; remove pits. Place halves, cut side up, on lettuce-lined platter. Top them with fish mixture; decorate with egg slices. Refrigerate until ready to serve. Makes 6 servings.

* Cooked diced chicken, turkey, or shrimp may replace fish.

UMINTAS
(*Baked Corn*)

About 4 ears fresh corn (3 cups kernels)	1½ teasp. flour
1 tablesp. salad oil	½ teasp. salt
¼ teasp. chili powder	3 eggs, beaten
⅛ teasp. anise seed	¼ lb. process Swiss or goat's-milk cheese slices

About 1 hr. and 15 min. before serving:
1. Start heating oven to 350°F. With sharp knife scrape kernels from corn into medium bowl. In small skillet heat salad oil, stir in chili powder, anise seed, flour, and salt. Sauté 1 min., while stirring. Add to corn with eggs.
2. Pour half of this mixture into greased 1-qt. casserole; over it arrange cheese slices. Pour on rest of corn mixture. Bake 55 to 60 min., or until golden and custard is set. Serve as a vegetable dish. Makes 6 servings.

Brazil

Precisely the kind of warm-flavored dish so welcome on winter evenings. Pork shoulder—roasted, stuffed, and topped with a spicy blend of tomatoes, raisins, onions, peppers, and olives.

PORCO RECHEIADO
(Roast Stuffed Pork)

¼ cup salad oil
1 cup chopped onion
1 clove garlic, peeled, minced
½ cup chopped green pepper
3 cups diced fresh tomatoes
⅔ cup golden or dark raisins
¼ cup sliced ripe olives
2½ teasp. salt
1 teasp. chili powder

½ teasp. pepper
4- to 5-lb pork shoulder—cushion roast
2½ cups cold cooked rice
2 lb. whole white onions, peeled
6 carrots, pared, halved
Butter or margarine
Parsley or water cress (optional)
Hot fluffy rice

About 3½ hr. before serving:
1. Start heating oven to 325°F. In salad oil, in skillet, sauté onion, garlic, green pepper, till tender; add tomatoes, raisins, olives, 1½ teasp. salt, chili powder, ¼ teasp. pepper. Simmer, covered, 5 min., stirring occasionally.
2. Meanwhile, sprinkle inside of pocket in pork with 1 teasp. salt, ¼ teasp. pepper.
3. Then, in bowl, toss cold cooked rice with ½ cup tomato mixture; use to fill pocket in pork; skewer securely. Cover remaining tomato mixture; set aside.
4. Arrange stuffed pork shoulder on wire trivet in roasting pan. Insert roast-meat thermometer into fleshy center of roast. Roast 1 hr., then remove drippings from pan. Next, top pork with rest of tomato mixture; cover with foil.
5. Continue roasting 1½ to 2 hr. longer, or until roast-meat thermometer reads 185°F. Remove foil.
6. Meanwhile, cook onions and carrots until tender-crisp; season; keep warm.
7. Place roasted pork on heated large platter; remove skewers. Then arrange buttered, cooked whole onions and carrots along one side of pork. Garnish with parsley or water cress. Serve, along with bowl of hot fluffy rice. Makes 6 servings.

South America

Mention Brazil, and coffee springs to mind. But seafood is typical too. So why not serve a double-feature luncheon—the shrimp salad and coffee custard below?

MAYONNAISE DE CAMARÃO E LINGUADO
(Shrimp-and-Flounder Mayonnaise)

2 tablesp. butter or margarine
⅔ cup lemon juice
6 tablesp. snipped parsley
1 tablesp. sugar
1 teasp. salt
6 whole peppercorns
2 bay leaves
Two ½-lb. flounder fillets
¼ teasp. seasoned salt
2 doz. large, cooked, deveined, shelled shrimp

3 hard-cooked eggs, shelled
Mayonnaise
Rolled anchovy fillets
Bottled capers
Romaine leaves
Sour-pickle slices
6 pickled-beet slices
12 pitted ripe olives
Celery leaves

1. In large skillet melt butter or margarine. Add ⅓ cup lemon juice, ¼ cup snipped parsley, sugar, salt, peppercorns, and bay leaves; bring to boil.
2. Lay flounder fillets in mixture in skillet; cover; simmer 5 min. Refrigerate in skillet.
3. Combine ⅓ cup lemon juice, 2 tablesp. snipped parsley, seasoned salt, and cooked shrimp. Refrigerate.
4. Halve hard-cooked eggs lengthwise; top each with ¼ teasp. mayonnaise, then a rolled anchovy fillet with caper center.
5. Slice 1 doz. of the refrigerated shrimp and add 1 cup finely sliced romaine and ¼ cup mayonnaise.
6. Arrange 6 beds of romaine leaves around edge of large platter. Cut each fish fillet into thirds; lay one third on each romaine bed. Top with sliced-shrimp mixture and ½ cup mayonnaise.
7. Garnish each with sour-pickle slices and 2 whole shrimp.
8. In center of platter arrange egg halves, pickled-beet slices, and pitted ripe olives. Garnish with celery leaves. Makes 6 servings.

FLAN DE CAFÉ DE MOCHA
(Coffee Custard)

3 cups milk
1 cup light cream
6 to 8 tablesp. instant coffee
2 teasp. grated orange rind
4 eggs
1 egg yolk
½ cup granulated sugar

1 teasp. vanilla extract
1 teasp. almond extract
½ teasp. salt
Nutmeg
1 cup chopped Brazil nuts
1 egg white
3 tablesp. guava jelly

1. Start heating oven to 325°F. In saucepan scald milk with

Argentina's Boiled Beef Dinner (Puchero de Carne), page 209

cream. Then add instant coffee and orange rind; stir well; cool 10 min.

2. Meanwhile, in small bowl, with electric mixer at low speed, slightly beat eggs and egg yolk with sugar.

3. Now slowly add coffee mixture, then vanilla, almond, and salt; blend well. Strain through fine strainer.

4. Pour mixture into 6 custard cups; sprinkle each with nutmeg. Place cups in shallow baking pan; fill pan with cold water up to ¾" from tops of cups.

5. Bake 1 hr., or until knife, inserted in center, comes out clean. Cool, then refrigerate.

6. Just before serving, with small spatula, remove each custard from cup and arrange, upside-down, on serving dish. Sprinkle with Brazil nuts.

7. Beat egg white quite stiff; then beat in guava jelly until stiff. Swirl over nuts. Makes 6 servings.

World-famous Brazil nuts are used extensively in Brazil, too. Family and guests are sure to beg for repeats on this luscious cake.

TORTA DE CASTANHA DO PARÁ
(*Brazil-Nut Cake*)

6 eggs, separated
Granulated sugar
Instant coffee
½ teasp. salt
2 tablesp. pkgd. dried bread crumbs

1 tablesp. brandy
2 cups finely ground Brazil nuts (about ¾ lb.)
1½ cups heavy cream
¼ cup slivered Brazil nuts

Early on the day:
1. Start heating oven to 350°F. Grease, line with wax paper, then grease again bottom of 2 8" layer-cake pans.

2. In large bowl, with electric mixer at high speed, beat egg yolks with ⅔ cup sugar until thick and fluffy—about 10 min. Now beat in 1 teasp. instant coffee, salt, bread crumbs, and brandy, then fold in ground nuts.

3. Beat 6 egg whites until stiff, but not dry; fold them gradually into nut mixture. Pour into prepared pans, then bake 35 min., or until cake tester, inserted in center, comes out clean. Cool in pans.

About ½ hr. before serving:
1. Loosen layers around edges and turn out on rack; remove wax paper.

2. Whip cream until stiff. Dissolve 2 tablesp. instant coffee in 1 tablesp. water; fold, with 3 tablesp. sugar, into whipped cream. Use to fill and frost cake. Garnish with slivered nuts. Refrigerate until serving time. To serve, cut into 12 wedges.

Chile's Flank Steak, Rolled and Filled
(Chilean Malaya), page 216

Chile

Next time you see a special on flank steak in your market, make up this famous Chilean meal-in-one, with its flavorsome vegetable filling, for the family's supper.

CHILEAN MALAYA
(*Flank Steak Rolled and Filled*)

1 2-lb. flank steak
½ teasp. salt
½ teasp. dried thyme
⅛ teasp. pepper
1 medium onion, peeled
3 tablesp. snipped parsley
3 tablesp. red wine vinegar
½ cup fresh bread crumbs
½ cup chopped cooked spinach

½ cup cooked or canned peas
¼ cup finely grated carrot
1 tablesp. grated Cheddar cheese
1 hard-cooked egg, chopped
3 cooked bacon slices, crumbled
2 tablesp. salad oil
1 10½-oz. can condensed con-
    sommé, undiluted

Evening before:
1. Wash and dry flank steak; with sharp knife score one side of it in diamond pattern.
2. Then sprinkle both sides with salt, thyme, and pepper. In large bowl place flank steak with onion, parsley, and vinegar. Cover dish with foil; refrigerate about 20 hr.

About 2 hr. before serving dinner:
1. In large bowl lightly combine bread crumbs, spinach, peas, carrot, cheese, chopped egg, and bacon; spoon onto scored side of steak, then pat it till it nearly extends to steak's edges. Then roll up, jelly-roll-fashion and tie securely, at 1" intervals, with string.
2. In hot salad oil, in Dutch oven, brown rolled steak well on all sides—about 15 to 20 min. Add onion-vinegar mixture in which meat marinated, also consommé. Simmer, covered, at least 1½ hr., or until steak is fork-tender.
3. Arrange steak on heated platter, remove strings, and serve sliced. Skim surface fat from gravy and pass. Makes 6 servings.

Chileans are justly proud of their fine fish and shellfish, including langosta; their avocados and their game, too. Corn and beans appear often in their hearties.

PASTEL DE CHOCLO
(*Meat-and-Vegetable Bake*)

Olive oil
1½ cups sliced, peeled onions
1 lb. chuck beef, ground
Salt
¼ teasp. crushed red pepper
1 teasp. ground cumin seeds

⅓ cup chopped stuffed olives
¼ cup seedless dark raisins
2 cups fresh or canned whole-kernel corn
1 large tomato, chopped

About 45 min. before serving:
1. Start heating oven to 400°F. In medium skillet heat 2 tablesp. olive oil; in it sauté 1 cup sliced onions until golden; then add beef and brown, turning frequently.
2. Stir in 1 teasp. salt, red pepper, cumin seeds, olives, and raisins. Spread over bottom of 8" x 8" x 2" baking dish.
3. In same skillet heat 2 tablesp. olive oil; in it sauté ½ cup sliced onions until golden. Stir in corn, then sauté 5 min., stirring frequently.
4. Next, stir in tomato and 1 teasp. salt. Spread over meat mixture. Bake 15 to 20 min., or until bubbling. Makes 6 servings.

Colombia

Colombians are very fond of spice and pepper, but don't let that deter you from trying their vegetable salad and skillet chicken with its chick peas.

ENSALADA DE LEGUMBRES
(*Vegetable Salad*)

3 sweet Italian or Spanish sausages (or ¼ lb. salami, thickly sliced)
1 8-oz. can whole-kernel corn
1 cup cooked green beans
2 medium tomatoes, sliced
¼ cup snipped parsley
¼ cup snipped scallions

3 cups lettuce, torn into pieces
5 tablesp. olive oil
2 tablesp. vinegar
1 teasp. salt
¼ teasp. pepper
1 small clove garlic, peeled, minced

About 2 hr. before serving:
1. Sauté sausages in a skillet until light-brown; drain on paper

toweling, then cool. Cut into thin crosswise slices (if salami, cut into small cubes).

2. Place them in large bowl together with corn, green beans, sliced tomatoes, parsley, scallions, and lettuce. Cover, then refrigerate until serving time.

Just before serving:
In small bowl beat together olive oil, vinegar, salt, pepper, and garlic. Pour over salad and toss together well. Makes about 6 servings.

POLLO AL CAZADOR
(*Chicken, Hunter's Style*)

Salt
¼ teasp. pepper
2 tablesp. flour
1 3-lb. broiler-fryer, cut up
¼ cup olive oil
2 medium onions, peeled, quartered
1 large tomato, cut into 8 wedges
¼ lb. fresh mushrooms, sliced

1 medium green pepper, seeded, sliced
½ teasp. crushed red pepper
¼ teasp. dried orégano
1 bay leaf, crushed
1 cup red wine
1 1-lb.-4-oz. can chick peas, drained

About 1 hr. before serving:
1. Mix 1 teasp. salt, pepper, and flour; use to coat chicken pieces. In large skillet or Dutch oven, heat olive oil; in it brown chicken well on all sides.
2. Now stir in onions, tomato, mushrooms, green pepper, red pepper, orégano, bay leaf, 1 teasp. salt, and wine. Simmer, tightly covered, 40 min., or until chicken is almost tender.
3. Stir in drained chick peas and cook 5 min., or until peas are heated through and chicken is tender. Makes about 5 servings.

The markets in Colombia are laden with an abundance of tropical fruits—perfect partners for their Cocoa Cupcakes at dessert time.

PASTELES DE CACAO
(*Cocoa Cupcakes*)

½ cup butter or margarine
1 cup granulated sugar
3 eggs
1 teasp. vanilla extract
¾ cup cocoa

1½ cups sifted all-purpose flour
3 teasp. double-acting baking powder
⅔ cup milk

Make early in day, or about 1 hr. before serving:
1. Start heating oven to 375°F. Grease 12 2¾" cups of muffin

pan (measured across top). In medium bowl, with electric mixer at medium speed, beat butter with sugar until creamy. Add eggs, one at a time, beating until light and fluffy; then beat in vanilla extract.

2. Sift cocoa with flour and baking powder; with electric mixer at low speed beat into butter mixture alternately with milk until well blended.

3. Divide cupcake batter evenly between muffin cups. Bake 20 min., or until cake tester, inserted in center, comes out clean.

4. Set pan on rack for 10 min., then remove cupcakes from pan.

5. Serve warm for dessert, with vanilla or coffee ice cream as an American touch. Makes 12.

Peru

Peruvian soups have a deliciously spicy twist—especially the hearty chowder type made with fish or shrimp.

CHUPE DE CAMARONES
(Shrimp Chowder)

3 tablesp. salad oil
2 cloves garlic, peeled, minced
1 large onion, peeled, chopped
2 large tomatoes, cut into eighths
2 cups small raw potato cubes
½ teasp. ground chili pepper
1½ teasp. seasoned salt
2 teasp. salt
¼ teasp. crushed red pepper

Few drops Tabasco
Water
1¼ cups milk
3 medium flounder fillets
¼ cup cream cheese (2 oz.)
½ lb. shelled, cleaned, raw shrimp
1 12-oz. can whole-kernel corn
Few sprigs fresh mint

About 45 min. before serving:

1. In Dutch oven heat salad oil; in it sauté garlic and onion until golden—about 10 min.

2. Now add tomatoes, potatoes, chili pepper, seasoned salt, 1½ teasp. salt, red pepper, Tabasco, 3 cups water, 1 cup milk; stir occasionally, while bringing to a boil, then simmer, covered, 20 min.

3. Meanwhile, in 1½ cups water and ½ teasp. salt in skillet, simmer flounder fillets 6 min., or until fork-tender but still moist. Also, beat cream cheese with ¼ cup milk until very smooth.

4. Now stir cream-cheese mixture, then shrimp and corn, into soup; cook over medium heat 5 min.

5. Next drain flounder fillets, divide each in half crosswise, then place a half in each of 6 soup plates. Spoon hot soup over fillets, garnish with mint sprigs and serve at once. Makes 6 servings.

Their potato salad is different—delightfully so—the layer of tender potato slices being masked with a spicy, hearty, cottage-cheese dressing.

PERUVIAN POTATO SALAD

2 lb. medium new potatoes	1 teasp. salt
3 hard-cooked eggs	2 tablesp. heavy cream
2 8-oz. containers creamed cottage cheese	⅓ cup olive oil
	¼ cup minced onion
¼ teasp. red pepper	¼ cup snipped parsley
Few drops Tabasco	Lettuce leaves
⅛ teasp. pepper	8 ripe olives
1½ teasp. seasoned salt	Few sprigs parsley

Early on the day:
Wash, then cook potatoes in boiling water about 30 min., or until just tender. Drain, peel, then cut into ¼"-thick slices; cool, refrigerate.

About ½ hr. before serving:
1. Shell eggs; cut in half, then remove yolks, chop whites and set aside.
2. In small bowl, mash egg yolks, then add cottage cheese, red pepper, Tabasco, pepper, seasoned salt, salt, and cream; beat, with electric mixer at medium speed, until smooth.
3. Gradually add olive oil while continuing to beat; blend in onion and parsley.
4. Around sides of large chop plate or platter, arrange lettuce leaves; heap potato slices in center; spread with cheese salad dressing, covering potatoes completely. Garnish with chopped egg whites, olives, and parsley sprigs. Makes 8 servings.

Their doughnuts are extra light and fluffy with a crisp crust, and mingling flavors you'll like knowing. They're served with a Rum-Caramel Sauce.

BUÑUELOS
(Peruvian Doughnuts)

1 cup granulated sugar	½ teasp. anise seeds
¾ cup boiling water	½ cup milk
2 tablesp. rum	½ cup water
1 cup sifted all-purpose flour	5 tablesp. butter or margarine
1 teasp. double-acting baking powder	1 teasp. grated lemon rind
	3 eggs, separated
1 teasp. salt	Salad oil

Few hours before serving, make up Rum-Caramel Sauce:
In medium skillet melt sugar until it forms a golden syrup, stir-

ring occasionally; add water and stir until sugar is dissolved. Remove from heat, add rum; cool.

About 1 hr. before serving:
1. Sift together flour, baking powder, and salt; blend in anise seeds.
2. In medium saucepan place milk, water, butter or margarine, and lemon rind. Bring to a rolling boil; add flour mixture, all at once, then stir until smooth. Cook, stirring, until mixture leaves sides of pan in ball. Remove from heat, let cool slightly.
3. Now add egg yolks, one at a time, beating smooth after each addition. Beat egg whites till stiff, then, with large spoon, stir into egg-flour mixture.
4. Into large deep skillet or Dutch oven pour salad oil to a 1½″ depth; heat to 370°F. on deep-fat-frying thermometer.
5. Meanwhile, with teaspoon, cut off a small part of dough; then, on well-floured board, form it, with hands, into a roll about 10″ long and ½″ thick; cut roll in half, then twist the two strips around each other, form into a circle and press ends together. Place on greased wax paper. Repeat with rest of dough.
6. Now drop these doughnuts, a few at a time, into hot oil and fry until golden-brown on both sides. With slotted spoon transfer to paper towel to drain.
7. Pile up doughnuts on serving dish; serve warm with Rum-Caramel Sauce spooned over them. Makes about 20.

Uruguay

Uruguayans love food, and use great care in seasoning it—especially the chicken, beef, and fish which they serve so abundantly.

POLLO GUISO CON VEGETALES
(Chicken-Vegetable Stew)

Butter or margarine
3 medium onions, peeled, sliced
2 large carrots, pared, diced
½ lb. fresh mushrooms, sliced
1 tablesp. flour
Pepper

Salt
1 3- to 3½-lb. broiler-fryer, cut up
¼ teasp. powdered mace
2 tablesp. snipped fresh chives
1½ cups dry white wine
1 hard-cooked egg, shelled, sliced

About 1 hr. and 10 min. before serving:
1. In large skillet or Dutch oven, heat 3 tablesp. butter; in it sauté onions, carrots, and mushrooms until golden—about 10 min. Stir in flour, ¼ teasp. pepper, and 1 teasp. salt; remove vegetables.

2. To skillet add 3 tablesp. butter. Rub chicken pieces with 1½ teasp. salt and ½ teasp. pepper; place in butter in skillet, then brown well on all sides.
3. To browned chicken pieces add mace, chives, wine, and sautéed vegetables. Cover tightly and simmer 45 to 50 min., or until chicken is tender. Transfer to large platter and serve, garnished with egg slices. Makes about 6 servings.

While these Egg-and-Spinach Squares are usually served hot or cold, as an hors d'oeuvre, your lady guests will enjoy them as a luncheon main dish, too.

TORTA PASCUALINA
(Egg-and-Spinach Squares)

2 cups sifted all-purpose flour	Pepper
Salt	¼ teasp. powdered nutmeg
3 egg yolks	½ lb. process Swiss cheese, cut
Olive oil	into small pieces
4 to 5 tablesp. cold water	6 eggs
2 10-oz. pkg. frozen chopped spinach	

About 1 hr. and 15 min. before serving:
1. Into medium bowl sift flour and 1 teasp. salt; add egg yolks, 3 tablesp. olive oil, and water. Toss together, form into a ball, then knead on board until smooth and pliable. Refrigerate 10 min.
2. Meanwhile, cook spinach as label directs; drain well. Stir in ½ teasp. pepper, nutmeg, and cheese. Set aside.
3. Now cut dough into 4 equal pieces. Roll each piece into a rectangle to fit bottom of oiled 13" x 9" x 2" baking dish. Start heating oven to 375°F.
4. Place two of the dough rectangles on bottom of baking dish; on them spread spinach mixture to within ½" of edges. Make 6 "nests" in spinach mixture, placed equidistantly. Into each nest break 1 egg. Sprinkle eggs with ½ teasp. salt and ¼ teasp. pepper.
5. Cover with remaining two rectangles, pressing edges together. With back of knife or pastry wheel outline 6 equal squares (1 egg in each square). Brush top with olive oil.
6. Bake 20 to 30 min., or until eggs are of desired doneness. Serve, cut into 6 individual portions, as a luncheon dish, with a tossed mixed salad. Makes 6 servings.

Venezuela

Venezuela's Hallacas, with their corn-meal wrappings, are a version of tamales. Stuffed with a tasty meat filling, they're served as the main dish or as an hors d'oeuvre.

HALLACAS
(*National Corn-Meal Dish*)

1 lb. boned pork shoulder	1 tablesp. vinegar
Salt	½ teasp. crushed red pepper
2 tablesp. olive oil	1 tablesp. bottled capers, chopped
½ cup chopped onions	¼ cup seedless dark raisins
2 cloves garlic, peeled, minced	¼ cup chopped stuffed olives
1 small green pepper, seeded, chopped	1½ cups diced cooked chicken
	2 cups white corn meal
2 medium tomatoes, chopped	½ cup butter or margarine
¼ cup snipped parsley	1 egg, beaten

About 3 hr. before serving:

1. Cook pork in 2 cups water with 1 teasp. salt until almost tender—about 45 min.
2. Meanwhile, in medium skillet, heat olive oil; in it sauté onions and garlic until golden; then add green pepper, tomatoes, parsley, and vinegar and cook over low heat until tender—about 10 min.
3. Next, stir in 1 teasp. salt, red pepper, capers, raisins, olives, and chicken. When pork is done, drain and cut into small pieces; add to vegetable-chicken mixture, blending well.
4. Bring 3 cups water and 1 teasp. salt to a boil; slowly stir in corn meal, then cook a few minutes over low heat, while stirring in butter. Remove from heat and stir in egg.
5. Cut 8 10" squares from aluminum foil. On each square place about ½ cup corn-meal mixture. Pat into 6" square. Now spread about ½ cup meat-vegetable mixture over one half of each square. Fold other half of corn meal, with foil, over stuffing; wrap foil securely around each Hallaca.
6. Drop them into a kettle of boiling salted water and simmer 1½ hr. To serve, unwrap. Nice with a mixed salad. Makes 8.

P.S. Steps 1 through 5 can be done early on the day, or day before; then Hallacas may be refrigerated until ready to boil.

South America

Your meat-and-potato family will vote this meat loaf a treat—the spicy, fresh tomatoes in which it bakes give a rare touch.

CARNE MOLIDA VENEZOLANA
(Venezuelan Meat Loaf)

½ cup fresh bread crumbs
1½ lb. beef, ground
2 eggs, beaten
½ cup grated natural Swiss cheese
Salt
Pepper

Olive oil
2 cups chopped onions
Flour
¼ teasp. dried thyme
¼ cup snipped parsley
3 medium tomatoes, chopped

About 1 hr. and 15 min. before serving:
1. In large bowl place bread crumbs, beef, beaten eggs, cheese, 1¾ teasp. salt, and ½ teasp. pepper. Start heating oven to 375°F.
2. In medium skillet heat 2 tablesp. olive oil; in it sauté ½ cup chopped onions until golden. Add to meat mixture, then mix until *well blended*. On lightly floured board shape mixture into loaf, then place in 12" x 8" x 2" baking dish.
3. In same skillet, in 3 tablesp. hot olive oil, sauté 1½ cups chopped onions golden; stir in 1 teasp. salt, ¼ teasp. pepper, thyme, parsley, tomatoes.
4. Pour this mixture around meat loaf in baking dish. Bake 50 min., or until meat is done. Serve, cut into slices, with baked white or sweet potatoes and a mixed salad. Makes about 6 servings.

When the dinner main dish is to be on the light side, choose this rice pudding for dessert. Its flavors are so refreshing.

ARROZ CON COCO
(Rice-and-Coconut Pudding)

3 cups water
1½ teasp. salt
¾ cup uncooked regular white rice
1½ cups milk
½ cup granulated sugar

Flaked fresh or canned coconut
1 tablesp. grated lemon rind
Powdered cinnamon
Fresh oranges and grapes (optional)

Early on the day:
1. In medium saucepan bring water and salt to a boil; then stir in rice and cook, uncovered, 10 to 15 min., or until water is absorbed.
2. Now stir in milk, sugar, and ¼ cup flaked coconut. Cook over low heat, stirring occasionally, 10 to 15 min., or until milk is absorbed and rice is tender. Stir in lemon rind.

3. Rinse a 1-qt. mold or casserole with cold water; into it pour rice mixture. Refrigerate until well chilled and set.

Just before serving:
Unmold rice on serving dish; sprinkle with ½ to 1 teasp. cinnamon and 2 tablesp. flaked coconut. Serve as is or garnished with orange sections and small bunchlets of grapes. Makes about 6 servings.

WHEN YOU MEASURE

AMERICAN MEASUREMENTS

All the recipes in this book have been checked and rechecked in the *Good Housekeeping* Institute kitchens, using the standard measuring tools below. All measurements are level.

Measuring Cups:
For dry ingredients: Use a standard set of 4 graduated measuring cups, consisting of a ¼-cup, ⅓-cup, ½-cup, and 1-cup measuring cup.
For liquid ingredients: Use a standard 1-cup measuring cup whose rim, with pouring lip, is above the 1-cup line, to avoid spilling. Standard 2-cup and 1-quart measuring cups are also available.

Measuring Spoons:
Choose one or more of the standard measuring spoon sets that come attached to a ring, or hang on a special holder; these include a ¼-teaspoon, ½-teaspoon, 1-teaspoon, and 1-tablespoon measuring spoon. In a good set, 16 tablespoons or 48 teaspoons should equal 1 cup.

ABBREVIATIONS

cup = cupful	pt. = pint
°F. = degrees Fahrenheit	qt. = quart
1″ = 1 inch	tablesp. = tablespoon
lb. = pound	teasp. = teaspoon
oz. = ounce	

TABLE OF EQUIVALENTS

Speck, dash, or pinch	Less than ⅛ teaspoon
3 teaspoons	1 tablespoon
2 tablespoons	⅛ cup
4 tablespoons	¼ cup
5 tablespoons + 1 teaspoon	⅓ cup
8 tablespoons	½ cup
10 tablespoons + 2 teaspoons	⅔ cup

TABLE OF EQUIVALENTS (*continued*)

12 tablespoons	¾ cup
16 tablespoons	1 cup
1 cup	8 fluid ounces
2 cups	1 pint (16 fluid ounces)
2 pints	1 quart (32 fluid ounces)
1 quart	4 cups
4 quarts	1 gallon
16 ounces (dry measure)	1 pound

CAN AND JAR SIZES OF CANNED FOODS

Approximate Net Weight or Fluid Measure on Can Label	Approximate Equivalent in Measuring Cupfuls
8 oz.	1 cup
10½ to 12 oz.	1¼ cups
12 oz.	1½ cups
14 to 16 oz.	1¾ cups
16 to 17 oz.	2 cups
1 lb. 4 oz. *or* 1 pt. 2 fl. oz.	2½ cups
1 lb. 13 oz.	3½ cups

TIPS ON OVEN TEMPERATURES

If recipe calls for:	You may know it as:
275°F. up to 325°F.	Slow oven
325°F. up to 375°F.	Moderate oven
375°F. up to 425°F.	Moderately hot oven
425°F. up to 475°F.	Hot oven
475°F. up to 500°F.	Very hot oven

ENGLISH LIQUID MEASUREMENTS

¼ Imperial pint, or 1 gill	=	½ cup + 2 tablespoons
½ Imperial pint, or 2 gills	=	1¼ cups
1 Imperial pint, or 20 fluid ounces	=	2½ cups
2 Imperial pints, or 1 quart	=	5 cups

CONTINENTAL MEASUREMENTS

If Dry Ingredients:

1 ounce	=	28.35 grams
3½ ounces	=	100 grams
1 pound	=	453.58 grams
1 pound, 1½ ounces	=	500 grams (1 European pound)
2 pounds, 3 ounces	=	1 kilogram (2 European pounds)

If Liquid Ingredients:

3 tablespoons + 1 teaspoon	=	½ deciliter
6 tablespoons + 2 teaspoons	=	1 deciliter
½ cup + 1 teaspoon	=	1.25 deciliters (⅛ liter)
13 tablespoons + 1 teaspoon (or ¾ cup + 4 teaspoons)	=	2 deciliters
1 cup + 2 teaspoons	=	2.5 deciliters (¼ liter)
2 cups + 4 teaspoons	=	5 deciliters (½ liter)
1 quart + 2 tablespoons + 2 teaspoons	=	10 deciliters (1 liter)

EQUIVALENT AMOUNTS

Food	American	English	Continental
Apples, 3 medium	3 cups, sliced	1 pound	450 grams
Bananas, 3 medium	2½ cups, sliced	1 pound	450 grams
Bread crumbs, fresh	1 cup, packed	3 ounces	84 grams
Butter or margarine	½ cup	4 ounces	113 grams
Cheese:			
American or Swiss	2 cups, grated	8 ounces	225 grams
Cottage cheese	1 cup	8 ounces	225 grams
Cream cheese	6 tablespoons	3 ounces	85 grams
Chocolate, unsweetened or semisweet	1 square	1 ounce	28 grams
Coconut, flaked	1 cup	3½ ounces	98 grams
Consommé or beef broth, condensed	1 10½-ounce can	10½ ounces	3 deciliters
Corn meal	3 cups	1 pound	450 grams
Cornstarch	½ cup	2¼ ounces	63 grams
Dates	1¼ cups, cut up	7¼ ounces	205 grams
Flour:			
All-purpose flour	4 cups, sifted	1 pound	450 grams
Cake flour	4¾ to 5 cups, sifted	1 pound	450 grams
Whole-wheat flour	3½ cups, unsifted	1 pound	450 grams

EQUIVALENT AMOUNTS (*continued*)

Food	American	English	Continental
Honey	1 cup	12 ounces	336 grams
Lemon (1 medium)	3 tablespoons juice		
Lemon (1 medium)	1 tablespoon grated rind		
Lentils, split peas, or dried beans	1 cup	8 ounces	225 grams
Nuts:			
Shelled almonds	4 cups	1 pound, 2 ounces	506 grams
Shelled Brazil nuts	3 cups	1 pound	450 grams
Shelled pecans	4 cups	1 pound	450 grams
Shelled walnuts	4 cups	1 pound	450 grams
Potatoes	3 medium	1 pound	450 grams
Raisins	3 cups, not packed	15 ounces	420 grams
Rice	1 cup	8 ounces	225 grams
Salad oil	1 cup	8 ounces	225 grams
Sugar:			
Brown sugar	2⅓ cups, firmly packed	1 pound	450 grams
Confectioners' sugar	4½ to 5 cups, sifted	1 pound	450 grams
Granulated sugar	2¼ to 2½ cups	1 pound	450 grams
Tomatoes, fresh	3 medium	1 pound	450 grams

INDEX

Index

Murgh-i-musallam (Pakistan), 146-147

Murgi curry (India), 134

Mush, corn-meal (Italy), 68

Mushroom Dishes
Baked mushrooms (Finland), 25
Beef tenderloin and mushrooms in wine (France), 30
Mushrooms with sour cream (Poland), 76
Rice and mushrooms (Haiti), 165

Napfkuchen (Germany), 46

Nargisi kofta (India), 133

Nasi goreng (Indonesia), 139

New England boiled dinner (United States), 199-200

New Zealand's Dishes
Double-spice muffins, 181
Melon-cream pie, 180
Stuffed steak, New Zealand style, 179
Tomato-cheese pie, 180

Nibblers. See Appetizers

Norsk nøtt brød (Norway), 73

Norwegian Dishes
Bløt kake (Layer cake), 73
Fersk suppe og kjøtt (Two-course dinner dish), 71-72
Fyrste kake (Prince cake), 74
Julekake (Norwegian holiday bread), 74-75
Kongesuppe (Royal soup), 72
Norsk nøtt brød (Norwegian walnut bread), 73

Nut cookies (Lebanon), 117

Nut filling for Danish pastries, 17

Oatmeal squares (Canada), 191

Ökörfarok ragú (Hungary), 56

Omelets. See Pancakes and Omelets

Onion pie (Sweden), 94-95

Open sandwiches (Denmark), 15-16

Oriental nibblers (Polynesia), 183

Oriental roast pork (China), 128

Öszi barack tészta (Hungary), 59-60

Oven-fried chicken (Hungary), 57

Oxtail ragout (Hungary), 56

Oxtail soup (England), 19-20

Paella (Spain), 89

Pakistani Dishes
Eggplant-sour-cream salad, 147
Firni (Rice pudding), 147-148
Murgh-i-musallam (Stuffed chicken), 146-147

Paltas rellenas (Bolivia), 212

Panamanian Dishes
Ensalada de rabanos (Radish salad), 196-197

Panamanian Dishes (continued)
Pescado con alcaparros (Baked fish with caper sauce), 196
Sancocho (Meat-and-vegetable stew), 195-196

Pancakes and Omelets
Ginger pancakes with crab meat (Polynesia), 184
Javanese omelet (Indonesia), 138
Potato pancakes (Germany), 44
Swedish pancakes, 97
Viennese pancakes, 6

Parsley-stuffed veal rolls (Sweden), 94

Paskha (Russia), 86

Pasta
Baked beef and macaroni (Greece), 49-50
Lasagna al forno (Italy), 64-65
Manicotti (Italy), 67-68

Pastel de choclo (Chile), 217

Pasteles de cacao (Colombia), 218-219

Pastitsu (Greece), 49-50

Pastries. See Cakes

Pâté de pommes de terre (France), 33-34

Patties, beef-and-beet (Sweden), 93

Pea soup (Holland), 52

Peachcake (Hungary), 59-60

Pecan pie (United States), 204

Peking ja (Duckling) (China), 127-128

Pepper pork (Bolivia), 211-212

Pepperpot (Jamaica), 167

Peruvian Dishes
Buñuelos (Peruvian doughnuts), 220-221
Chupe de camarones (Shrimp chowder), 219
Peruvian potato salad, 220

Pescado con alcaparros (Panama), 196

Pescado Español (Spain), 88

Pesto Genovese (Italy), 64

Philippine Dishes
Chicken adobo, 181-182
Escabeche (Fish, Philippine-style), 182

Pieczen hazarska (Poland), 75-76

Pies and Tarts
Almond pie (Greece), 51-52
Banketletter (Holland), 55-56
Beefsteak-and-kidney pie (England), 21
Beefsteak pie (Canada), 189
Blueberry cream tarts (Belgium), 10
Boer chicken pie (South Africa), 158-159
Cheese torte (Italy), 69-70

Index

Index

Spritz cookies (Sweden), 96
Squash with dill (Hungary), 58
Steaks
  Beefsteak with pizza sauce (Italy), 67
  Flank steak, rolled and filled (Chile), 216
  Steak with mushrooms and bean sprouts (Polynesia), 184
  Stuffed steak, New Zealand style, 179
Steamed sea bass (China), 127
Stegt svinekam med aebler og svesker (Denmark), 14-15
Stewed chicken (Portugal), 78
Stews
  Beef stew (Argentina), 210
  Beef stew with peas (Morocco), 158
  Guinean beef stew, 155
  Guinean chicken stew, 154
  Irish stew, 60
  Lamb-and-chicken stew (Morocco), 156-157
  Lamb-okra stew (Sudan), 161
  Meat-and-vegetable stew (Panama), 196
  Tennessee Brunswick stew (United States), 197
Strawberry snow (Finland), 26
Strufoli or pignolata (Italy), 70-71
Stuffed boneless chicken (Russia), 85
Stuffed breast of lamb (Arabia), 113-114
Stuffed chicken (Pakistan), 146
Stuffed chicken à la Morocaine, 157
Stuffed green peppers (Mexico), 193
Stuffed lamb (Greece), 50
Stuffed rock-lobster tails (South Africa), 159-160
Stuffed steak, New Zealand style, 179
Sudanese Dishes
  Bani-bamia (Lamb-okra stew), 161
  Chicken-potato skillet dish, 162
  Salada (Cool-and-crisp salad), 162
Sukiyaki (Japan), 140-141
Summer soup (Finland), 24
Suomalaiset puikot (Finland), 26
Superb poached fish with tomato (France), 32
Swedish Dishes
  Biff à la Lindström (Beef-and-beet patties), 93
  Ellen's pepparkakor (Ellen's gingersnaps), 96-97
  Ellen's valnöts tårta (Ellen's walnut torte), 95
  Ester's spritsar (Ester's spritz cookies), 96
  Kalops (Swedish braised short ribs), 93
  Kalvrulader (Parsley-stuffed veal rolls), 94

Swedish Dishes (continued)
  Mrs. Linder's lök paj (Mrs. Linder's onion pie), 94-95
  Plättar (Swedish pancakes), 97
  Sweden's köttbullar (Swedish meat balls), 92
Sweet-and-sour meat balls (China), 129
Sweet-potato loaf (Haiti), 166
Swiss Dishes
  Chäs-tange (Cheese sticks), 102
  Cutlets of veal à la Suisse, 99-100
  Eierzopf (Swiss twist), 100-101
  Engadinertorte (Swiss walnut pie), 105-106
  Gugelhopf, 103
  Japonaistorte (Layered hazelnut torte), 104-105
  Kirschenkuchen (Cherry cake), 103-104
  Scampi mode semiramis, 98-99
  Soufflé glacé au Grand Marnier, 106
  Swiss fondue, 101-102
  Switzerland cheese-and-onion pie, 99
  Vegetable soup with veal roundels, 101
Székely goulyas (Czechoslovakia), 11-12

Tables of measurements and equivalents, 227-230
Tamale pie (Mexico), 192
Tart Ibiza (Spain), 90
Tarte aux fruits (France), 38-39
Tarts. *See* Pies
Teacakes, English, 23
Tejfeles pité (Hungary), 59
Tejfölös tökfözelék (Hungary), 58
Tempura (Japan), 141-142
Tennessee Brunswick stew (United States), 197
Teriyaki (Hawaii), 178
Thailand's Dishes
  Kai priao wan (Chicken sour and sweet), 148
  Kung yam (Shrimp salad), 149
Tien suan zou wan (China), 129
Timun salad (Malaya), 145
Toad-in-the-hole (England), 22
Tomato-cheese pie (New Zealand), 180
Torta de castanha do para (Brazil), 215
Torta di ricotta (Italy), 69-70
Torta pascualina (Uruguay), 222
Tortes. *See* Cakes and Pastries
Tournedos Medici (France), 30
Tourtière de Noël (Canada), 190
Toyaji-kogi wa tark-kogi (Korea), 143-144

244